Biblical Secrets

Why Some People Are Poor and Some People Are Rich

BIBLICAL SECRETS

WHY SOME PEOPLE ARE POOR AND SOME PEOPLE ARE RICH

BRIGHT OKOYE

ALABASTER HOUSE
PUBLISHING

Published by Alabaster House Publishing
P.M.B. 1865,
Onitsha, Anambra, Nigeria
www.alabasterhousepublishing.com
Tel: (+234) 703 427 7850

ISBN: 978-978-54670-1-7 (Hardcover)
ISBN: 978-978-54670-0-0 (Paperback)

Printed by CreateSpace, An Amazon.com Company

DEDICATION

This book is dedicated to our Lord Jesus Christ who gave up His riches in order that we might become rich.

For you know the grace of our Lord
Jesus Christ, that though He was rich,
yet for your sakes He became poor,
that you through His poverty might
become rich.

2 Corinthians 8.9 (NKJV)

CONTENTS

READER'S GUIDE

This book is divided into two main parts: part one and part two. Part one deals with the issue of poverty while part two deals with riches. I chose to handle the issue of poverty first because if people should do away with poverty, riches can add up on their own. You can consider a farmer who is pouring grain into a bag that is torn. Even if his harvest is the greatest in his neighbourhood, it will take only hours or days for poverty to stare him in the face. The first thing he needs to do is to mend the tear in the bag and then his grain will begin to accumulate. According to George Eliot, 'It's no use filling your pocket with money if you have got a hole in the corner.' Efforts will always end in futility when they are channelled towards solving problems that are outcomes of an error; the ultimate solution to an error is its correction. Thus I will advise that anyone who reads this book should start from part one before proceeding to part two.

Part One is like a list of problems. No matter how the problems are expatiated, it will only be a half way job if the remedies are not recommended. As a result, each chapter in this part comes with a section called 'Solution'. This section proffers the solution to the problem discussed. Since the Part One is meant to work like diagnosing a sickness and prescribing the medication, the Solution sections will have A Word of Advice and Practical Questions which the reader is expected to answer. And it is important that the answers be written down for clarity and for proper assessment.

Part Two is like a list of beautiful discoveries about riches. Leaving them like that can push some people to the extreme. Thus each chapter in this part comes with a section called 'Exhortation'. The Exhortation sections will have A Lesson from the Ants, Recommendation and Practical Questions which the reader is expected to answer in writing for clarity and for proper action. Each chapter of the book will also have A Verse for Inspiration from the Scripture. The verse will carry the message of the Solution or Exhortation for each chapter as the case may be.

Finally, I implore the reader to take each step prayerfully. My utmost desire and my sincere prayer is that anyone who reads this book will witness the life of abundance as revealed in the Bible.

INTRODUCTION

Discovering the Biblical Side of Finance

Do not let this Book of the Law depart from your mouth; meditate on it day and night, so that you may be careful to do everything written in it. Then you will be prosperous and successful.

Joshua 1.8 (NIV)

It is normal in every society to see both the rich and the poor. It is also normal to see the righteous rich ones and the righteous poor ones. Likewise, it is normal to see the unrighteous rich ones and the unrighteous poor ones. But have you asked yourself: why are some people poor and some people rich? Or is it all about coincidence? Is there any character common among the poor? Is there any character common among the rich? Are riches all about spirituality? Is there any physical aspect to riches? Is there any Biblical side to finance? By the grace of God, these questions and the likes are answered in this book.

The Bible, which is the Word of God, contains everything every human being needs to live a meaningful life. Any man that gives himself to the study of the Word of God, always have reasons to excel in life. Even a fool, when he studies the Word, he becomes wiser than his teachers and contemporaries. The riches in the Bible are not just for spiritual matters; they are also for physical matters—including financial matters. It is when people neglect this truth that they begin to grope in the darkness of poverty. That is why Jesus Christ said,

"You are in error because you do not know the Scriptures or the power of God.

Matthew 22.29 (NIV)

Elsewhere, the Bible also emphasizes the fact that corrections to errors could be made by the Word of God:

All Scripture is God-breathed and is useful for teaching, rebuking, correcting and training in righteousness.

2 Timothy 3.16 (NIV)

There can be no better place to learn about any issue of life (especially finance) than from the Bible. In the words of Smith Wigglesworth: This blessed Book, the Bible, brings such life and health and peace, and such an abundance that we should never be poor any more.

There are four basic aspects of our lives which we cannot neglect, namely: our spiritual lives, our marital or family lives, our health and our financial lives. The spiritual life comes first and every other aspect of our lives can be directly controlled on this platform. As could be seen from the Bible:

For whatever is born of God overcomes the world. And this is the victory that has overcome the world—our faith.

1 John 5.4 (NKJV)

Again, in another place the Scripture says,

For what will it profit a man if
he gains the whole world, and loses
his own soul?

Mark 8.36 (NKJV)

We can see that also in the case of Job. His wealth (financial life) was attacked, his family (marital life) was attacked, his body (health) was attacked but in all, it was his spiritual life that kept him standing.

It is not explicitly written in the Scripture which aspect of life comes second, though many Christians hold it to be the marital life. Indeed, the family is important and any man (or woman) with a troubled family is likely to be disturbed emotionally. Even his spiritual life, health and finances could be at risk. It is in the family that people are built from the cradle. Having a good family will go a long way in having a stable spiritual life, financial life and health. A lot of unstable people in the world today could be traced to an unstable family. And whenever any society or generation is about to be corrupted, the family is the first. Likewise, to build a society or a generation, the family is the first. The family life seems to have this edge over health and finances in the sense that it has to do with more lives. We may not be surprised that the first miracle of Jesus Christ was in a marriage feast and the relationship between Christ and His Church is compared to that of a marriage relationship.

Nevertheless, weighing the three aspects of life will give different results in different circumstances as regards to priority. However, giving priority to one aspect of life at any given time should not mean the neglect of others. Wisdom is needed to know which one to prioritise in any given situation. For instance, we will see that most of the miracles of Jesus on men's lives were on their health (healing). The miracles were not focused on people's marriage or finances. Again, in the case of Job, the last thing God allowed the devil to touch was Job's life (health) and the devil held it that Job would give in if his health was touched:

"Skin for skin!" Satan replied.
"A man will give all he has for his
own life. But stretch out your
hand and strike his flesh and bones, and
he will surely curse you to your face."

Job 2.4-5 (NIV)

Finally, when Job's health was attacked, his wife (his family), out of uninformed pity advised him to give up. No doubt, of the remaining three aspects of life, the closest to a man's spiritual life is his health. A man is made of spirit, soul and body (i.e. his health). Also, from the Scripture we can see that when one commits sin (i.e. breaking spiritual laws), his health will be affected in form of sicknesses.

On the other hand, according to the Words of Jesus Christ:

No one can serve two masters. Either
he will hate the one and love the other,
or he will be devoted to the one and
despise the other. You cannot serve
both God and Money.

Matthew 6.24 (NIV)

Jesus knows that what has been taking the greatest number of men away from the presence of God is not their marriage or family nor their health nor any other thing but money. Men ought to serve God and use money but out of ignorance many people want to serve money and use God. Also, St. Paul told Timothy:

...the love of money is a root
of all kinds of evil.

1 Timothy 6.10 (NIV)

We now see that for a man's spiritual life to stand, he must not serve nor love money. But at the same time, one can hardly do without money as long as he is living on earth. That is the reason why the proper understanding of money is needed in order to master it and not to serve nor love it. Anyone who neglects his financial life can end up frustrating his spiritual life, marriage or family and health. It is necessary that a man should take some financial decisions in his life even before getting married. It is necessary that a man should take some financial decisions in his life to give no room for compromise in his faith.

I want you to understand this: your financial life does not mean money. Rather, your financial life is you and your relationship with money. It is your way of living with respect to money. The money you have is just part of it. There are four aspects of our financial life: the first is our perspective on money, the second is how we make money, the third is how we spend money and the fourth is our financial worth. It is our perspective on money that directly determines the remaining two apart from our financial worth. It will determine whether one will open for business even on Sundays and forsake the gathering of the brethren; believing that faith is only in the heart and not in attending Church meetings. It will determine whether one will abandon his family in a bid to build a great business or career or whether one will close down his business, withdraw all his money and go on vacation with his family. It will also determine whether one will choose to die while working for a living. Finally, it will determine the things one can do for money and the things for which he will spend his money. Our financial worth is the product of the other three. It is not just the total money we have, but our financial value. If any man overcomes money, he will be closer to the kingdom of God.

I know that many books have been written concerning Christians and their finances. Many of them are good and I have learnt a lot from them. Nonetheless, I find it appropriate to write about some things concerning this same matter as shown in the Holy Scripture. Fortunately, all these things appear in our everyday life. Many ministers have presented this matter from the viewpoints that are not scriptural and ended up making the issue of finance look worldly in the eyes of some committed Christians. At a time in my life, I began to dislike the teachings which are commonly called 'Prosperity Messages' though I had believed and also taught others about prosperity. My resentment was that many ministers were manipulating the Scripture to prove their claims. But I came back to my right mind; for I will rather believe the Word of God as it is and not try to run away from the reality just because someone else is practising a lie. I tried to keep the belief within me and for those around me who would care to know but it continued to burn within me whenever I see people living in what I call 'Avoidable Poverty'.

On the other hand, I have seen Christians who struggle with finances when there ought not to be any reason for such and I mean no reason for such. Some enter into such struggles in the name of faith but it is actually because of lack of understanding. Today, many negative things have been said about money by true Christians but having a wrong opinion about anything can be disastrous, whether such things are good or bad on their own.

Thus, I decided to write on this matter of a Christian and his finances from the Biblical point of view. The points are not my own lest I should be responsible for their validity but they are all lifted from the Bible. The Bible is the Word of God, which is the Revealed Will of God. Just as a consumer will get the best of a product by keeping to the user's manual provided by the producer, our success depends on the Bible. It is our life's manual provided by God, the maker of everything. It is when we discover the things written in it and apply them in our lives that we have holistic success. The Bible says,

It is the glory of God to conceal a matter, But the glory of kings is to search out a matter.

Proverbs 25.2 (NKJV)

The essence of this book is to give the proper teaching of the Bible with regards to finance. The points treated in this book are matters of principles—not exceptions.

Shalom.

PART ONE

WHY SOME PEOPLE ARE POOR

Jesus answered…You will always have
the poor with you…

John 12.7-8 (NCV)

Presently (as of the time of writing this book), about half of the world's population is poor. They are poor in the sense that they cannot provide their basic needs. Though it could be said that some people are born into poverty, some acquire poverty and some have poverty forced on them. With regards to Christians, sometimes it seems that being a true and committed Christian is synonymous with a struggling financial life. But looking into the Scripture one would see a lot of promises which are true. God also watches over all His Words to see them fulfilled (Jeremiah 1.12).

Having seen that the Lord is good (Psalm 34.8), then it seems to be a contradiction seeing the people of God struggling with their finances. That truly calls for more insight. When God told Moses that His name is 'I AM', He revealed His capacity to do anything in that name. It is what anyone believes God to do in his life that He will do for him. A great number of the Israelites were not able to enter the Promised Land because they did not believe in God's ability to take them into the Promised Land. It is what we expect from God with faith that He does for us. A look at some passages in the Bible will reveal more about this issue:

However, there should be no poor among you,
for in the land the LORD your God is giving

you to possess as your inheritance, he will richly bless you.

Deuteronomy 15.4 (NIV)

There will always be poor people in the land. Therefore I command you to be openhanded toward your brothers and toward the poor and needy in your land.'

Deuteronomy 15.11 (NIV)

These are two verses in a chapter and they refer to the same people. If anyone chooses to be the person to be blessed, it will be so with him. If anyone chooses to be the poor that would be helped by others, it will be so with him. God knows that even in the midst of all the promises and blessings, some will still find themselves poor. The Bible also says,

Therefore, [inheriting] the promise is the outcome of faith and depends [entirely] on faith, in order that it might be given as an act of grace (unmerited favor)...

Romans 4.16 (AMP)

With all these Bible passages, then there are avoidable reasons why some people are poor. And such reasons must also have their solutions from the Bible. This book might not capture all of them but it will touch a good number of them. Only one of these reasons is enough to keep somebody in poverty.

However, there are those who are poor for a moment in their lives because they are in a transition period, but such people are not victims to any of the reasons that would be discussed in this book.

CHAPTER

1

Justification of Poverty

Do you see a man wise in his own eyes?
There is more hope for a fool than for him.

Proverbs 26.12 (NKJV)

Justification is giving a good reason or explanation that provides an acceptable support for something. On the other hand, poverty is the condition of having little or no money or possessions. Thus, justification of poverty is giving a good reason or explanation that provides an acceptable support for the condition of having little or no money or possessions.

When a man finds acceptable reasons to be poor, he will either become poor or will remain poor. Anything a man justifies, he cannot stop—including poverty. The greatest problem many Christians have with regards to poverty is seeing it always as the will of God. In all aspects of human life, the beginning of the solution to any problem is the acknowledgement of that problem. No matter how long a problem stays in a place (and people get used to it), it is still a problem. There are some problems that have stayed for a long time that you see people arguing that it is part of the system. In many cases, some fight anyone who tries to restore the normal situation. And the same is true with poverty.

Even now, in many places among Christians, anyone who is very rich is counted to be worldly. And as long as such an opinion thrives, no move would be made to depart from poverty. But the irony of it is that a good number of people with such mentality would still go to those rich ones to seek financial help. Such people can go to school to study finance but once finance is mentioned in the Church they would become disturbed. They can spend some time praying for God to send them a financial help but at the back of their mind they still believe that poverty is part of the Christian faith.

I will like to share some of the reasons why people justify poverty.

Ignorance

A lot of people live in ignorance. Greater percentage (more than 90%) of all the problems that we see in the world today could be avoided by knowledge, especially the knowledge of the Word of God. God says,

My people are destroyed for lack of knowledge.

Hosea 4.6 (NKJV)

This is God Himself speaking. He calls them 'My people'. These are people called by His name. God is always waiting to show Himself great on their behalf (2 Chronicles 16.9) but they are comfortable with a life of mediocrity. We as human beings feel insulted whenever someone takes us to be incapable of doing what we can do with ease. Can't we also think that it is sin for us to believe that God is in the business of keeping His people poor?

Ignorance is darkness and the light of knowledge puts away such darkness. There is an old saying that goes like this: 'He who knows that he knows not is a wise man but he who knows not that he knows not is a complete, complex and complicated fool.' Whenever a man is in ignorance, it is difficult for him to believe so until he decides to try knowledge. There is no single time (considerable) enough for a man to live in ignorance. The Bible says,

Also it is not good for a soul to be
without knowledge…

Proverbs 19.2 (NKJV)

The Word of God gives us revelation into many principles of life. Most of these principles apply to anyone who obeys them. In the Scripture, you will see a lot of words like 'Whosoever', 'Anyone', etc. Just the same way they apply to anyone that obeys; they don't apply to anyone that does not obey. Thus, living in the ignorance that poverty is part of every true Christian's life will not change the Word of God. Anyone given to such an opinion can die in Christ and still go to heaven but why will someone give himself to the temptations of poverty (Proverbs 30.9).

People living in this time of human existence should have nothing to do with ignorance of this nature especially when the Bible is all over the place and in different formats. The Bible was the first major book to be printed in human history. People worked hard to invent the printing machines with the belief that when the Bible is mass produced many living souls would be enlightened when they read it. Today with a cheap phone, one can access hundreds of Bible translations. But in all these, people still live in ignorance. They give reasons why they can't read the whole Bible. In just the same manner, they give reasons and justify why they are poor.

False Doctrines

What a man hears in the name of doctrine or sermon or teaching is like a mould that shapes that man. A pattern of words a man pays attention to consistently can change his mindset even when he is not aware of it. That is the reason why big companies spend a lot of money to flood their prospective customers with their adverts until those people begin to think the adverts. In the same way, if a man continues to hear the wrong things about wealth in the name of the Word of God, he will justify poverty and grope in its darkness. Jesus says,

...Take heed what you hear.

Mark 4.24 (NKJV)

And again,

"Therefore take heed how you hear.
For whoever has, to him more will be given;
and whoever does not have, even what he
seems to have will be taken from him."

Luke 8.18 (NKJV)

As what you hear is important, the person you listen to is also important. Even your heart will tell you that a message is as credible as the messenger. Now the issue is; how do you know a credible messenger? The answer is still the Bible. Jesus says that if the blind leads the blind, both will fall into a ditch (Matthew 15.14). He did not say that only the leader will fall but both. A lot of people preach the Word of God according to their own experience. If they are rich, they would preach that God makes rich. If they are poor, they would preach that poverty is a sign of true Christianity. They would link their life experiences wrongfully with some Bible passages to support their claims. But the Bible warns,

Knowing this first, that no prophecy of
Scripture is of any private interpretation,

2 Peter 1.20 (NKJV)

Even though having riches comes with its own temptation (likewise poverty), the Bible does not equate riches with worldliness. It is only when some people are wrongly informed that they believe that riches are meant to be enjoyed in sinful ways. As a result, when such men stumble into wealth; they abandon their faith. Being poor or in lack does not imply that one must encourage poverty in his preaching. Doing so can make one to be credible before his (weak) audience but not before God. If one preaches the Word of God as it is written in the Scripture not minding his financial status, it is the Spirit of God that would go on to convince his listeners. If a preacher shows his audience that he is a credible messenger of God, they will believe the Word of God he preaches. But if he tries to show himself credible on his own, he may not succeed if his audience should weigh him on their own financial standard. If a bank messenger goes to a man to deliver a cheque of large sum, the only thing the customer needs to do is to verify whether the messenger is truly from the bank and not whether the messenger is rich enough to carry such a cheque. The same applies to a minister of the gospel: his credibility lies in whether he is a true man of God and not on whether he is rich enough.

Many preachers that encourage poverty today in their preaching do so because they count themselves unworthy to talk about riches when they are living in lack. But that is lack of faith and understanding. The Bible says,

For we walk by faith, not by sight.

2 Corinthians 5.7 (NKJV)

Unfortunately, because they encourage poverty, they themselves continue to live in poverty. When Paul was in prison, it did not stop him from writing to the Philippian Church about the goodness of God. See what he wrote:

I can do all things through Christ who strengthens me.

Philippians 4.13 (NKJV)

As if that was not enough for a man in prison he went on to say,

And my God shall supply all your need according to His riches in glory by Christ Jesus.

Philippians 4.19 (NKJV)

He did not consider that the Philippians would question his authority to talk about divine provisions while he himself was a receiver in a prison. He was not bothered for he was not preaching his own theories: he was declaring the Word of God.

No matter who is preaching or teaching to encourage poverty, believing him will only justify poverty in someone's life. But that is not the good future God is planning for His own beloved children (Jeremiah 29.11). Hear the words of Benjamin Warfield: The real question, in a word, is not a new question but the perennial old question, whether the basis of our doctrine is to be what the Bible teaches, or what men teach. The Bible also says,

But Peter and John answered and said to them, "Whether it is right in the sight of God to listen to you more than to God, you judge. For we cannot but speak the things which we have seen and heard."

Acts 4.19-20 (NKJV)

Wrongful Acceptance

Many people have come to settle down with poverty as the will of God for their lives because of many things they have witnessed in life. In their own eyes, they have done everything possible thus they say 'It is the will of God.' As I mentioned in the introduction of the first part of this book, some people can be in a transition period but such periods are not forever. And such people do not contribute to it. A closer look at many people that justify their poverty as the will of God reveals the actual cause of their poverty. Some would continue doing the same thing the same way over and over and expect a different favourable result. The Bible says,

Some people ruin themselves by their own stupid actions and then blame the LORD.

Proverbs 19.3 (GNT)

You can consider a university student who is not interested in his studies; he can end up graduating with a poor result. In a world where many people with good results are looking for job, such a person may spend a good number of years in unemployment. When poverty strikes him, he may acknowledge God and the next thing he may do is to justify his poverty as the will of God.

Any man that is in Christ and is passing through financial difficulty whether he is the cause or not, should continue to press on until it is over. There is no place in the Scripture where God commands us to be at home with poverty. Even some people who experience poverty in line with God's plan for their lives continue in such a situation, even when they are supposed to have passed that stage. For example, the Word of God to Abraham was that his descendants (Israelites) would be strangers in a land that is not theirs and be treated as slaves for four hundred years (Genesis 15.13). But the Israelites ended up spending four hundred and thirty years in Egypt (Exodus 12.40).

One thing about being in lack in line with God's plan is that it doesn't last forever and God has a reason for that as could be seen in Deuteronomy 8.2-3. And another thing is that the opening date and the closing date are not clearly known. Thus, no man should relax, fold his hands and justify his poverty. A look at those who come out of their transition periods with testimonies will reveal that the foundations of their success are laid in those transition periods.

Generalization

People justify poverty when many people around them are poor. The tendency to relieve one's mind by generalization is common among human beings. And the case of poverty is not an exception. This issue contributes a lot in collective poverty whether it is in a Church or in an ordinary community. Having this mentality of 'As long as the problem is for everybody, it is not a problem' will by no means reduce the impact of the problem unless something is done about it. When an epidemic plagues a community, it does not stop on its own just because its victims are much. And it does not become ineffective and friendly just because it is affecting many people in the community. But in the case of poverty, people feel at ease and justify themselves because they think that it has no immediate harm. Nonetheless, in essence, poverty is also an epidemic. It is not just like other epidemics but wherever it thrives it can sponsor any disease to become another epidemic.

Fortunately whenever people rise to fight epidemics they succeed even if it takes time. In some cases, it takes only a sincere cry for help and a willingness to accept the help. Dealing with some epidemics may involve injecting vaccines donated by different organizations but the communities must be willing to accept the vaccines and the pains of injections. Unfortunately, many don't see poverty as an epidemic as long as it affects everybody in the neighbourhood. And in many cases, they are not willing to accept the painful sacrificial measures that will take them out of poverty. However, while such measures may be seen as painful by many, a man of understanding would receive them with joy.

The truth remains that poverty has a cause. For an entire community to be living in poverty simply means that something must be wrong with all the individual households in the community. Justifying the poverty won't keep away its effects such as hunger, lack, etc. from the individual families. Yet many don't bother themselves since the hunger and lack are evenly spread.

A better understanding could be seen from the Scripture:

And the mixed multitude among them [the rabble who followed Israel from Egypt] began to lust greatly [for familiar and dainty food], and the Israelites wept again and said, Who will give us meat to eat?

Numbers 11.4 (AMP)

While the meat was yet between their teeth, before it was consumed, the anger of the Lord was kindled against the people, and the Lord smote them with a very great plague.

Numbers 11.33 (AMP)

From this place, the Israelites did not hesitate to justify their demand for meat which was aroused by the mixed multitude that followed them. And that was in essence accepting the depravity or poverty of the mind displayed by others. Nevertheless, when the wrath of God came, it smote everybody.

There are many other reasons why people justify their poverty that are covered in this book but they are treated in separate chapters.

In conclusion, no matter how reasonable or unreasonable arguments may be to justify poverty, the point still remains that they only help in perpetuating poverty. Poverty is not a delight to any normal living soul. And to stop it, the yoke of its justification must first among other things be broken.

SOLUTION

A Word of Advice

It is time for you to disabuse your mind that being a faithful Christian translates to a life of poverty. Never accept poverty for your life. If you do so (i.e. rejecting poverty), God will complete it.

Practical Questions

1. Do you believe that the promises of God as written in the Scripture are true?
2. Are there reasons for which you think that poverty could be justified?
3. Do you believe that God is bigger than those reasons, if any?
4. Do you think it's a bad idea for you to live without a trace of poverty?
5. Do you believe that God is on your side?

A Verse for Inspiration

For I know the plans I have for you,
declares the LORD, *plans to prosper you*
and not to harm you, plans to give you
hope and a future.

Jeremiah 29.11 (NIV)

CHAPTER

2

Blame and Complaint

Don't always be asking, "Where are the good old days?" Wise folks don't ask questions like that.

Ecclesiastes 7.10 (The Message)

To blame is to hold somebody or something responsible for an unfortunate occurrence. On the other hand, complaint is to express dissatisfaction about something.

Any man who is given to blaming others and complaining for everything hardly takes responsibility for his actions, and that includes his finances. Having this kind of mindset also gives a man the reason to justify his poverty. Such a person don't only blame men for any problem in his life but he even blames God and accuses Him of many things. Even when he decides to pray, he will spend all his time complaining. One thing about such people is that they have ungrateful hearts. The best revelation they like to hear is that they are not the cause of their problems. They will always like to be presented in the good picture but will not be willing to pay the price. They love to be men of great value without responsibility. But in actual sense, the value of a man is the measure of his responsibility. For a man to be of value or to move out of poverty, he must accept the responsibility of everything happening in his life. It is as simple as that; any man who blames others for his poverty is running away from taking responsibility for his life. He could as well be said to be irresponsible. People with such weak minds think that others would understand their stories and thus they feel comfortable and satisfied telling the stories. The truth is that many people who hear them and understand them would only have pity on them. But that won't remove their poverty. On the other hand, a good number of people who hear them are not interested in their stories.

Having a good understanding of the enormous cost of blaming others and complaining all the time can help in taking one out of the dungeon. I will like to consider some of the things that make people to live that kind of life with ease.

Self-Exoneration

People resign to the life of blame and complaint when they feel that they are not the cause of their problem. Though it is true that some people are born into poverty and many also have poverty imposed on them, anyone who wishes to break away from its yoke is free to do so. The Bible says,

...the yoke will be broken because you
have grown so fat.

Isaiah 10.27 (NIV)

This also includes the yoke of poverty. Persistent growth becomes too big for a yoke to hold, and that breaks the yoke. People given to blame and complaint usually have pitiable stories and many of them die telling such stories. Many of such spend their lives harbouring hatred and bitterness; some against their parents, some against their relatives, some against their government, some against their society and some against anything around them. Such people don't realize the fact that their problem is irresponsibility and not because they don't have a one-time deposit of large sum into their bank accounts. Even if they get such a one-time deposit, without responsibility they will go back to poverty within a very short time. On the other hand, somebody without money, if he should accept responsibility, he will definitely walk out of poverty. It may take little steps at a time but walking out of poverty is certain. Truly, many people are not poor because they don't have money; many people don't have money because they are poor. In the words of Henry Ford, 'If money is your hope for independence you will never have it. The only real security that a man can have in this world is a reserve of knowledge, experience and ability.' We can see the Scriptural comparison between responsibility and money:

Wisdom is good with an inheritance,
And profitable to those who see the sun.
For wisdom is a defense as money is a
defense, But the excellence of knowledge is
that wisdom gives life to those who have it.

Ecclesiastes 7.11-12 (NKJV)

We should not fail to understand that responsibility is an act of wisdom. Responsibility makes one to seek for the solution to his problem and not to waste his time harbouring bitterness. A life of abundance is like a destination. A man who is born into riches can walk to it in less time. Likewise, a man who is born into poverty can walk to the same destination but may take a longer time. The main thing is that for anyone to get to the destination; he must walk to it. In the Gospel according to John, Nathaniel asked if anything good could come out of Nazareth (John 1.46). He was a sincere man as confirmed by the Lord Himself. The actual fact was that Nazareth was a place for lower class citizens in those days. Nevertheless, Jesus rose from that same environment to all-time greatness.

Really, there are people who are good and hard-working; nonetheless, trouble comes from nowhere to impose poverty on them. When such a thing happens, they can choose to spend the rest of their lives lamenting their story or to walk out of poverty and tell their testimony. As long as a man is alive, God has given him authority to subdue the earth (Genesis 1.28). The Bible also says,

But for him who is joined to all the
living there is hope, for a living dog
is better than a dead lion.

Ecclesiastes 9.4 (NKJV)

If any would learn how to say, 'I am responsible for anything happening in my life,' he would be on his way to greatness, and that includes living above poverty. Every man should make a conscious decision to stop the act of blaming and complaining if he is actually willing to walk out of poverty. He must believe that every condition in which he finds himself contains all the necessary things he needs to survive. In actual fact, most of the world's innovations and technologies were borne out of needs. It only takes responsible men to seek for the solution to such needs. And when they meet such needs, people will pay them for it. It is said that adversity is the mother of invention.

Blaming and complaining are simply disguised acceptance of failure. Failure actually does not exist until it's accepted. Just a life of gratitude will solve the problem of blame and complaint. It was only when Jonah expressed gratitude to God that God commanded the fish and it vomited him onto dry land (Jonah 2.9-10). Even when gratitude seems to be difficult, God is always there to help as long as you pray for help. Remember that the greatest anointing in God's anointing shelf is the anointing of gladness (Psalm 45.7 and Hebrews 1.9). Choose a life of happiness and responsibility, wherever there is a will, there is a way. Winston Churchill once said, 'He who wants to dig will find a spade somewhere.'

Unhealthy Sympathy

Many people continue with a life of blame and complaint when they receive enough sympathy from others. This kind of sympathy does not help but it only encourages the receivers to justify their poverty. People who extend such sympathy do so out of goodness and it does not occur to them that they are not doing the best. Even though one is not expected to trouble a poor man as Job's friends did, the sympathy should be accompanied with a positive advice. Again, the victim must be willing to listen and to accept the advice; lest the potential adviser will lack the courage to give his advice. People in this category don't mind spending all their lives depending on others and if any man tries not to show any sympathy, he would be termed an enemy. They won't mind using the Scripture to attract more sympathy. They can quote; "*Give, and it will be given to you…*" (Luke 6.38 - NKJV) but will never think of being givers. When they are young, they will look for Bible verses that talk about parents taking care of their children. But when they begin to advance in age, they will look for Bible verses that talk about children taking care of their parents. They can tell the story of the Good Samaritan but will always accept to play the role of the victimized traveller.

A good number of people, once they develop this kind of mindset, do spend their entire lives accepting sympathy. Sometimes it takes a harsh rebuke from a passionate or violent adviser to throw such people out of their comfort zone. And when many of such people make a step out of their comfort zone, they wonder why they spent a reasonable part of their lives accepting sympathy.

It is good for a man to accept sympathy if he meets any misfortune but he shouldn't allow the misfortune to dictate the rest of his life. He should disabuse his mind from keeping a list of sympathizers for that is where the problem starts. If the sympathizers are not forth coming, bitterness will enter. On the other hand if enough sympathizers continue to troop in, that would build a comfort zone of irresponsibility. Sometimes you even see people who would stop going to Church and attending fellowships just because they did not receive enough visits when they had a tragedy. In most cases, such people would not call their priest or pastor or fellowship leader or fellow members. They would assume in their minds that everybody ought to know about their tragedy by I-don't-know-how. Having the mind of a giver rather than that of a receiver will go a long way to deliver people in this category. Jesus says,

…'It is more blessed to give than to receive.'

Acts 20.35 (NKJV)

Erroneous Lifestyle

A good number of people believe that blaming others and complaining all the time is an effective way of achieving their aims. Even though lodging complaints might be needed in certain circumstances to call proper attention; that should not become a lifestyle. Essentially, a Christian can make a complaint concerning a matter but he should not feel at home with blaming people. Even if such people are at fault, taking up blame as a song could be irritating and would end up not solving the problem. Once a point is made and the person at fault sees his wrong; that should be enough. Repeating the blame will only be an act to fill the mind of the offender with guilt. Even when the offender acts to the pleasing of the person singing the blame song, he does so out of fear and guilt, not out of love. Using such a tool for manipulating others is only a characteristic of the devil himself. In the Bible, he was called

…the accuser of our brethren…

Revelation 12.10 (NKJV)

Consequently, when people continue in such a lifestyle, hoping to have a financial breakthrough from its outcome, they will be disappointed. For the Bible says,

A man cannot be established through wickedness…

Proverbs 12.3 (NIV)

Some people who take to this path may succeed for one or two times and then return to a worse condition. Whereas some people do it intentionally, others get involved in it out of ignorance. But the same outcome awaits them both when it comes to finance, and that is poverty. Even when a complaint is made to a godly man and he attends to it with kindness, if such complaints continue to come from the same source, the godly man will become tired of it. Some folks won't mind telling their stories of how their complaints in the past were attended to with immediate effect but presently, no one seems to be concerned. It does not occur to them that people are tired about their complaints. To such folks, the word 'Improvisation' is only a grammatical construction. Such people would rather die complaining than lift one finger to do anything for themselves, especially when they have a situation where complaint had attracted an immediate action. The Bible says,

A little sleep, a little slumber, a little
folding of the hands to rest—and poverty
will come on you like a bandit and scarcity
like, an armed man.

Proverbs 6.10-11 (NIV)

Poverty never asks why you are folding your hands before attacking you. Even if you just sent the ninety-ninth petition concerning your finances to the appropriate authorities, poverty will still strike as long as you are found folding your hands and doing nothing. If a man can write petitions concerning his problems to the appropriate authorities, it is good. But it would be better if by the time the authorities are receiving his letters, he would have solved his problems by himself. In actual life, many complaints on personal finances do not come in form of a letter but verbally. And in many cases, the person to whom the complaint is being made is not under obligation to attend to the complaint. Who knows whether such a person has his own personal problems and another man somewhere is relaxing on his bed hoping that his own problem would be solved first by the same person?

Bandwagon

Many people are carried away by a life of blame and complaint when the majority of people are doing the same. It works like justifying poverty; people easily follow the band wagon. There is a great relationship between blame and complaint, and the justification of poverty. Once people can do away with blame and complaint and take the responsibility for their lives, they will stop justifying poverty. And that is the first step out of poverty.

If we consider the case of the Israelites again, we will see that the complaint for meat was not raised by the Israelites but by the mixed multitude (Numbers 11.4). The Israelites had been following the ways of the Lord as they journeyed in the wilderness. It never came to their mind that they had not tasted meat for long and they never suffered from any deficiency disease for lack of meat. But the mixed multitude that only saw signs and wonders in Egypt but never knew God, reminded the Israelites about meat. The mixed multitude was made up of people whose life had not been so good in Egypt and they saw the exodus of the Israelites as an opportunity to try a new life. They were people who had tasted frustration in their lives and were seeking comfort. They were people whose histories were not well defined and their future not certain. Why then would the Israelites turn to listen to their reasoning? One thing you should understand is that it is easy to lay blames and make complaints. And if you are not careful, you will see yourself ranting blames and complaints in the company of people who do not know their left from their right. This could be taken care of by knowing the kind of people you move with. Moving around with people who will never accept their responsibility can be risky. Even when you try to improvise a solution, they can encourage you to wait for the solution to come from somewhere else. The Bible says,

Be not deceived: evil communications
corrupt good manners.

1 Corinthians 15:33 (KJV)

One question you will always ask yourself is: 'This crowd that is raising blames and complaints, what kind of life do they live?' You can decide to tread the easy path and become like them or you can decide to walk out of the comfort zone of laying blames and complaints. One thing that is common among such crowd given to blame and complaint is that they are always self-centered and none is willing to make any sacrifice for the common good. But in essence, where there is love and unity, and people are willing to help one another, not counting whose duty it is to render such help, they will see themselves out of poverty. The Bible says in Psalm 133.3 that God commands blessing for such a place.

In conclusion, accepting the responsibility for one's life is the best he can do for himself to move out of poverty. Forgiving all the people he thinks have contributed to his poverty including himself is necessary. There is not enough time to be wasted on blaming others. Even if a complaint is made, that shouldn't be enough reason to fold one's hands doing nothing. Taking the responsibility for your life is like starting a journey with a right step in the right direction.

SOLUTION

A Word of Advice

It is time for you to live a life of gratitude. Never waste any time in bitterness and grudges. Many have spent their lives in blame and complaints but gained nothing from it. No matter the difficulty, taking up the responsibility for your life is the key to greatness. Of course, it's the key to keeping away from poverty.

Practical Questions

1. Do you think that people should hold those who make them poor responsible for their poverty?

2. After holding such people responsible and they are doing nothing about it, do you suggest that the poor people should spend the rest of their lives in poverty?
3. Have you seen children born into riches who grew to be poor?
4. Have you seen children born into poverty who grew to be rich?
5. If yes, what do you think makes such people rich?
6. Do you believe that responsibility plays a role even in the midst of God's blessing?

A Verse for Inspiration

In everything give thanks; for this is the
will of God in Christ Jesus for you.

1Thessalonians 5.18 (NKJV)

CHAPTER

3

Procrastination

"I'll just take a short nap," he says; "I'll fold
my hands and rest a while." But while
he sleeps, poverty will attack him
like an armed robber.

Proverbs 6.10-11 (GNT)

Procrastination is to postpone or delay doing something especially as a habit.

Not doing things as and when due makes people to lose opportunities that may never come again. You won't be surprised to see that many people who are poor hardly do things when they are due. They hardly repair things when the damage is minimal only to spend heavily when it gets worse. They will always say 'tomorrow' without taking thought that today was the tomorrow they wished for yesterday. They rarely believe that a little thing they neglect today can lead to their poverty tomorrow. It is easy for such people to think that everything could be done at any other time. But in actual sense,

To everything there is a season…

Ecclesiastes 3.1 (NKJV)

There are some things that can't wait. If you fail to do them when they are due, there might not be another good time to do them again. There are things a man should do in the days of his childhood. There are things a man should do in the days of his youth. There are things a man should do when he is married. There are things a man should do when he is old. If a man fails to do any of these at its proper time, he may not have the opportunity to do them again. In the words of John Mason, 'Procrastination is a grave in which opportunity is buried.' Even those who come to realize themselves later, have to pay higher prices for such things. The same rule applies to finances. God does not want us to be hasty in our dealings especially when it comes to financial matters, He wants us to consider such matters very well but whenever we have reached our decisions He does not expect us to procrastinate our actions for no good reason. The Bible says,

Whatever presents itself for you to do,
do it with [all] your might, because there
is no work, planning, knowledge, or
skill in the grave where you're going.

Ecclesiastes 9.10 (GW)

God always provides opportunities for the prosperity of His children but He won't come down from heaven to compel them to take action. Thus, we don't expect Him to be pleased when His children miss such opportunities only for them to come back for another. However, there are things that promote procrastination.

Lack of Seriousness

Many people are given to procrastination because they are unserious about their lives and finances. People in this category believe that what will be will be. They are so carried away that they can argue that hard work is not a factor if one must walk into the life of abundance. Even when God answers their prayers and grants them opportunities, they would treat it with levity, believing that if that one does not work God will provide another. With such a mindset, those people don't mind postponing their actions. Right from their school days, they will always be among the last to enter the classroom. And of course will always sit at the back. They will always be among the last to submit their assignments (that is when they submit at all). They will always postpone their studies until the examination comes very close. Even after school, they will always come late to appointments. Their spiritual lives are also not spared. They can postpone their personal Bible studies until they forget about it. They can postpone their prayer times until they have to resolve to say only 'The Lord's Prayer'.

A person in this kind of life would easily say, 'I don't allow anything to bother me.' The word sounds good and spiritually mature, but the truth is that for him; it is a matter of an unserious individual. No serious individual takes delight in dealing with unserious individuals. If you pick out any great or successful man, not only in terms of finance but in other aspects of life, you can count hundreds of people he had interacted with through his life. And if you check those people you will see that at one point or the other they had the same opportunities with the great man, only that the man made use of his opportunities.

Premature Rest

People easily procrastinate if they think that there is still time. This kind of assumption can be very costly. Even when everything is saying that there is time, it is better you do what is before you immediately and rest later. As long as you are not God, you don't have the complete knowledge of what will happen next. And whenever God presents any opportunity before you, He is not interested in procrastination. God does not do things early, neither does He do things late; He does everything at the right time. The Bible says,

He has set the right time for everything.

Ecclesiastes 3.11 (GNT)

Something can come up and you think that you have up to three weeks to do it. So you decide to rest for two weeks before doing it. In your mind, you may think that you are smart since you will be one week ahead of time but that might be something for which God allocated only one week for you. When such is the case, immediately that one week is over, you will find out that it will be difficult to make it. Now, think of this, will it be better to tell your children how you did many things on time and rested later or will you take delight in listing to them many things you would have done—but never did.

The reason why I will emphasize that you are not God even when you seem to know the future is that God not only knows the future but He is the one that makes the future. You can be a smart person, you can be a man of faith, but you should know that you are only one out of billions of people on earth today. You can talk about being another Elijah that held the whole earth to ransom through prayer or like Joshua that held the solar system to ransom through prayer. You should also remember that God has poured out His Spirit on all flesh. If you pray that it should not rain for one week only in your city because you want to procrastinate, do you know the number of men of God in that locality, even with higher anointing, who will fast and pray for it to rain because they need it? The men of faith you see in the Bible prayed out of necessity and not for the sake of procrastination. According to Henry Ford, 'Success comes to the man who does today what others thought of doing tomorrow.'

Whenever God places something before you and gives you the ability to do it; that is the time He wants you to do it. Don't think you can still do it sometime later. That time may never come. God asked Job,

Have you commanded the morning
since your days began…

Job 38.12 (NKJV)

Many people die and go to hell without accepting Christ because they think that there is still time for them. In the same way, many people continue to live in poverty because they failed to do what they were supposed to do when they had the opportunity, thinking that there is still time.

Looking for the Perfect Time

Many people procrastinate because they are waiting for the perfect time to act. This is not a call for hasty living, but when matters that need action come up, they usually never come with perfect times for actions. This is always typical of beautiful opportunities. For such opportunities, you have to create the time for actions yourself. The Bible says,

Those who wait for perfect weather
will never plant seeds; those who look
at every cloud will never harvest crops.

Ecclesiastes 11.4 (NCV)

One thing you should know about good opportunities is that they don't come with perfect time open to everybody. Again, whenever good opportunities come with a relatively good time, they are taken immediately, but such ones are not seen all the time. What a wise man does in his life is to learn principles and acknowledge exceptions. But it is unfortunate that many people spend their lives looking for exceptions. In all the miracles Jesus did in the Bible, there was always an exhibition of faith at least from a third party. Nevertheless, there were exceptions where Jesus made the first move Himself out of mercy. An example was the man at the pool of Bethesda in John chapter 5. However, you should also know that the man spent thirty eight years before receiving the miracle. The point is that if you wait for a perfect time, you are likely to end up doing nothing. The Scripture admonishes:

Make good use of every opportunity you
have, because these are evil days.

Ephesians 5.16 (GNT)

Some people will come with the excuse that they don't want to be hasty. They say they like to take their time before making decisions but that is different from taking time before actions. Though we commonly count making a decision to choose and making a decision to act as the same, they are not. Making a decision to choose is all about accepting or rejecting an opportunity. It might be based on moral ground, spiritual ground, ability, etc. This is where the core decisions are made and maturity plays an important role on how fast or slow the decisions are made. It is here that people will either get it right or wrong. The next stage is making a decision to act. Once an acceptance has been made, there ought not to be any reason for delay. At this stage, there is no need to wait for a perfect time. A perfect time only exists for an opportunity when it meets a man who is prepared. Those opportunities that seem to come with relatively good times are simply those that require less preparation. And I will say again that such don't come all the time. Even when they come, they are taken immediately by those who are first to meet them.

Meanwhile, you should know that perfect times never exist objectively. It is only a matter of perception. To the wise, the only thing they need is to find an acceptable opportunity, and then they will create the perfect time. This is how many people languish in poverty; waiting for a time when they will see an angel that will come and tell them that the perfect time has come for them to act upon the opportunity God has given to them.

Purposeless Life

When people don't have any purpose or goal in life, they procrastinate habitually. It is said that for a man who does not know where he is going, any door could lead to his destination. A lot of people have surrendered their lives to fate and confess with their mouth that it is faith. Meanwhile, faith looks on towards something. The Bible says,

Faith means being sure of things we hope for…

Hebrews 11.1 (NCV)

For faith that brings provision to be in existence, there must be something you are hoping for. When people look up to God for healing, with faith they receive their healing. In the same way, when people look up to God for financial healing, with faith, they receive it. It is when people are not expecting anything that they can easily postpone their actions when the opportunity comes around. It is simply because they can't even identify the opportunity. It is the purpose a man has in his heart that motivates him. It is very difficult to discourage a man of purpose. For even when he is not where he is going to, he knows the path, and the goal encourages him to move on. For such a man, immediately he sees the door of opportunity, it will be difficult for him to procrastinate taking the right step. The Scripture makes us to understand in the book of Hebrews 12.2 that Jesus Christ endured the shameful death on the cross because of the joy that was set before Him. He knew what He was looking up to. He knew His purpose while on earth. Thus, He did not procrastinate His preaching, His teaching, His miracles and the rest of His good works. He knew that He did not have eternity to do His good works on earth for His goal to be achieved. He was termed demon-possessed. He was termed a mad man and His own family came to take Him home. Perhaps, they even went with chains to bind Him. He was accused of a lot of things but the vision of His goal was always before Him. In the Gospel of John when His brothers tried to question His vision,

…Jesus told them, 'The right time for me has not yet come; for you any time is right.'

John 7.6 (NIV)

Any time can do for people without vision but not for people with vision. Many people keep on praying for God to grant them financial breakthrough. They can recount their fasting and their prayers over time, which seem to have no answers. But if you ask God, He will tell you that He had been sending answers only that the supposed recipients do push them aside. They always do so because they have no vision of what they are looking for. The Bible says,

Where there is no vision [no redemptive revelation of God], the people perish…

Proverbs 29.18 (AMP)

Now, whenever the word 'Vision' is mentioned, three things come to mind. One is the physical eye sight. And of all physical challenges, blindness is the worst. Then the next is a goal one is looking forward to. It is the mental creation of the future one is looking for. This is where a lot of wise people dwell. But for Christians, there is another level which is revelation. This one is God's guidance for one's purpose or goal. It is having one's goal in line with the will of God. Or simply put: having one's goal inside the will of God. It is having insight into the will of God. And when one follows this level of vision, God will watch over him to fulfill it. This level of vision is beyond human goals; it is all about God.

In all, vision enables one to identify an opportunity when it comes and to act upon it without delay. God's Word as revealed in the Scripture gives us a clear vision for life and godliness. Not just for godliness alone but for life also. And that includes our financial life. A look at the words of Peter will make us to see it better:

As His divine power has given to us all
things that pertain to life and godliness,
through the knowledge of Him who
called us by glory and virtue,

2 Peter 1.3 (NKJV)

In conclusion, procrastination has never been a good idea. We can see in the book of Genesis that God worked before resting. And the same is expected for men. Time is precious, make good use of them. Take time to consider opportunities but when you accept them, do not waste time to act.

SOLUTION

A Word of Advice

It is time for you to start utilizing the opportunities God is sending your way without procrastination. It is better for you to tell your testimonies while you are resting than for you to recount your regrets just because of a little delay. Get serious with your life and do away with postponement of your actions.

Practical Questions

1. Do you have anything you have accepted to do but have postponed the action?
2. What is actually your reason for postponing the action?
3. Have you ever missed any opportunity because of delay?
4. Do you believe that one can miss an opportunity because of delay?
5. Can you change times and seasons?
6. Do you believe it is a good idea to work before resting?
7. Do you believe that God expects you to act whenever He sends an opportunity on your way without delay?
8. Are you ready to move into action now?
9. If no, why not?

A Verse for Inspiration

I must work the works of him that sent me, while it is day: the night cometh, when no man can work.

John 9.4 (KJV)

CHAPTER

4

Faulty Goals

For which of you, intending to build
a tower, does not sit down first and
count the cost, whether he has enough
to finish it—

Luke 14.28 (NKJV)

Something is faulty when it is structurally incomplete or contains mistakes, and it ends up not working well. On the other hand, a goal is a result that someone wants to achieve. Thus, goals become faulty when they are structurally incomplete or contain mistakes, and they end up not being achievable.

It is good to set big goals but when they become unreasonable, there will be no capacity to achieve them. When people venture into such financial goals, they are bound to fail and after many fruitless efforts they won't only be discouraged but would be frustrated as well. In some cases, immediately people set such goals they will see the big mountain and be discouraged even without taking a step. And such people usually resign to fate believing that they can't achieve anything, though the problem was with their goal setting. There is a great need for wisdom, knowledge and understanding in effective goal setting. Knowledge is awareness of facts. It is having the right information and in this case, concerning the financial goal you want to set. Understanding means knowing the relationship among those facts. It involves knowing how they come about, how they behave and how they interact with each other. And finally, wisdom is the right application of knowledge. It involves making good judgement.

Now, the three things work together; knowledge acquires information, understanding interprets the information and wisdom applies the interpreted information. Wisdom also entails acquiring more knowledge and the cycle goes on and on. Looking at the Scripture will throw more light on these three things:

Through skillful and godly Wisdom
is a house (a life, a home, a family)
built, and by understanding it is
established [on a sound and good
foundation], And by knowledge shall
its chambers [of every area] be filled
with all precious and pleasant riches.

Proverbs 24.3-4 (AMP)

We can see from this Bible passage that wisdom has to do with building which is application. Understanding has to do with establishment which is solidification or comprehension. Knowledge has to do with filling which is acquisition. When all these three are applied to a financial goal, there won't just be success but an established success. When the three are not complete, success might not be said to be guaranteed. Zeal without knowledge can lead to progress in the wrong direction. Progress without understanding can be a temporary affair. Progress without wisdom can lead to disaster. All three apply to every aspect of human life including finance and financial goals. When the three are available, they enable a man to calculate his goals aright and know whether he could go for it. He will also know whether the benefit is worth the cost. In many circumstances wisdom is used to refer to all. And when wisdom is lacking, a man may work hard but may not be effective. The Bible says,

The labor of fools wearies them, For they do not even know how to go to the city!

Ecclesiastes 10.15 (NKJV)

Though such individuals labour themselves until they are wearied, they cannot get to their destination. They cannot achieve their faulty financial goals. The Bible calls it 'the labor of fools.' As it is important for a man to be zealous, energetic and full of faith in order to achieve his financial goals, it is essential that his goals be set in wisdom. We can take a look at another Bible passage:

If the ax is dull, And one does not sharpen the edge, Then he must use more strength; But wisdom brings success.

Ecclesiastes 10.10 (NKJV)

Now, there are many reasons for which a goal could be said to be faulty.

Undefined Goal

A goal that is not well defined is like an invisible target. People set goals both consciously and unconsciously. However, people only achieve their goals consciously. Setting goals unconsciously is a daily affair common to mankind but such goals are usually minor goals. Their achievement is usually automatic and the time frame is also short. When you talk about meaningful financial goals, they may not be necessarily long term but they are not the short automatic ones. An example of the ones I call short automatic goals is a man who wakes up in the morning to discover that his car does not delight him any longer. Then he thinks of selling the car, he picks his mobile phone or laptop to put it on sale on the internet. Maybe in a matter of hours or days he can sell the car. That morning, selling the car was the man's goal but it was automatic and he might not be conscious of the fact that he had set a goal. Nevertheless, it was achieved. But if the man had woken up in the morning to think of starting up a car sales business, the goal setting would be definitely conscious. Another example is a woman that wakes up in the morning and thinks of preparing breakfast for her family. She can achieve the goal unconsciously but if she thinks of starting up a restaurant, she will need a conscious planning.

Now the first problem people face about goal setting is trying to treat their financial life goals like the short automatic goals. Some people's financial goal is simply to become rich but they can't say how rich they want to become. They just have it as a thought and nothing more. Though goal setting starts in the form of a thought, it cannot be actualized like that without having a clear vision about it especially on sensitive matters like one's financial life goals. It is common for every business owner to be thinking of increasing the size of the business but having it as a mere thought would be the same as leaving it to fate. In the same way, a worker who earns monthly salary and thinks of becoming rich, if the thought is only kept like that in his head, he would likely end up like others who have retired from that same job.

What makes a thought to become a goal is its definition. It is the definition that gives life to the goal. It gives the goal direction. It moves the goal from a general statement to a distinctive statement. If you are looking for a man, you don't just enter his street and tell anybody that you are looking for a man. It can be possible that the first person you will meet in the street will be a man. It's obvious that you cannot meet a man and ask him that you are looking for a man. For you to find the man you are looking for, you must describe him. You must describe his height, his complexion, his age bracket and so on. The more of his features you know the easier for you to find him. Besides, knowing his name will do a lot better. The same rule applies to financial goals, the more characteristics you know and specify about the goal, the easier for you to achieve it. There are qualities that must be considered in order to have an effective and efficient goal. The first is giving the goal a unique name. It is not just inventing a name but calling the goal by its name. Every form of ambiguity must be dealt with and every spade must be called a spade. If at this time you feel ashamed of the name of the goal, then you better think twice. What makes this part of goal setting more effective is writing. See what the Bible says about it:

The Lord gave me this answer: "Write down clearly on tablets what I reveal to you, so that it can be read at a glance.

Habakkuk 2.2 (GNT)

The same God who gives you the idea of a goal in the form of a thought is the one who demands that you write it down. Writing it down gives you a stable focus on the goal. It keep's you from ignorantly changing the goal from one time to the other due to memory issues. Even when you think that you have the goal intact in your memory, there can be little attributes of the goal that can escape your mind over time. Again writing it down according to the Bible passage helps to clarify the goal and its characteristics. It helps to avoid general statements: instead of a business owner wishing to be rich, he can clearly state that he wants to increase the net worth of his business by hundred percent. He can state that he wants to increase his turnover by two hundred percent and so on. On the side of a worker who receives monthly salary, he would be able to state the things that mean riches for him instead of wishing to be rich. He can state that he wants to live in his own house. He can state that he wants to be taking care of his family needs without struggles. He can state that he wants to have more than enough such that he can be supporting missionary works, education, etc. with specific amount of money annually. He can state that he wants his net worth to be a certain amount of money. He can state the amount he wants to be receiving every month. The clarifications go on and on but at the end, they will make the man to think well. They will make the worker to see clearly whether he could achieve his goal only with his salary or to add another stream of income.

The main thing about this part of goal setting is that everything must be called by a definite name. Instead of saying 'a long distance', you say 'ten kilometers'. Instead of saying 'a long time', you say 'one year'. Instead of saying 'a large sum of money', you mention the definite figure. Nothing should be taken for granted, everything should be counted.

Having known how to call a spade a spade, the second thing to consider in defining a goal is the scope. You have to consider the actual scope and use the naming process to make it alive. The scope is all about the size of the goal. It defines the boundaries of the goal. It defines the things that are part of the goal and the things that are not part of the goal. It is only when the scope is clearly defined that one can measure his progress. And if a man is able to see his progress, he would always be encouraged to move on. Just consider a man who is heading for a destination of unknown distance, if the vehicle breaks down after many hours on the journey he could be easily tempted to join another vehicle going back to where he was coming from if many people are doing so. But let's say the destination was a five hundred kilometer journey and the vehicle breaks down after four hundred and ninety nine kilometers, the man would easily use his legs to complete the remaining distance. And it would be extremely difficult to discourage such a man simply because he knows the scope of his journey. If you ask some poor people, they will narrate to you how they missed out on some opportunities just because they dropped on the way very close to the end.

Again, having a definite scope helps a man not to waste his resources. He will know the things that are directly related to his goal and focus on them. Many poor people do learn by experience after wasting their resources, only to discover that some things are not actually necessary for their goal to be achieved. Furthermore, having a definite scope makes a man to know when his goal is achieved.

Finally, the third thing to consider while defining a goal is its timing. Having given a definite name to the scope of a goal, it won't make any sense if the effort would be endless. Having a definite timing also helps to measure progress. If you are in a vehicle going on a hundred kilometer journey and you are still on the way after one day, you will definitely know that something is wrong somewhere. In such a situation it will be better for you to use your legs. Again, definite timing will discipline you to do things as and at when due for the goal to be achieved. Without definite timing, you can achieve some goals but their usefulness would have passed. Think of fire fighters coming to a fire scene hours after the fire has destroyed everything. In fact, if a man sets a goal without timing, he is simply resigning to fate.

Miscalculated Cost

A goal is bound to fail if the cost is not well calculated. It is clearly spelt out by Jesus Christ our Lord in the introductory verse of this chapter. Setting big and good goals is not bad at all but God expects us to consider sowing as well as reaping. In the Bible God says,

...Seedtime and harvest...Shall not cease.

Genesis 8.22 (NKJV)

He did not say, '(only) harvest shall not cease.' But He said, 'seedtime and harvest shall not cease.' Ordinarily, a goal focuses on the end which is the harvest but for it to be achieved the proper seed must be sown. If your goal is to build a tower, God will help you so that it does not collapse during construction but you must count the cost yourself. You can now ask, 'Where is the place of faith?' Yes, faith works, but on what you have sown. The Bible says,

Then Isaac sowed in that land, and
reaped in the same year a hundredfold;
and the LORD blessed him.

Genesis 26.12 (NKJV)

Now, you can see that Isaac sowed before God multiplied his harvest. Even though you may have a big dream, it is the seed God has placed in your hands that He wants you to sow. The problem is that many people will like to become wealthy instantly without thinking of what to offer. In many cases, you will see where God intends for a man to go through seedtime and harvest for three times before coming to his goal with the seed in his hands. But the man will want the goal immediately. Consequently he will waste his resources and be frustrated. On the other hand, most people that are poor usually look up to a goal of becoming rich but they would never like to think of the commensurate cost. They will always want God to do everything for them. When they are in school, they will like to pass their exams very well. But they will not study hard; instead they will like God to do a miracle for them to pass with just a little study. For some people, the cost of their goal might be sleeping for four hours a day for one year. But they can never sacrifice their sleep; they will rather give up only one hour of their normal eight hours of daily sleep assuming that it will be enough. For some people, it might be walking for long distances every working day to meet potential customers at the initial stage of their business. But they cannot sacrifice their relaxation and will rather choose short distances.

In all this, it is only when one has properly calculated the cost of his goal that he would know whether to continue or not, lest he would be frustrated on the way. It may require that he should reduce the scope of his goal for the moment and increase it later. It may require that he should go and acquire more skills. It may require that he should go and raise more funds. The main thing is that it will prevent him from being frustrated when he is half way into the pursuance of his goal. No goal comes without a cost and until the cost is paid the goal can never be achieved.

Unreasonable Goal

Goal setting must be with proper reasoning lest it will only be a big wish. Now a goal is an aim someone is looking forward to achieve. And goal setting involves the conceptualization of that aim and the plans for its achievement. When a man has a goal before him, it motivates him to carry on and gives him a sense of responsibility that he is not running aimlessly. However, all such aims must be reasonable. Even in the presence of faith, reasoning is not suspended. Faith is only a higher level of reasoning. Faith is not arbitrary.

One big mistake many poor people make is having an unrealistic target. They always want to get all in one fell swoop. But the Bible tells us that our walk of righteousness is from faith to faith (Romans 1.17). The same applies in finances. It is from one stage to another. Many times, you see people setting goals that could be compared to a nursery school pupil aiming to acquire a PhD degree in one year. For such people, their aims are right but their timing makes it unreasonable.

On the other hand, many people set goals that have nothing to do with reasoning. One can easily laugh at the story of some old communities that tried to bring down the moon. I don't need to tell you whether they succeeded or not. But in our present world, people still set goals that could be compared to that. Sometimes you see people starting up a business with exaggerated projection of profit margins. By the end of the day, they will spend heavily in anticipation of a heavy profit which will not come. The Bible says,

...the one who chases unrealistic dreams
has no sense.

Proverbs 12.11 (GW)

Sometimes you see people without skills that want to manufacture things that need high technology on their own and end up manufacturing toys. Nonetheless, a closer look at many of such goals that seem to be unrealistic shows that for a greater number, the problem is not with the aims themselves but how to go about their achievement. And that includes the capacity to achieve them.

In conclusion, a man can dream big, but let him start within his capacity. Optimism is good but knowledge makes it effective.

SOLUTION

A Word of Advice

It is good that you always dream big dreams but make sure you plan for its achievement very well. Make sure you count the cost before making the first step. Understand that dreaming big does not imply dreaming wild. People around may not understand your dream but let it agree with the Word of God.

Practical Questions

1. Do you believe that you can achieve great dreams with little steps, each at a time?
2. Do you believe that you are to launch out for the pursuance of your dreams and take whatever that comes out of it?
3. Do you believe that God wants us to plan even when he has given us a goal to achieve?
4. Is every goal achievable?
5. Is there any room for reasoning in goal setting?
6. What do you think can frustrate the achievement of a goal?
7. Is anything holding you from launching out for your financial goals?

A Verse for Inspiration

Prepare your work outside, and get
things ready for yourself in the field.
Afterwards, build your house.

Proverbs 24.27 (GW)

CHAPTER

5

Idle Wishes

Indolence wants it all and gets nothing;
the energetic have something to show
for their lives.

Proverbs 13.4 (The Message)

Something can be said to be idle when it is not doing anything. In this context, as it relates to human beings, a man can be said to be idle when he is not doing anything, especially when he is unwilling to do anything. On the other hand, a wish is a desire for something. Thus to have an idle wish is to desire something while doing nothing and unwilling to do anything to achieve it.

Many people are poor today because they spend their lives expecting to reap from where they did not sow. Such people imagine beautiful things of life and are encouraged by the joyful mental pictures but they never think of walking towards them. All their expectation is that those beautiful things will just come their way anyhow anytime. This kind of people is quite different from those that set faulty goals. For those with faulty goals, some get discouraged when they see the mountainous goals they have set. And some get frustrated along the line while executing those goals. But for those with idle wishes they only dream about beautiful things of life and nothing more; they just want the dreams to come true, that's all. You can say that they set goals but never plan for its achievement. They can spend a good time talking about such goals or dreams but when the question comes, 'How do you plan to achieve it?' they will either become speechless or take offence. They believe so much that what will be will be, no matter what happens. They believe that life is all about luck. It is very easy for such people to go into the life of lottery and gambling. They only care for the end and not the means. Even the Christians among them will quote the Scripture where it says,

'Everything is possible for one who believes.'

Mark 9.23 (NIV)

They will gladly give an unwholesome interpretation to the word 'Believe'. They fail to see that the same Scripture says,

In the same way, faith by itself, if it is not accompanied by action, is dead.

James 2.17 (NIV)

One thing about people in this category is that they can easily give in to temptations. Since they have the mental picture of the good things of life, their unconscious minds desire them but their conscious minds make no effort to get them. Thus, any opportunity that presents itself is usually accepted whether good or bad.

Most of the time, many people find themselves in this kind of life and they wallow in it without knowing it. Meanwhile, it does not just happen; many things cause it to be.

Knowledge without Action

Laziness knows good things but cannot go after them. This chapter's introductory verse says that indolence (which is habitual laziness) wants it all and gets nothing. A lazy man can do a lot of things as long as it is not work. He can talk a lot as long as it is not a work. He can dream a lot as long as it not a work. Of course, he loves to sleep and will always want to have everything on his own terms. In the same way he will always want to have his desires on his own terms (which will mean having them without working for them). However, the Bible says,

Be not deceived; God is not mocked:
for whatsoever a man soweth, that
shall he also reap.

Galatians 6.7 (KJV)

If a man sows nothing, he will also reap nothing. If a man sows wishes he will also reap wishes. There is a saying that you cannot build something on nothing and expect it to stand. Idle wishes never come to reality. Idle wishes are always idle for they are always found in idle minds. They perish in idleness for there are no active hands to push them into reality.

Misinterpretation of Success Stories

People wallow in idle wishes when they misinterpret the success of others. Testimonies abound on how God blesses His people. He raises poor people from nothing all the time. But in all these, everyone's destiny and relationship with God is unique. It is usually easy to desire the beautiful sides of people's testimonies without thinking about the difficult sides. But is essence, it is the difficult side that produces the beautiful side. The Bible says,

Those who sow in tears will
reap with songs of joy.

Psalm 126.5 (NIV)

Normally, a man can cry in the secret and sing for joy in the open. Now, it behooves anyone who wants to sing like that man to ask of how he cried while sowing his seeds. Sitting down to wish for a man's success just because he is a Christian and you are a Christian may not bring you any good. Everything must be taken into consideration. It is good to ask questions. It is good to know the different steps successful people took if one is interested in their success. And such a person must be ready to pay the price they paid.

Wishful Thinking

Wishful thinking easily degenerates into idle wishes. As I have explained before, to have idle wishes is having imaginations of good things and nothing more. There is no plan to achieve them and there is no willingness to pay any price for their achievement. On the other hand, wishful thinking is planning to achieve things on one's own terms rather than based on reason or reality or laid down principles. Unlike a lazy man whose terms is always to have his desires without working for it, many people in this state of life can be willing to plan for the achievement of their financial goals. And also, they are willing to pay the price but the problem is doing everything on their own terms. This is when a man thinks subjectively instead of thinking objectively. If a man desires to build a tower, it will be a good idea but he cannot do that on shallow sand and expect it to stand; no matter how he loves sand. By the end of the day, the man indulging in wishful thinking will become a brother to the man indulging in idle wishes.

Moreover, a man indulging in wishful thinking can move his mind between paying less the right price for the achievement of his goal and paying nothing. And when it is at the point of 'nothing', it simply becomes idle wishes. However, when people waste their lives in wishful thinking over time, they tend to settle with idle wishes.

Misinterpreting the Bible

Wrong interpretations of some Biblical teachings send people into idle wishes. The Bible says,

…the desire of the righteous shall
be granted.

Proverbs 10.24 (KJV)

But the Bible in no way declares that a righteous man should sit back in his house desiring good things without making a move. Many people tend to hang on a Bible passage like this to give themselves over to idle wishes. The difference between a righteous man and a wicked man is that the righteous commits his plans to God, and God helps him but not so with the wicked. The Bible did not say that the righteous only desires but rather, his desires are granted because God blesses his work. God don't bless idle wishes. The Bible says,

The soul of the sluggard desireth, and
hath nothing: but the soul of the
diligent shall be made fat.

Proverbs 13.4(KJV)

The second issue on this is the fact that our lives are determined by what and how we think. The Bible says,

Be careful how you think; your life
is shaped by your thoughts.

Proverbs 4.23 (GNT)

Many people hang on this fact and spend their lives in idle wishes. Even though your thoughts attract a lot of things to your life, you must make a step to receive those things. The totality of your thoughts should also include how you intend to work, in other words, what you intend to give in return. It is wrong for people to teach and believe that you can only think for good things while sitting back in your house and they will locate you even when you have done nothing. Truly, I can tell you that God still sends manna from heaven. Nevertheless, you must go out to gather it according to God's rules for manna collection.

In conclusion whatever a man harbours in his mind finds its way out in the man's action. Even if he tries to cover it up it must still show up. Thinking of good things only will not be of benefit to anyone. In such thinking, adding plans for the achievement of such goals will go a long way to help, since everything will then be manifested in action; i.e. the good things and the plans to achieve them.

SOLUTION

A Word of Advice

Thinking about a good financial life is the first step in setting your financial goals. Nevertheless, if you don't make plans on how to achieve them and what to give in return for their attainment, everything will remain in that first step. So, as you think of good things of life make plans for their achievement and begin to put the plans into action. With God on your side, you will begin to see such wishes coming into manifestation.

Practical Questions

1. Are there good things of life or financial status you are looking up to?
2. Do you think that those things will just come, merely because you are thinking about them?
3. Do you think that most of the poor people you see don't think about good things of life?
4. If poor people think about good things of life, why are some people still dying poor?
5. Can you now begin to consider how to achieve that financial status of your dream?
6. Are you now ready to start making the necessary moves?
7. If no, why not?

A Verse for Inspiration

Commit your works to the LORD,
And your thoughts will be established.

Proverbs 16.3 (NKJV)

CHAPTER

6

Dishonesty

Dishonest money dwindles away,
but he who gathers money little
by little makes it grow.

Proverbs 13.11 (NIV)

Dishonesty is the quality of being characteristically deceitful.

Many people are poor not because they never had opportunities but because they abused their opportunities. It always looks easy and simple to make money through the back door but a little thought of wisdom will keep one out of it. A little wisdom will show you the consequences. But the devil has blinded the eyes of many people that when they get opportunities to build their finances, they will like to get everything in one fell swoop. Once such a thing happens, they will close that channel. The bad thing there is that not only the channel will close, but all other channels known to that particular channel. No matter how much a man makes from dishonesty, he will continue to spend it until it is all spent, besides, God Himself opposes such a fellow.

Many people lose their jobs simply because of dishonesty. And no matter how they repent later or the level of their skills, their employer may not consider taking them back. The Bible asks,

Will the wild ox be willing to serve you …
Will you trust him because his strength
is great? Or will you leave your
labor to him?

Job 39.9,11 (NKJV)

Everything a man does in his life is a test for something higher. No one can tell who is watching. Even in little things (I mean things that are negligible), your honesty counts. Faithfulness in such little things can open doors for great prosperity. But it is common for many people to neglect such little things and display dishonesty, hoping that when bigger things come their way, they will display honesty. But in essence, they will remain where they are, for nobody will consider them for anything of greater financial commitment. Jesus says,

Whoever can be trusted with a little can
also be trusted with a lot, and whoever
is dishonest with a little is dishonest
with a lot.

Luke 16.10 (NCV)

It is not a new thing to see businesses closing down simply because the owners are dishonest and are cheating their customers. The news of cheating a customer spreads faster than when a customer is satisfied. But when customers are satisfied over time, the business will build a good reputation. Good reputation is an asset to a business and it is sometimes termed 'Goodwill'. The same is true whether the business is a large corporation or a one-man business.

Having seen the disadvantages of dishonesty, one may begin to ask, 'Why are people still dishonest?' Understanding the answers to this question will help people not only to build their financial lives but their whole lives.

A Life without Christ

Many people are dishonest simply because they have not given their lives to Christ. One good thing everyone should know is this; when a man gives his life to Christ, his life will become a gift to others. People struggle with many sinful habits and many have tried with many man-made rules all to no avail. Those who seemed to have done well can only be termed 'good men'. But being a good man is all about morality. And morality is a function of time and place. I once read of a Christian missionary that went to New Guinea. And it happened that the people he met were not interested in the good things he was teaching. They only enjoyed the story of how Judas betrayed Jesus Christ. For them at that time, to be a dishonest man meant a smart person. That is just an example of morality. You should also know that in a city of liars, half-truth would be celebrated. Jesus also talked about a man having his light to be darkness (Matthew 6.22-23). Such a man can be dishonest but in his own eyes, he is good enough. That is why the Bible says,

The people who walked in darkness
Have seen a great light…

Isaiah 9.2 (NKJV)

In this place, the prophet was prophesying about Jesus Christ for He is actually the true Light which gives light to every man (John 1.9). And when Jesus came into the world He said,

Come to Me, all you who labor and
are heavy laden, and I will give you
rest.

Matthew 11.28 (NKJV)

He said this to people labouring under the yoke and burden of sin. He said it to people labouring under the yoke and burden of (struggles with) moral rules. One thing you should understand is that when a man has a good moral standing, he could be called a good man which is relative. But when a man is in Christ Jesus, he will become a righteous man. And righteousness has godly morals as one of its outcomes. Now the Scripture says,

For when we were still without strength, in due time Christ died for the ungodly. For scarcely for a righteous man will one die; yet perhaps for a good man someone would even dare to die.

Romans 5.6-7 (NKJV)

From this passage, it becomes obvious that Christ died both for the ungodly sinner and the morally good man. A man can only be completely honest if he is in Christ. You may not need to trust the man but you can trust the Christ in him. Once you can identify Christ in a man, you don't need to bother about his facial look or his race or level of education; such a person can be trusted. The Bible says,

...if anyone is in Christ, he is a new creation...

2 Corinthians 5.17 (NKJV)

The Word is true for anyone. If dishonest people who are struggling or living with poverty can give up dishonesty and embrace Christ, He will give them a new life. Then they can prove their honesty with new opportunities that will come their way. Only one act of honesty can be enough to lift a man to a good financial standing.

The kind of honesty Christ brings about in a man is the kind that is consistent. Come rain, come wind, come flood, it can never be moved; for it is founded on the Rock which is Christ (Matthew 7.24-25). If you have not given your life to Christ, you can just do it now and receive a new honest heart.

False Principle

A lot of people believe that dishonesty is the only way to make wealth. It is a common belief among many folks that every rich man is corrupt. Those that are struggling with poverty would easily conclude that to break the yoke of poverty, one must compromise his faith. On the other hand, those that acquire their riches through dishonest means would always think that honesty does not pay. From the Scripture, we can see many people questioning 'Why do the wicked prosper?' In Psalm 73, Asaph said,

But as for me, my feet had almost
stumbled; My steps had nearly slipped.
For I was envious of the boastful,
When I saw the prosperity of the wicked.

Psalm 73.2-3 (NKJV)

The same has also been the opinion of many righteous Christians today. But going a little further in the same Psalm 73, Asaph said,

Until I went into the sanctuary of God;
Then I understood their end.

Psalm 73.17 (NKJV)

The only reason why people engage in dishonest activities to make money is because they fail to see the end. They only see the end of acquiring the riches and nothing more. They fail to see the ultimate end itself. They see the riches but fail to see the sorrow. The Scripture says,

The blessing of the LORD makes one rich,
And He adds no sorrow with it.

Proverbs 10.22 (NKJV)

The riches made through dishonesty bring sorrow with it. And in essence, such riches are not true riches. No matter how many people that made or are making riches through dishonesty, a Christian should not be moved. A Christian sees better and should not fret because of dishonest men who don't have the vision of Christ in their lives. The worst state of mind is not when a man has committed a sin but when a man has lost the vision of Christ. Such a man can do anything for money. And the more a man commits nasty things for money, the more he is hardened to commit more evil. The Bible says in Romans 1.28 that God gives people over to a depraved mind when they reject Him. He will definitely bring such people to judgement.

In the first instance, dishonesty usually seems to be a fast way to make riches but such riches are not permanent; they all end in poverty. It is only honest riches that abide.

Temptation

Many people become dishonest when they cannot withstand the temptation. It is a general knowledge that temptation is not sin but when one gives in to temptation, it becomes sin. Some temptations could be withstood easily but some seem to come with great pressure. However, I want you to understand one thing; no one overcomes temptation when it comes, you overcome temptation before it comes. In many cases of financial dishonesty, people tempt themselves by their love for money. The Bible says,

But people are tempted when their
own evil desire leads them away and
traps them.

James 1.14 (NCV)

Yielding to financial dishonesty starts with a great desire for more money, and then to little negligible acts until it gets to the actual financial dishonest act. We learnt from the Scripture that Judas betrayed his Master for money but we must not forget that he had been helping himself with the apostolic fund. If a man should rid his mind of inordinate desire for money by all means, that will be a step in the right direction. Again, a man should make up his mind (and seal it) not to take any money by dishonesty. He must make the decision before the *temptation-money* comes around. We can see in the case of Daniel:

But Daniel purposed in his heart that he would not defile himself with the portion of the king's meat, nor with the wine which he drank…

Daniel 1.8 (KJV)

Without a prior determination, it will be difficult not to give in to financial temptation especially when you need money. Remember that the devil only tempted Jesus with bread when Jesus was hungry. Don't be surprised that it is when a Christian is in true financial need that *temptation-money* will come dancing around his table. It can be when his child is sick and the doctor insists on receiving a certain huge amount before further treatment. It can be when the house rent is due and the landlord insists on ejection if the house rent is not paid. The list can go on and on. It is not when a man is in a situation like this and a dishonest offer is standing before him that he would go and start studying the Bible or to pray for the ability to overcome the temptation. Jesus did not tell the devil, 'Wait I will study the Scripture before giving you an answer.' Rather, He used the Word immediately.

Sometimes, some people would say, 'Let me compromise just once.' But they never know that all corrupt individuals started with only one act of dishonesty. You should know that faithfulness can only be called faithfulness if it is consistent. When people bow to pressures of financial temptation, they may get a temporal relief but the sorrow will follow. And one bad thing about poverty of dishonesty is that no one will be willing to give anything to such a man (as was the case of the prodigal son in Luke 15.16). Prepare your mind; believe in the Word of

God and hold on to your integrity. Pressures of financial temptations will come and go but you will have a good testimony.

Unholy Normality

Many people are dishonest because they think it is part of a normal life. Normality is a function of time and place. And it could be true that whatever the majority of the people are doing in any setting is normal. Nevertheless, a Christian lives by the Word of God and not by normality. Whenever the devil wants to finish a man, he gives him a lie to believe in. The devil can make a man to think that everybody is involved in one act of dishonesty or the other while the man is actually among the few if not the only dishonest person in the neighbourhood.

Jesus tells us that the devil is the father of lies (John 8.44). And whenever a man believes that dishonesty is part of life, it will be difficult for him to change. Such a man can be in the Church even as a Church worker but it will not occur to him to desist from his dishonesty. Even when his dishonesty hits him down to poverty, he will classify himself among those suffering for Christ's sake. He can pray and wait upon God for a breakthrough and when it comes, he will continue with his dishonesty. That is one of the reasons why you see many people who are Christians and are committed in the things of God but are struggling with poverty. Some will try to defend it as giving to Caesar what is Caesar's and giving to God what is God's. But in essence, Christ was referring to government (Caesar) and God. No matter how people look at it, no one will like to commit his finances to a dishonest person. For wealth to be created in any circumstance there must be a trace of trust. Wherever you see people having dishonesty as part of their lives; poverty will not be lacking. The Scripture says,

Righteousness exalts a nation, But
sin is a reproach to any people.

Proverbs 14.34 (NKJV)

In conclusion, dishonesty will always result in poverty. No matter the number of people involved or how long it is practised. Following God's way is all about faith. Faith will make a man to be satisfied with only his just profits while he watches the unjust gain slip away. But at the end, his just profits will accumulate into a big fortune for him. On the other hand, a man who believes that dishonesty is part of life will like to take his just profit as well as the unjust gain. But at the end, the unjust gain will cover his finances in darkness such that even the just profits will no longer be available. The earlier a man gives up dishonesty in totality, the better for him.

SOLUTION

A Word of Advice

The Hebrew word 'Shalom' which means 'Peace' also means 'Wholesomeness' and 'Prosperity'. In other words, prosperity is only wholesome when it comes with peace. A dishonest man is a wicked man and the Bible makes us to understand that there is no peace for the wicked (Isaiah 48.22). In this context, you can say that there is no true prosperity for the wicked. Focus your mind on the ultimate end of the kind of riches you desire and begin to live a life of honesty as an act of faith. It will be only a matter of time and you will be surprised at how far you have gone financially.

Practical Questions

1. Are there people you know that were once rich and dishonest but are now poor?
2. Do you think that those people were not smart enough or that they are reaping the fruit of their dishonesty?
3. Do you think a man can fool others forever?
4. Can you commit your money in the hands of a dishonest person?
5. Do you think other people will like to commit their money in the hands of dishonest persons?

A Verse for Inspiration

So let us not become tired of doing good; for if we do not give up, the time will come when we will reap the harvest.

Galatians 6.9 (GNT)

CHAPTER

7

Laziness/Idleness

Laziness throws one into a deep sleep,
and an idle person will go hungry.

Proverbs 19.15 (GW)

A man is lazy when he is unwilling to work. And a man is idle when he is not working or unwilling to work.

It is as simple as that; anyone who does not work will suffer lack. Even if a man should pile up riches and stop working, it will only be a matter of time; he will likely go below the poverty line. Moreover, God created human beings to be working. Even in the Garden of Eden, before the fall of man, God gave work to man. If you take a closer look at the society, you will discover that when people retire from active service and go home to stay indoors without doing any other thing, they tend to die faster.

Actually, laziness and idleness are not the same but they are twin brothers; they have the same outcome which is lack of income and essentially, poverty. Laziness is the state of being unwilling to work, whereas idleness is the state of not working. Whether a man is unwilling to work or he does not have work to do, the point is that he is not working. And it is not unusual to hear the word, 'No work, no pay'.

In chapter 5 of this book, 'Idle Wishes' was treated but 'Idle Wishes' is not the same as idleness. An idle person is a man who is not doing anything. It might be caused by laziness or any other thing. On the other hand, 'idle wishes' is all about when a man conceives a goal but is unwilling to work towards it. Nevertheless, all of them lead to the state of not doing any work.

Of all the causes of poverty, idleness and laziness guarantee zero income. This is no longer a matter of doing the right work or proper management; it is a matter of empty pocket. It is not the will of God that any man will only be living as a parasite without contributing to his society. Essentially, a man's income is his payment for his contribution to his society. With a greater contribution, he will earn a higher income. And with a small contribution, he will earn little income. Thus, with no contribution, he will earn nothing. The Scripture says,

For even when we were with you,
we gave you this command: Anyone
unwilling to work should not eat.

2 Thessalonians 3.10 (NRSV)

Many idle people can argue that they are not lazy, but a close examination of their cases will show evidence of laziness. Idleness is not the same thing as when a man is doing something but is not yet making income from it. Not having a stable job does not mean idleness; idleness is doing no job. And the chief cause of idleness is laziness. A further examination will reveal more on idleness and laziness.

Disdain for Certain Jobs

Many people are idle because they are not willing to take the available jobs. This idea may not be bad for a young fresh graduate, but when that freshness begins to turn sour, he should take what is available until the desirable comes. Now, in a case like this (i.e. in the sour state), such a person will say that he is not lazy and it seems so. But going by the definition of laziness, which is the state of being unwilling to work, such a person might not be exonerated from the word 'laziness'. Whether it is the laziness of the first order or fifth order or last order or lower order, etc., the individual has something to do with laziness since he is not willing to do the available work. No matter how knowledgeable, skillful and qualified a man is, nobody will pay him when he has done no job. The Bible says,

In all labor there is profit, But
idle chatter leads only to poverty.

Proverbs 14.23 (NKJV)

This has been a major problem with many people who are highly skilled or those who have higher educational qualifications. They always find it difficult to do those things they deem so little for their qualifications. And that is the simple reason why you can see some skilled and educated people with empty pockets. The Bible encourages us to be involved in one labour or the other, for that will guarantee an income. The Bible also encourages starting a work even if it is small:

The people should not think that
small beginnings are unimportant.

Zechariah 4.10 (NCV)

Actually, if God's promise to bless the work of your hands will be accomplished, your hands must be doing something whether big or small. Edmund Burke once said, 'Nobody makes a greater mistake than he who did nothing because he could only do a little.' Another important verse in the Scripture concerning this matter is in the book of Job:

Though thy beginning was small,
yet thy latter end should greatly
increase.

Job 8.7 (KJV)

Many people see the available works staring at them as eating a humble pie but who knows whether that is the place from which God will lift such a person. In any field where you see people doing well financially, you are bound to see people struggling with finances in the same field. In fact, it is in those fields that you will hardly think that people are not struggling with finances that you will find those whose accounts are in red, i.e. those in debts, even big debts. What I want to bring out here is that no matter the field available to you, you can do your work in an extraordinary way. You can go a step further than others. If you start in that small measure available to you, profits may not start flowing in immediately but with time, you will forget the early days of dryness.

Many highly skilled and educated people have spent some years in idleness. But think of it, if they have started something however small, they will not be counting wasted years. Rather, they will be recounting their financial growth.

Wrong Focus

A lot of people are idle because they focus on the big things they cannot do. People in this category can be counted among those who belittle the available opportunities but this category goes further to include people who are afraid of the big task in the opportunities before them. It is easy to notice them among the young people. When they see people who have gone to school, the big books they have studied and the discomforts of studying, they will make up their mind not to go to school. Of course they will conclude that they cannot do it. Among the adults, such folks won't mind reciting the hard tasks that would be involved in the opportunities before them. They are not ready to sacrifice their comfort all in the name of making money. Nonetheless, they need the money. Such mindsets always emanate from laziness. Even when they have the most powerful guns at their disposal and many soldiers as their guards, they will always envision the lion on the road to the gold mine. This kind of people always long for easy life. Even if you take them into a gold mine with a thought that the fear of a lion has been conquered, they will remind you of the news of miners being trapped in the mines. If you decide to take them to a surface mine; they will remind you of miners who died from a sickness caused by the vibrations of the drilling machines. One thing with this kind of people is not just that they hate the difficult tasks; they always love pleasure and easy life. They always like to enjoy life even more than those doing the hard work. The Bible says,

Whoever loves pleasure will become poor. Whoever loves wine and expensive food will not become rich.

Proverbs 21.17 (GW)

Of course, whoever loves pleasure will not like to disturb himself doing what he calls a hard job. Even men that are already working, whenever they begin to love pleasure they will begin to squander their resources.

Another set of individuals in this category of idle people are those who neglect the available jobs because they seem little to their class and then keep on looking for big jobs they are not qualified to do. They look on for the big jobs that will bring the big money without thinking about their own capacity. In the words of Adolphe Monod: 'Between the great things that we cannot do and the small things we will not do, the danger is that we shall do nothing.'

Faulty Childhood Foundation

The laziness and idleness in some people started from their childhood. It is not abnormal to see children who will not like to do anything. It can only become a problem if the child is allowed to grow with it. Children are like fallow grounds, anything can grow naturally in them but their parents or guardians, like farmers, can determine what will grow in them. Let's take a look at the Bible,

Children just naturally do silly,
careless things, but a good
spanking will teach them how
to behave.

Proverbs 22.15 (GNT)

This is where discipline comes in. The Word of God clearly tells us that discipline is needed in bringing up children. There are times to use words of instruction and there are times to use the rod of correction. God knows better than we can imagine. His ways are higher than our ways. And His thoughts are higher than our thoughts (Isaiah 55.9). If God should demand the use of the rod for correction, no human philosophy can be a better option.

Some children can exhibit lazy tendencies when they are still small but that also could easily be changed when they are still small. There is a saying that it is better to train a child than to repair an adult. For the training to be effective as Christians, it must be with the Word of God. From the premise that the Word of God commands many kinds of discipline including the use of words and the use of rod; the words of instruction should involve the Bible (the Word of God). Besides, it should be done with love and wisdom. The discipline must start from the tender age. It shouldn't be postponed till any future time. The Scripture says,

Train up a child in the way
he should go: and when he is
old, he will not depart from it.

Proverbs 22.6 (KJV)

When people are allowed to grow with lazy character, it becomes part of them. And such a character is usually difficult to drop. That contributes a lot to the reason why many adults find it difficult to work even when the opportunities are before them. Nevertheless, any time a man comes back to his right mind, he can begin a new life.

Envy and Jealousy

Envy and jealousy empower idleness. Whenever people start becoming envious or jealous of others, they will no longer have time to work for their own progress. They will spend their time thinking evil about other people's progress and will have no time to think about their own progress. They will also waste their energy working against other people's progress and have no time to work for their own progress. What makes envy and jealousy to be dangerous is that they open up a gateway for the devil to come in. And at the same time, they close the gateway to godly inspirations. It is not unusual to see folks who are slaves to envy and jealousy to move together, as the saying goes that birds of a feather flock together. Even those that seem to have work, whenever they give themselves to envy and jealousy, they tend to forget their work while discussing and criticizing others. Meanwhile, those they are criticizing are oblivious of their acts and thus, continue with their progress. And the more they progress, the more the envious and jealous ones waste their time in idleness—talking for no good purpose.

On the other hand, people that are hard-working have no time to be envious or jealous of others. They believe that the world is wide enough for anyone who cares to spread hands in prosperity. When they see others progressing, they will only get more inspiration. They don't have enough time for their own work let alone spending it on criticizing other people's progress. The Bible has this to say about such people:

Blessed is the man who does
not walk in the counsel of the wicked

or stand in the way of sinners
or sit in the seat of mockers.

Psalm 1.1 (NIV)

Mockery, negative criticisms, backbiting and all similar vices emanate from envy and jealousy. They end up making their victims unconsciously idle and finally, poor.

Perpetual Dependency

A lot of people are easily given to laziness and idleness when their needs are supplied by others. It is not uncommon to see people who are not bothered about their lives and will gladly linger on their beds as long as their basic needs are met. They don't see such provisions as a cushion while they engage themselves in one work or the other. Rather, they see the provisions as an opportunity to relax and enjoy life without working for it. That is also one of the reasons why many countries of the world are very poor today, for they have made up their minds to depend on financial aids. People in this category see a good life as having one's basic needs provided. And as long as those needs are provided, they don't mind how they are provided. Even if they are adults, they don't mind if a child does the provision. Even the men in this category don't mind if their wives do the provision. Likewise, the young adults in this category don't mind if their great grandparents are doing the provisions. To such people, the Bible says,

Go to the ant, you sluggard!
Consider her ways and be wise.

Proverbs 6.6 (NKJV)

It is good for a man to accept a fish to eat in order to quench his hunger. But it is wrong for him to spend his life accepting fishes without learning how to fish. It is not good for a man to live as a parasite, for a parasite eats without contributing to the good of its host.

If its host dies, it will also die. Actually, a parasite contributes to the death of its host.

Resignation to Fate

Many people become idle and lazy when they resign their lives to fate. One of the important things a man should not lose in his life is hope. That is why the Scripture says,

So these three things continue
forever: faith, hope and love.

1 Corinthians 13.13 (NCV)

Any man who has not given up on hope can still make it in life because he will continue trying until there is a breakthrough. One thing common with many poor people is that they give up on hope very easily. And when that happens, they will cease making attempts. We should not be ignorant of the fact that an idle man is a man who makes no attempt. And it is obvious that when no attempt is made nothing could be achieved. Nonetheless, many people do not understand this fact. They make up their mind to sit and fold their hands to see what life will offer them. Consequently, they spend their days in idleness and their years in poverty. Christians should be careful not to count hopelessness as patience. Patience continues to make attempts, believing that one day things will work out but hopelessness makes no attempt. It does not believe that things will work out. If there is anything hopelessness believes, it is; 'what will be will be'. Thus, it does not bother to work again.

In conclusion, idleness (laziness) seems to be the most visible cause of poverty. If any people, whether individually or collectively want to step out of poverty they must be willing to work. And they must make sure that they are working.

SOLUTION

A Word of Advice

If you must be out of poverty, you must be doing something. You must be busy with a work. Once you are faithful to God, He will surely bless the works of your hands. Don't accept to be idle for any reason. You can do little things in great ways and they will eventually become great things. If you can start with great things, that will be fantastic. The point is this; whether small or great just make sure you are doing something so that God will see something to bless. Remember that God raises a poor man who works in a waste bin and also lifts the needy who works in an ash heap (Psalm 113.7-8).

Practical Questions

1. Have you seen people who became rich by just staying idle?
2. Have you discovered that a lot of people who are poor are not doing anything?
3. Do you think you can achieve anything when you try nothing?
4. Do you believe that it is essential that every man must have a work?
5. Do you believe that what makes a difference in any work is how you do it?
6. Do you believe that if you try something and it doesn't work, that you should continue trying until something works out?

A Verse for Inspiration

If you love to sleep, you will be poor.
If you stay awake, you will have
plenty of food.

Proverbs 20.13 (NCV)

CHAPTER

8

Pride

First pride, then the crash—
the bigger the ego, the harder
the fall.

Proverbs 16.18 (The Message)

Pride in this context is an excessive perception of one's own superiority which usually manifests in contempt for others and self-deceit.

Many people go about pretending that all is well and would even reject any opportunity if it appears to be a small one. Nevertheless, they go about in lack. Pride makes a man to place himself where he is not supposed to be. The problem is that those at that level will not find him worthy and those at the level he ought to be will not even see him. It is like a lost sheep wasting its time in the midst of shepherds. Such a sheep cannot be allowed to enjoy the benefits meant for shepherds and it will also miss the good things meant for the sheepfold, simply because of its absence.

Pride is a by-product of self-centeredness. It makes a fellow to be busy looking only on himself and he will not even know that he is actually blindfolded. Pride is so subtle that some of its victims are not even aware of it. That is why you can easily see a poor man given to pride criticizing a proud rich man. Traditionally, once you mention pride, people will think of the rich ones. But in reality, pride contributes to the poverty of many folks. Pride is not exclusive to the rich or poor; pride thrives wherever there is self-centeredness. For a self-centered man, he is the only person that could be found in his heart; he exists alone. And that hampers his productivity. The Bible says,

I assure you, most solemnly I
tell you, Unless a grain of wheat
falls into the earth and dies, it
remains [just one grain; it never
becomes more but lives] by itself
alone. But if it dies, it produces many
other and yields a rich harvest.

John 12.24 (AMP)

Sometimes, one should ask why the lowest ranking soldiers are called 'privates' while the high ranking ones are called 'generals'. For a man to move into prosperity, he must break out of the shell of himself which is made of pride. Every human being should be checking himself constantly against pride because it stalks like a subtle thief (1 Corinthians 10.12). If a rich man faces any misfortune and the devil wants to keep him poor forever; he will give the man pride as a gift. I will take a little time to expose some things about pride.

Threat of Shame

Pride usually comes with a threat of shame. One thing a lot of people don't understand is that nothing good can come out of the devil. Some people do say that the devil you know is better than the angel you don't know. However, they fail to know that every devil is evil whether you know him or not and every angel is a servant of God. Moreover, God is good. Thus, every angel is good whether you know him or not. What I want to bring out of this analogy is that everything from the devil will always lead to disaster. The normal way the devil works is by instilling fear into his victims. Thus, whenever he wants to give poverty to a man through pride, he will bring the threat or fear of shame. Then the victim will cover himself with shame not knowing that poverty will lay hold of him. And finally, his shame will be full of grief. The Bible says,

When pride comes, then comes shame;
But with the humble is wisdom.

Proverbs 11.2 (NKJV)

Whenever a man succumbs to the fear of shame, he will begin to hide himself even when no one is looking for him. He will always be thinking that people are laughing or will laugh at him even when no one is mindful of him. The reality is that responsible people don't laugh at other people's means of livelihood; rather, such things give them encouragement. Pride, working through the threat of shame will make a man to despise all opportunities that he deems shameful to his 'class'.

Now, think of it, if a man feels ashamed of his work, it will be only a matter of time and he will forget the shame (as long as he does not quit). When that work begins to give him enough money he will not like to quit again. On the other hand, when he makes enough money from the work he can change to another work. It only takes humility for someone to pass through such a stage in life but it will lead such a person out of poverty. The Bible says,

…For God sets Himself against the
proud… but gives grace (favor,
blessing) to the humble.

1 Peter 5.5 (AMP)

It only takes boldness to fight poverty face to face and tell the story later. But if a man decides to lift himself above what he is, poverty will eventually disgrace him. With humility, a man can attract God's blessing in any work his hands find doing.

False Appearance

Pride makes a man to look bigger in the eyes of those that are supposed to help him. People in this category can lie about themselves even before those that have come to help them. They can even pick offence when people try to treat them according to their real worth. They can be dying within themselves but will not disclose it to others. A good number of them will rather die than accept their actual worth. Their utmost interest is all about their public image. The Scripture says,

There is one who makes himself rich, yet has nothing; And one who makes himself poor, yet has great riches.

Proverbs 13.7 (NKJV)

People that are victims of pride don't mind borrowing to buy new clothes, shoes, cars and other things that will make them appear rich. One of the consequences is that those who would have assisted them financially will count them as rich enough. Pride is so bad that even when such persons have a little breakthrough their focus would be on displaying their wealth instead of maintaining the breakthrough. Sometimes you hear some folks discussing that their government should share their national treasures to every citizen but that would mean an introduction to chaotic existence. Nevertheless, if the government should decide to do that with the intention of ending poverty; it will take only a short time and poverty will start staring many people in the face again. One of the things that make it so is because some folks, immediately they get their own share of the treasures, they will begin to build their financial image which they thought had suffered all the while. They will do that ignorantly instead of building their financial lives. That is trying to build shadows instead of the substance. If a man's financial life is strong, his financial image will be strong as well and not the other way round.

Pride can achieve all these things in the life of a man because of ignorance. The truth is that pride is a form of ignorance. An ignorant man does not know when assistance is offered to him and thus will not accept it. Likewise, a proud man, even though he knows that assistance is being offered to him, pride will not allow him to be humble enough to accept it. Finally, you will discover that just in the same way an ignorant man does not know about his assistance, a proud man also does not know that he can get his assistance through humility. Thus, the financial assistance will elude the ignorant man who is below the platform of acceptance and also elude the proud who hangs above the platform of acceptance.

A Mind not Teachable

Pride makes a man to reject wise counsel. Pride makes a man to think that he knows everything even when he knows next to nothing (if not nothing). The Bible says,

> *Poverty and shame shall be to him*
> *that refuseth instruction: but he that*
> *regardeth reproof shall be honoured.*
>
> Proverbs 13.18 (KJV)

Many people have lost their fortunes not because they invested in the wrong businesses but because they failed to ask questions. Maybe, the person that supposedly had the answers was not educated enough. But the reality remains: whether the man was an illiterate or not; he had the answers. If people should humble themselves to ask questions before committing their finance, they will avoid a lot of problems; even if the person that has the answer is a child. It is not unusual to see that when financial seminars are organized, pride will not allow some folks to attend. Most times, by the time they finish analyzing the qualifications of the organizers and the speakers, they will find no reason to attend. Such folks also find it difficult to read books on finance. They end up developing minds that are not teachable. Whereas, according to Johann von Goethe, 'The man with insight enough to admit his limitations comes nearest to perfection.'

Pride can make a man to take a big risk with his finance and plunge his head into disaster just because he cannot humble himself enough to ask questions. Because of pride, he will think that asking questions reveals his level of ignorance and puts him under the person giving the answers. But the reality is that nobody knows everything and learning is a continuous process. Asking questions prevents one from making the mistakes of others who had been before him. If seventy per cent of business startups fail within their first three years in a particular field, asking the right questions and getting the right answers on the reasons why they fail can save one from losing his money. The answers will give him a clue on how to start up successfully. They will tell him the things to do and things not to do for the business to be successful. On the other hand, the answers may suggest that he should look for another line of business.

For the fact that pride is putting one's self above others; it does not give itself to objective reasoning. Its reasoning is only subjective. The Bible also calls such a person a sluggard:

The sluggard is wiser in his own eyes than seven men who answer discreetly.

Proverbs 26.16 (NIV)

In conclusion, pride makes a man to unconsciously choose poverty just in a bid to stay away from humility. Pride has done no good to any man in any aspect of human life. Thus, no man should expect pride to be of benefit in the area of finance.

SOLUTION

A Word of Advice

Don't allow pride to enter into your life for any reason. Besides being a destroyer of finances, it is a sin that attracts God's opposition. It will always come with a threat of shame but if you withstand it, it will flee from you. It will only take a little time for you to turn back and smile if you refuse to give in to pride. Moreover, you should also know that if anyone gives in to pride out of fear of shame, poverty will still overtake him with a greater shame.

Practical Questions

1. Have you seen a man that pretends to be rich only for you to discover that he is not?
2. Have you seen a man that is more interested in his public financial image than in his actual finance?
3. Do you believe that you don't know everything concerning finance?
4. Do you believe that humility makes it easier for people to render help to you when you need it?
5. Have you considered giving a financial help to a man you believe that is well richer than you?
6. Do you think that people will consider rendering a financial help to you when they count you to be well richer than them?

A Verse for Inspiration

A man's pride brings him low, but a man of lowly spirit gains honor.

Proverbs 29.23 (NIV)

CHAPTER

9

Lack of Savings

Wise people live in wealth and
luxury, but stupid people spend
their money as fast as they get it.

Proverbs 21.20 (GNT)

A man is said to be lacking something when he does not have it or when he does not have enough of it. On the other hand, savings refers to the money that is not used or wasted but set aside for the future. Thus, lack of savings means having no money set aside for the future or not having enough of it.

Anyone who does not save will either perpetuate his poverty or will become poor at any slightest interruption in his flow of income. This is one of the most visible causes of avoidable poverty. It is avoidable because the individual concerned is earning some money. It is only a financial management problem. Good knowledge of financial matters can go a long way in solving this kind of problem. Lack of savings has contributed a lot in making many people who were once rich to go down to poverty. It seems to be a general tendency among human beings to be spending their money according to how they get it. That is a normal practice but it behooves every individual to adjust his own settings. That means that he shouldn't leave his expenditure to be determined by the forces of demand and supply of money around him. The adjustment must be done consciously and explicitly. There must be a definite plan for savings if it must be actualized. I want you to understand that savings does not mean lack of faith as some Christians may think. This chapter's introductory text calls people who do not save 'stupid people'. Faith does not mean lack of planning. God does not pour all the money we would need in life at once into our hands; He does that bit by bit. And you will agree with me that there are certain financial needs you must meet by accumulating your earnings. And it is usually the case when you think of making investments. Remember the story of Joseph in Egypt. God gave him the revelation concerning savings for Egypt to become the world food center in his days. And he was also elevated to the position of a prime minister only for his godly counsel on savings.

However, sometimes you see individuals with the desire to save but they end up not doing so. There are many things that contribute to that and I will like to touch a good number of them among other things.

Faulty Scale of Preference

Many people put savings at the bottom of their scale of preference. This seems to be the number one cause of lack of savings especially among the people that have savings in mind. They always wait to spend all their income and intend to save the leftovers. But unfortunately, most times, nothing would be left. And I tell you the truth, with this mentality, even if a man should try to discipline himself he will only succeed in saving an inconsequential portion of his income. Savings must not be done at the end of the month or week as the case maybe. It must be considered even before the income is received. Just the way a Christian considers paying ten per cent of his income as tithe, he should also be considering the percentage of his income that will be saved beforehand. I cannot give you a fixed percentage for your savings. You are to ask yourself a lot of questions before coming to a good percentage. You can ask yourself: If I feast sumptuously today, can my savings ensure at least a normal meal tomorrow?

The truth is that there is no level of discipline you can apply to yourself to ensure good savings apart from setting the money aside immediately you receive it. It constrains your spending; it makes you to think only on the leftover after the savings. If you have all the money in your hands, you are likely to be moved to spend it not just only on your needs but on your wants also. But if you constrain your spending by setting aside your savings first; you will discover by the end of the day that some things that come up as pressing needs but are not met due to financial constraint are actually wants—not needs.

Come to think of it: if you are serious about saving let's say fifty percent of your income, won't it be advisable to set it aside immediately you receive it (when you can do it) rather than waiting for the end of the month (when you may not be able to do it)? You will agree with me that if you have any financial need that you meet regularly, you plan for it even before your income comes. And immediately you receive your income you set aside the money for that need. Why not do so also for your savings? I want you to see your savings as a pressing need. Until you see your savings as a pressing need; you won't be serious about it. You can take a look at the advice of Joseph to Pharaoh:

Let Pharaoh do this, and let him appoint officers over the land, to collect one-fifth of the produce of the land of Egypt in the seven plentiful years.

Genesis 41.34 (NKJV)

Note that Joseph was specific on the savings: one-fifth—which is twenty per cent. And they had to measure out that portion when the harvest was still complete, that is immediately after the harvest. I also want you to note that the twenty per cent was only the national savings besides individual and family savings. Thus, for effective savings, it must be done at the beginning by a specific percentage.

Risky Expectation

Many people don't take savings seriously because they believe that their income will continue to flow in. This is where many Christians get it wrong in the name of faith. It is good to have faith that your income will continue to flow in but that does not mean that you should discard the rules of financial management. Just as in the case of driving, a Christian should have faith that he is not going to have an accident but he should also learn how to drive obeying road signs. The same rule applies to all aspects of human life and finance is not exempted. Many things can cause interruption in the flow of one's income whether he has faith or not. In fact, it is his faith that will keep him going when such things happen. The Bible says,

Even though good people may be
bothered by trouble seven times,
they are never defeated…

Proverbs 24.16 (NCV)

An example of the things that can affect ones flow of income is market demand. Such might be caused by a shift in technology and so on. Just consider a Christian who is dealing in typewriters; it is likely that immediately demand starts moving towards computers his flow of income would be affected. That does not mean that he has no faith but a simple change in demand has occurred. Moreover, the change does not segregate between Christians and non-Christians. But believe you me, if such a Christian has no savings, this change in demand can dump him in the quagmire of poverty.

Another example is whenever there is a crash in the stock market, it affects everybody's money. It does not separate faithful Christians' money from non-faithful Christians' money. If a government fails to pay salaries, it affects everybody. The list goes on and on. The only thing that keeps people on their feet when such things happen is planning against it. And savings is one of such plans. I know some Christians will easily say that God will provide. Yes, God provides and

His provision starts with the income you are earning now. However, God also encourages you to save. The Bible says,

For riches do not endure forever, and
a crown is not secure for all generations.

Proverbs 27.24 (NIV)

Even if your job is a highly secured job, you will still retire someday. It is not a surprise to see some workers in big establishments with good salaries get frustrated just because their salaries get delayed for only one week. Such things can happen any time but it is always shameful to see high earnings individuals looking for where to borrow money within a short time just because they don't save.

Earn and Spend Character

Many people don't save because they want to enjoy their lives immediately without thinking of the future. Sometimes you see people make some money and become rich but in a little time you see them again becoming poor simply because they squandered their money. Such people are not given to prudence. They like to spend everything today and abandon tomorrow to fate. Whenever a man trains himself with such a mentality, any time money enters his hands 'Spend it! Spend it!' will begin to resound in his head. Most times I see people that worked for big establishments crying that their severance benefits had not been paid and they wallow in poverty. Though their benefits are ought to be paid as and when due but I do ask, 'What had they been doing with their salaries when they were in active service to justify their poverty?' It is even unfortunate to see many people in active service in such establishments still on a spending spree despite the condition of those ahead of them. After all the spending, they retire and join those below the poverty line (unless their benefits are paid on time).

On the other hand, you can see people working in establishments with low job security. Of course, most of such jobs attract high salaries but some people usually surrender themselves to squandering. And when they lose such jobs they fall into poverty. The same happens to those who are doing their own business. If they fail to save when the business is booming, if they fail to save when they are still young and strong enough to manage the business, poverty can be lurking at the door.

Prudence might not look fashionable to many people but it sustains a man who has it over time. Prudence does not in any way suggest that a Christian should be stingy but a prudent Christian also considers his giving when he makes his budget. The Bible uses the ant as an example of prudence in Proverbs chapter six, simply because it stores its provisions in summer even without a commander. The ant knows that the rainy season will come and thus does not go on with splurging. Then why will a human being, who is supposed to have more understanding, still go on with splurging?

It is not unusual to hear people say, 'I love shopping.' They are simply saying, 'I love spending' which can also mean 'I hate saving.' You can say, 'But every human being goes for shopping at one time or the other.' Yes, you are right. But when a man begins to love shopping, it is no longer a matter of need but of want.

Perceived Little Income

Many people don't think about savings because they consider their income to be too small. This is one reason that looks so genuine and justifies lack of savings. But truly, it is the other way round. As I said before; savings should be seen as a need and not as remnant from expenditures. In fact, a man whose income is small should be serious with his savings more than a man who is already out of the range of poverty. The reason is that when such a person who earns little income accumulates his savings over time, it will help to launch him out of the range of poverty. It might not be a pleasant experience to save in this kind of situation but it is like sowing one's seed in tears. After some time, the same person will begin to reap the harvest and will forget the pains he went through during the time of sowing. This kind of situation calls for deliberate sacrifice. There must be a deliberate move to cut down some expenses. It may be for a period of one year or two or three; it all depends on the situation. I know it will be easy for people to begin to think about the extremes like starvation or malnutrition but I will like you to see the true picture at the end. It may necessitate not buying clothes and shoes for the given period. In some cases, it can involve cutting down the feeding budget (though not for children or to the extreme of starvation). Of course, all expenditures on frivolities must stop.

One may think that a person who is earning a little income is already in a difficult situation, so why make life more difficult for him. The answer is that if such a person should continue in that situation without standing against it, he may end up with it. And I tell you the truth; poverty is worst at old age. It is common to see people denying themselves of pleasures, even eating less just because they want to gather money for new clothes, shoes, electronic gadgets and so on. So why can't individuals deny themselves of pleasures in order to cross the poverty line. Why not sacrifice (say) three years and live the rest of your life out of poverty than trying to take it easy with poverty for the rest of your life. Actually, you don't have to live your life by what you desire but by what the occasion demands (of course, not in the wrong or sinful sense). Paul the apostle, in his own time wrote:

I know how to be abased and live humbly in straitened circumstances, and I know also how to enjoy plenty and live in abundance. I have learned in any and all circumstances the secret of facing every situation, whether well-fed or going hungry, having a sufficiency and enough to spare or going without and being in want.

Philippians 4.12 (AMP)

People save in order to have something they can fall back on when the need arises. Again, people save to accumulate fund for investment. A man whose income is small should think more of saving to accumulate fund for investment. It is all about increasing his financial earnings in order to be out of poverty. Another thing I will like to mention is the fact that many so called small earnings are not actually small. In many cases, it is all about perception and management.

In conclusion, just make sure you are saving something each time you receive your income. It is an issue of self-denial and self-discipline. Do your best to plan for your savings even before the money enters into your hands. Savings can be a guaranteed means through which a man can finance himself to the life of financial independence.

SOLUTION

A Word of Advice

First among other things, I want you to see savings as a need. It is a need whether you are earning enough money; it will help to keep you out of poverty. It is a need whether you think you are not earning enough; it will help to lift you out of poverty. Another thing is that you will be careful about where you save. Don't put your savings into something that you are not sure of. Saving in a bank is advisable. And you must not save in one bank, at least three is recommended. Finally, have a vision of what you want to use the savings to do; that will prevent you from wasting your savings. Don't go about broadcasting your savings, it may attract unnecessary distractions.

Practical Questions

1. Do you save now?
2. If yes, is it regular?
3. When do you deduct your savings: when you receive your income or when you finish making your expenses?

4. Do you think it is easy to have a regular meaningful savings if you allow your expenses to come first?
5. Do you believe that lack of savings can make people who earn enough money to be frustrated whenever an emergency need arises?
6. Do you believe that a poor man should also save from his little income?
7. Is saving a necessity or a choice?
8. Do you believe that it is better to save than to have hope that somebody will raise fund for you someday?

A Verse for Inspiration

The LORD will command the blessing on you in your storehouses and in all to which you set your hand, and He will bless you in the land which the LORD your God is giving you.

Deuteronomy 28.8 (NKJV)

CHAPTER

10

Lack of Regular Financial Self-Examination

Be fully aware of the condition of
your flock, and pay close attention
to your herds.

Proverbs 27.23 (GW)

Something is lacking when it is not available or insufficient. An occurrence is said to be regular if it happens frequently especially with relatively definite or specific intervals of time. 'Financial' refers to finance or money. The word 'Self-' shows when something is to be by itself or oneself and examination is the act of inspecting something carefully. Thus, lack of regular financial self-examination means not frequently and carefully inspecting one's finances by oneself with specific or relatively definite intervals of time.

Any man who does not look into his finances from time to time may not know when things start going wrong except when they have gone substantially wrong. Be it a man working for himself—if he does not keep the proper financial records of his business, he can only notice a problem with his finances when things have gone wrong. On the other hand, a man who earns salaries; if he does not evaluate his income and expenditures from time to time, he is likely to see his error when things have gone wrong. Sometimes people enter into some financial commitments based on the assumption that they have enough to take care of them only to be frustrated at last. Naturally, most of our financial commitments come gradually; they don't come all at once. And in many cases, they come in little amounts that could be easily neglected. Nonetheless, when those little amounts come together they become huge amounts.

Many people are struggling with their finances today not because they are not working hard but because they failed to notice the little leaks in their finances before they turned into big financial crises. Sometimes you hear people blaming spiritual forces and it is always easy to do so. Truly, spiritual forces can work against people's finances but not at the extent people count it to be. Regular financial self-examination helps one to know when his income is no longer commensurate with his inputs. It helps one to monitor and manage his regular expenditures and his occasional expenditures. It does not just involve making a budget but monitoring the budget. Sometimes you see some people running around to raise money for an emergency financial need. But when you consider some of those needs called 'emergency' you will find out that they are not supposed to be called 'emergency' in any way. For instance, a man whose children are in school should not say that the school fees are emergency expenditures. They are regular expenditures with specific time frames. A man whose wife delivers in the hospital should not say that the hospital bill is an emergency. It is an occasional expenditure and it gives nine months' notice. A man who gets married should know that his expenditures will increase automatically. If he is the kind that feeds with half of his earnings, he should then ask himself if he feeds with one half and the wife feeds with the other half, will they have children. It is because the structure of his expenditures does not make any provision for children. It is not at all the will of God that we should fall into financial crisis or any problem before we realize ourselves. The Bible says,

Sensible people will see trouble coming
and avoid it, but an unthinking person
will walk right into it and regret it later.

Proverbs 22.3 (GNT)

From time to time we can stumble into some erroneous financial commitments but regular examinations will go a long way in saving us before it is too late. It will be nice to see how this lack of regular financial self-examination works to bring about poverty.

Negligence of Little Things

Many people are easily tempted to ignore the monitoring of their finances when the individual interacting factors seems to be small. As I have mentioned earlier, when the expenses are coming in little ways, there will be a tendency for one to assume that the changes are insignificant. What makes it more serious is when one is also having increase in his income which comes in various little ways. In this situation, he can assume that the increase in income will be cancelling the increase in expenditures. However, when it is negative, the assumption might be costly and such is usually critical when it happens over a long period of time. This kind of situation makes many people to think that they are doing well financially until the poverty land mine is activated. That is why the Bible says,

Catch us the foxes, The little foxes
that spoil the vines, For our vines
have tender grapes.

Song of Solomon 2.15 (NKJV)

All these assumptions of little increments and little expenditures work like little foxes. They can hide easily in the vineyard of your finances unlike the big foxes. Sometimes they might even look friendly for you to treat them like home grown puppies. But they are wild animals and could be dangerous. You must catch them and take them away. No level of expenditures should be neglected, however small, especially when such expenditures are meant to be repeated.

Unwritten Assessment

Some people who claim to be monitoring their finances fail because they don't write things down. Most times one could be tempted to use his head to do the calculations instead of pen and paper (or computer as the case may be). The problem with using your head is that you may not catch all the items in your calculations. At the same time, you will be at ease—that all is settled.

Writing things down is a principle one must not neglect if he is serious about regular financial self-examination. No business can really thrive consciously without it. One does not need to be a trained accountant to keep his records. Having some knowledge of accounting is good but where it is not available just make sure you write down your income in one place and then your expenses in another place. Then get their individual sums and compare. Writing things down will help you to compare your current financial activities (i.e. income and expenses) with the previous ones. It will help you to know whether you have grown over a period of (say) one year or not. But if you are using your head for monthly calculations, it will be difficult for you to remember all the figures for your incomes and expenditures for twelve good months, including their differences.

Writing down your financial activities is not a modern development; it had been since the days of old. If you look at the parable of the wise servant as told by Jesus Christ in Luke 16.1-13; when the servant found out that he would lose his job, he went to his master's debtors to change their records. If there were no records, he wouldn't have seen any record to change. Again, if writing down records was not practised in those days Jesus wouldn't have mentioned it in a parable.

It is also possible for someone to say that he does not know how to read and write. Then learning how to read and write should be the first step, since poverty doesn't ask questions before dealing with a man. When God gave Moses the Ten Commandments, He wrote it with His finger (Exodus 31.18). Even when Moses broke the first two tablets, God still wrote the Commandments again on another two tablets of stone.

Perceived Hard Labour

Some people see the act of regular financial self-examination as a heavy task. Someone might be of the opinion; if I have laboured to make my money, why trouble me again with self-accounting? Yes, it may look like trouble if you look at it from a distance. But when you begin to practise it, it might be a task of few minutes. If your financial territory is bigger, then it is likely to take you a longer time. Meanwhile, think of it: if one hour in a month can save you from a big financial frustration, why not give out the one hour peacefully for your own good. I will like to note again that one hour will be recommended only if your financial ground is quite big. For a simple salary earner or a man that runs a simple business, five to ten minutes might be too much for the examination.

No matter the time it will take you to do the examination, it is worth it. If the time is bigger, then it is likely that it will save you from a bigger financial quagmire. The truth about this financial examination is that for the first time you try it, it may take longer time. But the subsequent ones would likely take shorter times. It is when men find it to be a hard labour to do this little peaceful task that they give themselves to an unnecessary risk of financial problems. The Bible says,

The lazy man does not roast what
he took in hunting, But diligence is
men's precious possession.

Proverbs 12.27 (NKJV)

One may ask; hunting to catch a game and roasting the game, which is more laborious? The same question goes with working to make money and conducting a financial self-examination. As you know, roasting a game will preserve it for a longer time than keeping it fresh. Of course if you keep meat for one day it will start decaying. Nevertheless, a man can give himself the trouble of hunting down an animal but finds it a difficult task to preserve the meat by roasting it. The same goes with people who will work hard to make money but will find it a difficult task to preserve their earnings by conducting a regular financial self-examination.

In conclusion, if you can labour to make money, it behooves you to make out a little time for regular financial self-examination. This practice can save you from getting into financial difficulties. Initially, you can look at it as something trivial but when you begin to practise it, it will open your eyes into many serious things. You may not necessarily need a special book for this practice; getting a pen and a piece of paper can see you through within five minutes. This financial self-examination should be different from your business records. Meanwhile, if you have a business, you should be seeing yourself as a worker in the business for efficient accounting and management.

SOLUTION

A Word of Advice

Do not neglect any expenditure you are making especially the regular ones. Don't assume that the expenditures are too small and your income is too big. Regular financial self-examination can save you from the falling of the little stones that may degenerate into an avalanche. This practice could be likened to fire prevention rules and a fire service station. No one prays for fire but the fire service station will continue to exist as a safety measure (should fire come). However, it is safer to be applying fire prevention rules.

Practical Questions

1. Do you think that regular financial self-examination is not necessary?
2. Have you seen people with a stable job who usually get financially broke before their next pay day?
3. Have you seen people who woke up one day to discover that they are in a financial problem due to expenses made over a long period of time?

4. Do you believe that prevention is the best solution to any problem including financial problems?
5. Do you believe that financial problems can attack any man irrespective of his financial standing once there is an opening for them?
6. Will you like to taste financial problems?
7. Can anything stop you now from conducting a regular financial self-examination?

A Verse for Inspiration

Everything was counted and weighed,
and a complete record was made at
the same time.

Ezra 8.34 (GNT)

CHAPTER

11

Competition

We're not, understand, putting ourselves in a league with those who boast that they're our superiors. We wouldn't dare do that. But in all this comparing and grading and competing, they quite miss the point.

2 Corinthians 10.12 (The Message)

Competition in this context is trying to look more successful than others.

Whenever people begin to measure themselves financially with one another, they begin to squander their resources. In such a circumstance, they try to please everybody by their own expenditures on their own account. Margaret Thatcher once said, 'If you just set out to be liked, you would be prepared to compromise on anything at any time, and you would achieve nothing.' This lifestyle of comparison is supposed to be for unbelievers who do not know God but unfortunately some Christians drag themselves into it. At the beginning, many people get into it consciously because they want to keep up with the joneses. But after a long time, it becomes part of them and they become prisoners of themselves unconsciously. The

Bible did not tell us in any way to present ourselves as rich men unto God, rather it says,

I beseech you therefore, brethren, by the mercies of God, that you present your bodies a living sacrifice, holy, acceptable to God, which is your reasonable service.

Romans 12.1 (NKJV)

It is good for you to look good but you shouldn't be a prisoner of fashion just because you think somebody is watching. The same goes for the type of house you live in, the class of furniture in your house, the class of school your children attend, the class of car you use and the list goes on and on. Unbelievers can go on living like that because they are ignorant (Ephesians 4.18). But it shouldn't be so with Christians. Sometimes people pay heavily for inferior goods and services just because those things come with high prices (and thus, prestigious). And the premonition of such people will not allow them to consider the quality of what they are paying for. They do all such things simply because they want to please any one that sees them. Even when their finances are objecting to such spending, they will close their mind and continue spending until poverty comes around. Some will easily claim it is an act of faith, but it is actually a display of arrogance and insincerity. Faith does not call for competition. The Scripture says,

But you have not so learned Christ,

Ephesians 4.20 (NKJV)

It would have been possible for Christ to have been born in the best hospital in His time but He chose a manger. He had to borrow Peter's boat for His preaching. He borrowed a donkey to fulfill a prophecy of His triumphal entry into Jerusalem. He had to use another man's house for His Last Supper with His disciples. In fact, it was even prophesied by Prophet Isaiah that He would be buried in another man's grave and it happened like that. You may ask why. The Bible says,

For ye know the grace of our Lord
Jesus Christ, that, though he was
rich, yet for your sakes he became poor,
that ye through his poverty might be rich.

2 Corinthians 8.9 (KJV)

He lived this kind of life on earth to show you that you can live a successful life with contentment. He did not consider what people would say. He only considered what God would say. God expects us to live within our means. A man can apply faith whenever it becomes necessary. The main issue about applying faith is the motive behind it. Is the application of faith born out of competition or out of sincerity? We cannot hide our motives from God. If a man can embrace humility it will regulate his lifestyle and of course his spending caused by arrogance. The Bible says,

Have the same attitude that
Christ Jesus had.

Philippians 2.5 (GW)

It is the will of God to make you prosper financially. It is also His will to see you build your finances as He makes the provision. But it is never His will to see you spend recklessly all in a bid to please men. I will now take time to discuss how competition works as an agent of poverty.

Trying to Please Men

Many people spend beyond their limit when they want to please a particular group of persons. You will agree with me that whenever a man tries to please everybody with his finances, he is also planning for his poverty. But there is something I will like you to know, that word 'everybody' does not necessarily mean every human being in the whole world. It is usually a group of persons. It can be relatives or family members. Such a thing can happen when a Christian fails to present himself as a true child of God before his friends and relations. In some cases, you can see a man presenting himself to be richer than he is actually. In another, you can see a man who does not say 'no' to certain financial demands. The consequence of all these is that the relations will have certain expectations from him which might be too high for him. Some Christians continue in such life thinking that it is necessary for people to see them as true children of God. The reality is that you don't need man's approval for you to be a true child of God. Look at what the Bible says,

Does this sound as if I am trying to win human approval? No indeed! What I want is God's approval! Am I trying to be popular with people? If I were still trying to do so, I would not be a servant of Christ.

Galatians 1.10 (GNT)

God expects us to do our best in loving others but He does not expect us to spend our money unnecessarily just to please others. He does not expect us to bite our fingers buying expensive clothes, cars, etc. for ourselves just for our relatives to be proud of us. He does not expect us to sacrifice our finances on the altar of ourselves just to gain family members' approval. If you show yourself as a true child of God and spend your money accordingly, all such expectations will end.

Another group of persons that can drag a man into the unnecessary spending of competition is his friends. If you make wrong friends, they will make wrong demands from you and you will end up living a wrong life. And in this case, such a wrong life will lead to poverty. The Bible says,

Don't let anyone deceive you. Associating with bad people will ruin decent people.

1 Corinthians 15.33 (GW)

One may ask, 'But Jesus loves sinners?' The answer is 'Yes'. You can love sinners but not their sinful lives. Your friendship with sinners should be on different terms when compared to your friendship with fellow Christians. You should remember that even though Jesus loves sinners, His bosom friends were the apostles not sinners. He told sinners parables but revealed the secret things to the disciples.

I will like you to understand certain things about friendship so that you don't go into a wrong one. A friend is a loved one who is likely not a member of your family but shares the same views with you and you can trust that person. Now, there are six kinds of friends which you can have in life. They are: close friends, distant friends, true friends, false friends, good friends and bad friends. Somebody can be one of these kinds of friends to you. He might even be two of the kinds or at most three. Let me now give you the definitions of these friends so that you'll know when you meet them.

I will start with a close friend. A close friend is a friend that knows you very well and you also know him (or her) very well. He is to you such a person you can tell what you can't tell others. In many cases, the closeness can be physical, i.e. you like staying together. This is the kind of friend that other people easily recognize as your friend. When people say, 'Show me your friend and I will show you who you are,' this is the kind they refer to. Usually, this kind of friend is to an extent a replica of your own personality. And anyone who wants to gain access to you can easily come through this friend. Thus, it behooves you to be careful about the kind of person that plays these roles in your life. You can easily influence the life of your close friend and he as well can easily influence your life. It is only among your close friends that you can have your bosom or best friend. Thus, one can have more than one close friends but it is not good for them to be many lest your life will be as good as a city without walls. Though you may not necessarily have one person who you can call your best friend, close friends are usually there in our lives at one time or the other.

Another kind of friend is a distant friend. A distant friend is a friend that knows little about you and you as well know little about him (her). Sometimes they are close friends that had been separated by time or distance. Sometimes they might be people with whom you are developing a new friendship. However, you can have some people as distant friends for life. This is usually the case when you don't have anything much in common. If there should be any friendship with a Christian and an unbeliever, this is where it should fall into. This is a loose kind of friendship. It may not be easy for other people to identify this kind of friend in your life. It is even possible for you to be living in the same street with this kind of friend. Most times this kind of friendship dies a natural death and no one is hurt unlike close friendship.

Meanwhile, I will like you to understand that there are varying degrees of close friendships and distant friendships. I only gave a typical definition of both. A good example is Jesus and the multitude, then Jesus and the seventy disciples, then Jesus and the twelve apostles, then Jesus and Peter, James and John, and finally, Jesus and John. At one extreme of the friendship line you see the distant friends which in this case are the multitude. At the other extreme of the friendship line you see the bosom friend which in this case is John the Beloved Apostle. I will classify close friend and distant friend to be friendship by proximity.

Another kind of friend I will talk about is true friend. A true friend is that kind of friend that will always stand by you both in the time of abundance and in the time of need. When people say, 'A friend in need is a friend indeed,' they refer to this kind of friend. Most times, they are revealed in times of adversity. Though you don't have to rule out the times of abundance; for some friends can turn against you (maybe out of jealousy or whatever reason) when things begin to work well for you. Another word you can use to refer to this kind of friend is 'A Faithful Friend'. He (or she) will not disappoint you. The Bible says,

A friend loves at all times…

Proverbs 17.17 (NKJV)

In this place, it is referring to this kind of friend. He does not love at some times; he loves at all times. He is not faithful at some times; he is faithful at all times. In fact, a man can only be said to be faithful when he is consistent. You may not wait for a big disaster to take place before you notice that a friend is faithful. His faithfulness is manifested even in little things.

Then, another kind of friend is the false friend. This is a kind of friend who pretends to be a friend but he is not what he claims to be. He is a fair weather friend. He will always be with you when things are well with you but as soon as you have a misfortune he will take to his heels. Though in some cases, you will see such a friend coming to sympathize with you when you have problems, as soon as light shines on your way he will turn against you. You will also notice that he will be doing more of sympathizing with you—no other meaningful help. You may think he is a friend but he does not wish you well. On the other hand which is common, he will only want to take from you but will not be willing to give to you. He will like your relationship to continue as long as he remains a parasite to you. I want you to know that even if a man is poor he must have something to contribute to a friendship. It might not necessarily be in terms of money but he must have something to offer both in good times and bad times. One thing common with false friends is that they will always disappoint you when you need them most. A false friend will rather throw sumptuous parties instead of giving you a financial help. A false friend will rather sleep in his house throughout the day instead of coming to your aid when you need his presence. A false friend will like to know your secrets only to divulge them freely. See what the Bible says about this kind of friend,

Poor people's relatives avoid them;
even their friends stay far away.
They run after them, begging, but
they are gone.

Proverbs 19.7 (NCV)

The kind of friends the Bible refers to in this verse is false friends. They only think about their own goodness and won't bother themselves with any other person's problem. In fact, they enter into friendships to take advantage of their friends.

There are no varying degrees of true friendship and false friendship. It is either a man is a true friend or he is a false friend. I will classify true friend and false friend as friendship by faithfulness. Nevertheless, I will like you to understand that in life you reap what you sow. If you have a friend and you don't want to commit anything to the friendship; don't bother yourself expecting anything from the friendship. In such a case it might not necessary mean that the other person is a false friend; two of you are only having friendship without commitment. The Bible says,

A man that hath friends must
shew himself friendly…

Proverbs 18.24 (KJV)

Another kind of friend is a good friend. This person is first of all, a good person before becoming a friend. From the spiritual point of view, this person is first of all, a born again Christian before becoming a friend. He can be a close friend, he can be a distant friend; the point remains that he is a good person. He can only be a true friend; he can never be a false friend. He is always faithful in friendship just as he is faithful in other things. He can be trusted because of the fear of God in him. He can only offer godly advices. He is the kind of friend that will tell you the truth even when it hurts. He doesn't go into friendship because of what he expects to gain. Rather, he is always interested in what to contribute to the friendship. He is the kind of person that will advise you to forgive an offender even when others are instigating you to fight for your right. He is that person that will not laugh at you when you face financial challenges. He is that person that will try to stop you when you want to spend unnecessarily. Of course, it won't even come to your mind to spend in order to please him. In fact, having this kind of person as a close friend is pure friendship defined. He will help you to build your life, including your financial life. The Bible, in referring to this kind of friend says,

Faithful are the wounds of a friend, But the kisses of an enemy are deceitful.

Proverbs 27.6 (NKJV)

Even if he wounds you, you will eventually know that it is for your own good. Most times, in practical life, his wounds might not be physical on your body. It can be emotional wound. For instance, you want to borrow money from a bank to buy a new car because you think that your personality should be accompanied by such a car. A good friend will turn you down even if he is the only person qualified to sign as a guarantor. He will do that if he knows that such a loan can subject you to a protracted financial slavery. It may hurt you for the moment but it is for your own good.

Above all, a good friend brings you closer to God. However, there is one thing I will like you to know: if you will like this kind of person to be your close friend, then you must be a good friend yourself. If you want him to be your friend and he discovers that you are not good in yourself, the best he can give himself to you is a distant friendship (of course, he remains a good man and a good friend).

The Bible says,

Just as iron sharpens iron,
friends sharpen the minds of
each other.

Proverbs 27.17 (CEV)

Finally, another kind of friend is a bad friend. This person is first of all, a bad person before becoming a friend. From the spiritual point of view, this person is not a born again Christian. (Though a true Christian must be born again, I use the word 'Born Again Christian' for emphasis). This kind of person can be a close friend, he can be a distant friend; the point remains that he is a bad person. He can be a false friend and surprisingly he can also be a true friend. He can be trusted for some things but not for godliness. He lacks the ability to offer godly advices. He can only offer worldly advices. The Scripture says,

The good man out of his good treasure
brings forth good, and the evil man out of
his evil treasure brings froth evil.

Matthew 12.35 (RSV)

He can be by your side in time of need. Nonetheless, the main thing about this friend is that he can lead you away from God. He can be sincere with you but sincerely wrong. He is the worst kind of friend you can ever have. He is the kind of friend that will encourage you to spend beyond your means. He can do so because he wants to frustrate you and he can also do so because that is his own lifestyle. But whatever the reason, you will likely end up in frustration. The Bible says,

Keep away from angry,
short-tempered men, lest you
learn to be like them and endanger
your soul.

Proverbs 22.24-25 (TLB)

Here, it is giving an example of bad friends. However, I will like you to know that if you are a bad person in any measure, you will always attract bad people as friends; even people worse than you. The easiest way to keep away bad friends is to be filled with the Holy Spirit, because the Holy Spirit will either convert them or repel them. Hear what the Bible says,

An unjust person is disgusting to
righteous people. A decent person is
disgusting to wicked people.

Proverbs 29.27 (GW)

There are no varying degrees of good friendship and bad friendship. It is either a man is a good friend or he is a bad friend. However you can only differentiate a good friend from a bad friend in the light of the Word of God. Thus, you must have the Word of God in you for you to know who is good and who is bad. I will classify good friend and bad friend as friendship by personality.

Now, in all these classifications of friendship, the most important is friendship by personality. If you have a good friend, whether he is close or distant might not be a big issue. The issue is that you will get the best of friendship from him. Most times, we don't even choose our friends consciously. People are attracted to each other to become friends. Nevertheless, we have the power to discontinue a friendship whenever it proves to be a wrong one. If you allow an ungodly man or woman who is not faithful even to himself or herself to become your close friend, it may not only lead you to financial poverty but to spiritual poverty and even premature death and hell.

Fashion Driven Life

People go into competing with their finances when they give their attention to the trends of the world. It is not unusual to see people who want to be Christians but at the same time, they want to be up to date with the trends of the world. In our present world where there is heavy competition, new things come out every day. New innovations flood the market every day and any man that wants to be buying every good thing his eyes see will be ready to welcome poverty. The Bible says,

Not everything that the world offers—physical gratification, greed, and extravagant lifestyles—comes from the Father. It comes from the world.

1 John 2.16 (GW)

Every good manufacturer looks for a scintillating advert to advertise his products but it's left for any man to decide whether to buy the products or not. A wise man knows when he sees a product that he needs and goes for it but many people go for new products just because they are new and probably trendy. It is not unusual to see people buying what they have already just because another brand is trendy. As in many other wrong financial practices, you can see Christians claiming to show forth the glory of God with their extravagant lifestyles; meanwhile, they are only trendy with the world. At this point, I will like you to understand that anything a man gives his attention to can influence his decisions. In other competitions, people get a prize if they win. But for somebody competing with his expenditures, he wins nothing. Rather, after some time, he will discover that poverty is haunting him.

Rat Race

People compete with their finances when they want to show how successful they are. It is good for people to work hard to become successful. But whenever the motive is to compete with others, it tends towards a rat race. One thing about rat race is that it can lead to display of wealth. The rule is 'If you are rich; show it.' For you to show that you are richer than the other person, you have to spend money. In most times the expenditures are not on the need list lest it will be a good spending. Even in many cases, they are not necessarily on the wants list but just for display of wealth. For instance, a man might need a simple bungalow for a home he can comfortably afford. Moreover, his want might be a duplex. Yet, for the sake of display of wealth, he will go for a mansion more likely with a loan. This can be a man who doesn't like a mansion but he will go for it to show that he is successful. Moreover, he will live unhappily in the mansion forever after. The unhappiness would have been enough but poverty won't mind knocking at the door.

In most cases, it might not be only one big thing like a house that will take all the money, it might be many little expenditures that will come together to wreak the financial havoc. The Bible says,

...For everyone who exalts himself
will be humbled, and he who
humbles himself will be exalted.

Luke 18.14 (NIV)

In conclusion, it is good to work hard but do your best to measure your success with respect to your goal and not with other people. It is good and normal to spend your income but do your best to spend your money on the things you need and not to compete with other people.

SOLUTION

A Word of Advice

Be careful about how you present yourself to other people. If you present yourself to be very rich, they will push you into spending like those who are very rich. If you present yourself the way you are then they will only expect you to spend the way you are. Above all, be mindful about those that would likely influence your spending. And also know that the main person that will influence your spending is yourself. It is even a sin of pride to compete financially.

Practical Questions

1. Have you ever bought anything just because everybody around you was buying it at that moment?
2. Have you ever bought something trendy though you are not necessarily in need of it?
3. Are there people you know presently that shouldn't be richer than you?
4. Do you think that those people who cheer you up when you buy the big things you don't need will also cheer you up when you begin to sell the things you need?
5. Do you compare yourself financially with any one?
6. Do you buy anything of a particular class because that is the standard people are expecting from you?
7. Who are your friends?

A Verse for Inspiration

That is why I run straight for the finish line;
that is why I am like a boxer who does
not waste his punches.

1 Corinthians 9.26 (GNT)

CHAPTER

12

Premature Success

Then the younger son gathered up all that was his and traveled far away to another country. There he wasted his money in foolish living.

Luke 15.13 (NCV)

Something is said to be premature when it happens before the suitable time or time of maturity. On the other hand, success is the achievement of one's goal. Thus, premature success is the achievement of one's goal before the suitable time or time of maturity.

Success is a good thing, but when it comes before the right time, it can as well lead to poverty. I know that it may not sound so good for someone who is praying for success to hear that the same success can lead to poverty. Nonetheless, it behooves me to show you when success is premature and how it leads to poverty.

I will like you to consider the analogy of a pregnant woman and a new born baby. When a woman gets pregnant, it is expected that after nine months she will give birth to a baby. And when that happens, it brings joy. But if a pregnant woman should deliver before nine months, it becomes a premature baby. The truth is that many premature babies don't survive even with the technological developments in the medical sciences. And you should not assume that such modern equipment are available everywhere. From this analogy, you will see that there is time between conception and delivery. The same is true for success; there is a time for every level of success. The Bible says,

There is a time for everything,
and a season for every activity
under heaven.

Ecclesiastes 3.1 (NIV)

A successful life is a series of events and not a one-time event. For somebody to become a successful professor of Mathematics, he will first of all encounter the mountain of nursery school mathematics and come out successfully. Then he will conquer the primary or elementary school Mathematics, the secondary or high school Mathematics and then the university Mathematics. It is only when he has faced the PhD Mathematics and come out successfully that he will begin to think of being a professor of Mathematics. Now, if a child excels greatly in secondary school Mathematics and he is made a professor of Mathematics immediately, it will become a success story. Nevertheless, that will also mark the beginning of frustration for that child; for he has jumped a lot of steps.

Most times people clamour for instant success without process not knowing that it will lead them ultimately to frustration and poverty. Now, let me show you how this phenomenon works.

Low Capacity

Success can be premature when people lack the capacity to contain it. It is not unusual to see a man making his young child the managing director of his big company. And it is also not unusual to see such a company going down simply because the young man lacks the capacity to manage such a big company. If he must succeed, he must first of all learn the basics and he cannot do that very well sitting on the seat of the managing director. Many times, you see some people make a lot of money but before you see them again, they are struggling with poverty.

The simple reason is that they stumbled into the money and stumbled out. Gambling is a good window for that. What such money usually does in their lives is that it increases their spending habits before flying away. Thus, such people are always candidates for indebtedness. You will notice from the Scripture that whenever God wants to use a man, He will first of all increase the man's capacity. He changed the name of Abram to Abraham. That is from 'Exalted Father' to 'Father to Multitude.' And that was indeed the ministry of Abraham. He kept Moses for forty years before sending him back to Egypt. Jesus had to train the apostles for up to three years before departing for them to continue with the Church. If God observes this principle; why not men? God can use a donkey to deliver His message, and He did that when there was a need. Nevertheless, He takes men step by step. The Bible says,

And we all, with unveiled face, beholding
the glory of the Lord, are being changed
into his likeness from one degree of
glory to another; for this comes from
the Lord who is the Spirit.

2 Corinthians 3.18 (RSV)

It is in the process of moving from one level to another that your capacity is being developed for the success ahead of you. You might be saying, 'Just give me the big money and I will control it.' That had been the words of many before you but since the capacity was not there, they ended in frustration. Just think of God giving a helicopter to a man as a gift in the days of Joshua. They would call it names like 'iron bird', etc. And don't be surprised that they could end up worshipping it. Nobody would ever think of using it as a means of transport. In the parable of the prodigal, you saw that the younger son sought for his inheritance before the right time. Even though he got it, he wasted it because he lacked the capacity to contain it at that time.

In the track of success, some people crawl, some people walk, some people run and some people fly. If you must be among the fastest group, then you must learn how to run or fly but also bear in mind that flyers are the easiest group to move off track. If you must fly, you must be very careful not to fly off track.

Excessive Celebration

Success can be premature when it is wrongly celebrated. This happens in different forms when people are carried away by celebration. Here, celebration refers to the mindset of having made it in life. Such also can lead to sumptuous feasting and careless spending. I said before that success is not a one-time event but a series of events. Now, each of the events is a success on its own but not ultimate. Many times, people are tempted to be carried away in celebrating one of these events and forget to move on to the next. You can notice it easily when some students who are on top of their classes in their secondary or high school days begin to struggle with their academics in the university. This also answers the question why most of the students that excel in the universities end up working for those who graduate with low grades (i.e. if they graduated from any university at all). It will then appear that their early success has become a problem to them. One poet called Emily Dickinson said, 'Fame is a bee. It has a song—it has a sting—ah, too, it has a wing.' When it comes to finances, you will see some people when they make some money, they will forget the hard work and discipline that led to the making of that money. They will forget that they are going somewhere. The only time they come back to themselves is when the money is gone. In a good number of cases, if such people must get back again, they will have to start from the very humiliating humble beginning. And that is if the opportunity is still there. However, it is always difficult for someone who has reached a certain height of success to go back to such humble beginnings. Whenever such things happen, poverty takes over like an armed man.

Another way this kind of thing happens is when people are carried away when they have reached the end of a particular life goal. This kind of people seems to be more mature than the first kind. They understand very well that success is a series of events, thus they wait till the last event is accomplished. But at this point, I will show you a higher truth: a successful life is a continuum of success. For a man to say that he is financially successful, it should be continuous. It shouldn't be having one day of sumptuous feasting followed by a day of hunger. If you accomplish a financial goal, that shouldn't mark the end of your life. Even if you are to retire, you should plan well and retire successfully. Again, I will use the analogy of a student that wants to become a professor of Mathematics. After passing through many tests and examinations and becomes a professor of Mathematics, he won't say that his goal has been accomplished and then turns to go home. Rather, he will begin to set another goal.

It is good to celebrate any kind of success but care must be taken in order not to be carried away by it. The Bible says,

> *Woe to you, O land, when your king is a child, And your princes feast in the morning! Blessed are you, O land, when your king is the son of nobles, And your princes feast at the proper time—For strength and not for drunkenness!*

Ecclesiastes 10.16 (NKJV)

Pageantry Mindset

When people are interested in flaunting their success, they may end up with premature success. A man who is not interested in flaunting his success won't mind waiting till the success is fully developed. But someone who is bent on flaunting his success won't mind running wild at the sight of the first sign of success. He can run wild with the first cash but will come back to his senses when the cash is gone. Meanwhile, poverty must have broken and entered the house. Just think of a farmer who harvests his crops prematurely because he is in a hurry to display his bountiful harvest.

Sometimes, when people make a lot of money from a particular venture, they will forget that a bird at hand is worth more than two in the bush. They will start spending freely for others to see their prosperity. But as with many human endeavours, that initial income is what the individual should stand on to make further progress until he is established. It is not unusual to see that in many cases when that initial financial flow is abused, it might be very difficult to start again. It is also not unusual to see individuals in this category become frustrated in life when poverty comes upon them after they have experienced financial success. Moreover, poverty thrives very well on a frustrated or discouraged mind.

In conclusion, every man who is longing for financial success should also be prepared to receive it. At times, financial success can be intoxicating. Thus, the individual should prepare his mind beforehand. Even when other people come to pressurize, one must know that he is the driver of the vehicle. For when poverty comes, every man will go 'to his tent'.

SOLUTION

A Word of Advice

I will like you to know that financial success without character destroys the successful. It is better for some people to continue the way they are than for them to stumble into wealth only to crash into a serious poverty. Thus, be patient to move into financial success through the right steps. As you are planning for success, do well to increase your capacity to contain it.

Practical Questions

1. Have you ever seen people who suddenly became rich and also dropped down to poverty within a short period of time?
2. Have you seen people who started misbehaving because they became rich?
3. Do you believe that financial success can corrupt a man?
4. Have you seen rich people with good character?
5. Do you believe that you can be rich and still have good character?
6. What are you doing to improve your character every day?
7. Do you pray and read your Bible every day?
8. Do you think that financial success comes once and for all or that it is a continuous phenomenon?

A Verse for Inspiration

For the turning away of the simple
shall slay them, and the prosperity of
fools shall destroy them.

Proverbs 1.32 (KJV)

CHAPTER

13

Fear

A person's fear sets a trap
[for him], but one who trusts the
LORD is safe.

Proverbs 29.25 (GW)

Fear is an unpleasant feeling of anxiety caused by actual or perceived danger.

Fear is a multifaceted evil that does no man any good. Sicknesses thrive on fear, strife thrives on fear, and corruption also thrives on fear with many other vices. In the same way, poverty thrives on fear. A good number of the causes of poverty listed in this book thrive on fear. People compile reasons to justify their poverty out of fear of being challenged by others. People engage in many dishonest activities to make money out of fear of failure. Many people will rather remain idle out of fear of being humiliated. Many people will rather remain in their comfort zone of sustainable poverty out of fear of losing it all. Many people are afraid of taking risks but the truth is that there is no business venture that does not involve risks. The rule is the higher the risk, the higher the profit potential.

Wherever fear thrives, faith cannot be found. Fear is simply faith in the opposite direction. The Bible says,

Without faith no one can please God.

Hebrews 11.6 (NCV)

If you substitute 'with fear' for 'without faith' in this verse, you can read: With fear no one can please God. In the midst of the plethora of God's promises, a man can still live in poverty simply because of fear which is lack of faith. As long as fear works in a man's life, he will not even venture to walk out of poverty; for fear tells him that it won't work. The worst kind of fear a Christian can live in is the kind that gives him Bible quotations to defend his fears. He can claim to be a patient man. He can claim to be a humble man. He can claim to be in the shoes of some Biblical characters. He can claim a lot of things but if he should be truthful to himself, he will know that fear is withholding him. Even when some people want to exhibit their faith and still retain fear, they end up with wishes. It is only faith that goes with work; wishes don't. No one can have both faith and fear. They are opposite of each other. A good understanding of how fear works will help one to know whenever he derails into the tracks of fear.

Profit versus Loss

Fear makes a man to see the loss instead of the profit. Fear makes a man to see only why something will not work even though there are over hundred reasons why the same thing should work. Fear makes a man to see the Judas in a business venture even though there are other eleven faithful apostles in the same business venture. Meanwhile, for every Judas there is a Mathias to replace him. Fear can make a Christian to magnify an anthill into a mountain, instead of him to focus on his mountain-moving God.

Whenever you talk about loss, you are talking about failure—you are talking about discouragement. On the other hand, whenever you talk about profit, you are talking about gain or benefit—you are talking about encouragement. The work of fear is to cover the eyes of a man from seeing the encouragement in any business venture and open his eyes to the discouragement. The introductory verse of this chapter says that fear sets a trap. That implies that many people live in poverty not because they are destined to be poor but because their fear sets a trap of poverty for them and they are caught in it.

When the Bible warns us in Proverbs 4.23 to be careful about what we think, we should know that just as faith for profit attracts profit, fear of loss attracts loss. In the same way, just as faith for prosperity attracts prosperity, fear of poverty attracts poverty.

A man who is afraid of loss thinks about loss all the time. He will always avoid profitable ventures until hunger pushes him out. Then he will walk with fear until he falls into a loss. 'That is what I feared!' he would say. Thus, encouraging himself that his fears were true. The result is that he will go back into his shell of a poverty-stricken life that ventures into nothing. Then he will lose nothing and gain nothing. The Bible says of Peter,

But when he noticed how strong
the wind was, he became afraid
and started to sink.

Matthew 14.30 (GW)

The question one will ask is, 'Was the wind not there before Peter began to walk on the water?' The answer is that Peter took his attention off Jesus and saw the wind. However, his new knowledge only made him to sink. The same thing happens to people that are involved in any business venture. Whenever they begin to fear the risks, they will begin to fail in the same business they had been making progress. But at the end, they will see that most of their fears never existed. Winston Churchill once said, 'I remember the story of the old man who said on his deathbed that he had had a lot of trouble in his life, most of which never happened.'

Possessions versus Lack

Fear makes a man to see what he does not have instead of the things he has. It is a reality that God provides us with many things we need at every point in our life. The Bible says,

God's divine power has given
us everything we need for life
and for godliness.

2 Peter 1.3 (GW)

If you look at the verse very well, you will see that God does not make provisions only for godliness or spirituality but also for the physical life. However, a man can choose to look for the things God had already given to him—both on the outside and the inside of himself. I will like you to know that even if it seems that nothing is on the outside, something is always on the inside. Fear will make a man to believe that the reason why he will not succeed is because of what he does not have. And no man can succeed in anything if he does not believe that he will succeed in it. Meanwhile, the truth remains that if a man ventures into nothing, he will make no loss, neither will he make profit and that leads to poverty.

Good News versus Bad News

Fear makes a man to hear only the bad news and pay no attention to the good news. The Bible tells us that most of the Israelites that left Egypt could not enter the Promised Land because they decided to believe the bad news told by the ten spies, instead of the good news told by Joshua and Caleb. The good news and the bad news came at the same time but they decided to choose fear instead of faith. Any man that gives attention to fear will only hear the news of how many people that have failed in any business venture. And he won't even bother to ask why they failed. He will only conclude that the business is full of failures and that no one can succeed in it. Moreover, if such a man does not change from such an attitude, he will become obsessed with bad news of failures until his old age. The Bible says,

Loafers say, "It's dangerous out there! Tigers are prowling the streets!" and then pull the covers back over their heads.

Proverbs 26.13 (The Message)

Such men will not ask themselves, 'Why are others walking freely on the streets and not yet devoured by the animals?' The way such things happen for some Christians is that they see corruption in every business venture and thus decide to stay indoors. Such Christians will not ask themselves, 'How did Daniel and his three friends succeed in the pagan land of Babylon?'

A man should listen to good news as well as bad news. He should listen to bad news for information and learning. But he should pay more attention to good news not just for information and learning but for encouragement and edification.

Fear of Criticism

Many people fail in life because they fear criticism. Whenever people are given to fear of criticism, they will either spend the rest of their lives preparing for the perfect business venture, or they will spend their lives bemoaning the fact that the only business they could embark on would be severely criticized. However, one thing common with them is that they usually spend their lives doing nothing and that leads to poverty. I want you to know that a truly successful man looks for people that will analyse him critically. Every good book passes through editors who criticize it until it is done. Big organizations do employ professional hackers to try their websites and software applications before they are exposed to the public. It is only a weakness, born out ignorance, for people to fear criticism. Another truth is that nobody can keep away from criticism as long as he has been born into the world. Even if he decides to stay indoors, he will still be criticized. In fact, the more a man is criticized the better he becomes. The Scripture says,

And it happened, as He was alone
praying, that His disciples joined
Him, and He asked them saying,
"Who do the crowds say that I am?"

Luke 9.18 (NKJV)

Jesus also went on to ask His disciples about their own opinion concerning Him. However, all the answers did not stop the ministry of Christ. He still went ahead to accomplish His mission on earth.

It is a common practice with many business organizations to carry out periodic studies on the opinion of the public concerning their products. They don't go looking for people that will tell them sweet words, they look for people that will tell them the truth. And the truth, when it is critical helps such companies to improve on their products.

The fear of criticism is driven on the wheels of low self-esteem. Anybody without self-confidence can spend his life time in a shell. When God commissioned Joshua, He instructed him to be courageous (Joshua 1.9) and the same happened with Jeremiah (Jeremiah 1.17). David, in his own time said,

I will praise You, for I am
fearfully and wonderfully made;
Marvelous are Your works, And
that my soul knows very well.

Psalm 139.14 (NKJV)

These are not words of pride, but an affirmation that one knows how great God has made him. Self-confidence repels fear of any kind including criticism. One irony about fear of criticism is that those who spend their lives criticizing others are always afraid of criticisms.

In conclusion, when a man fears God, he will have nothing else to fear. Poverty thrives wherever there is fear. Thus, keep fear away from your mind.

SOLUTION

A Word of Advice

Do not let fear to be your teacher. Fear will always teach you how and why things cannot be done. Put your faith in God's ability, for that will boost your self-confidence. You acknowledge your faith in God by praying to Him. And a regular study of the Bible will help you to see life better. Believe that you can do all things through Christ and you will see it happen. God does not disappoint those that trust in Him.

Practical Questions

1. Do you fear God? (i.e. a reverential fear)
2. Is there any other thing you fear?
3. If you fear God why fear any other thing?
4. Are you too conscious of what people will say?
5. Do you think that every human being must be afraid of something (apart from God)?
6. Do you believe you can do all things through Christ?

A Verse for Inspiration

For God has not given us a
spirit of fear, but of power and
love and of a sound mind.

2 Timothy 1.7 (NKJV)

CHAPTER

14

Addiction

They promise freedom to everyone.
But they are merely slaves of
filthy living, because people are
slaves to whatever controls them.

2 Peter 2.19 (CEV)

Addiction is the condition of being unable to stop taking or using or doing something habitually despite its negative consequences.

Addiction has to do with destruction. If anything or habit becomes addictive, then it is destructive. Whenever the word 'addiction' is mentioned, things like drugs and alcohol come to mind. However, the domain of addiction is uncountable. In most cases, addiction demands time and money—two important factors that when a man loses them he will settle down with poverty. No man is born an addict except in spiritual cases which are few in number. Addictions are usually learnt (through bad influence) and they start gradually until they grow strong like a tree with deep roots.

Addiction is a respecter of no man. And the best way to deal with it is by not allowing it to enter in the first place. In the beginning, addiction may appear innocent and harmless but at the end it bites like a poisonous snake. It preys on the mind and in most cases; it takes the hand of God to break the yoke of addiction. That is why the Bible says,

Don't give the devil any
opportunity [to work].

Ephesians 4.27 (GW)

Addiction does not just make a man poor; it can destroy a man's spiritual life, marital or family life and also his health. It can kill a man and cause him to end up in hell. Poverty is only one of its numerous children. Its mission is only for destruction. If it is addictive; it is destructive. As a Christian, you should monitor the things that take your time and money regularly. It can be sports, it can be television, and it can even be lying down on the bed. The list goes on and on.

Anything that takes your time takes your money as well; for time is money. Having a proper knowledge of how addiction works can help you to know whether you are into one, whether you are about to enter into one or whether one is knocking at your door.

Quest for Comfort

People go into addiction in quest for comfort but end up in poverty and frustration. It is not bad for people to seek comfort, but when they seek it from the wrong place they end up with the wrong result. It is like seeking the living among the dead. There are many things that could be found in this quagmire but there are three nefarious brothers that dominate it, namely: drugs (and tobacco), sexual immorality (and pornography) and alcohol. They are so domineering that many people now believe that every man must have at least one of them as a master. But that is a great deception that has kept many people in bondage. As I have said before; all addictions (except spiritual cases) are learnt, thus they could be unlearnt. They all start gradually, thus they can be avoided. Since they are not part of a man at birth, they can all be stopped. Even the spiritual cases can also be stopped spiritually. However, many physical addictions grow beyond physical management and thus could only be handled spiritually.

The use of drugs, tobacco and a host of stimulants is rampant because people claim that they are passing through stress or depression. Now, it is written in the Scripture,

God said to them, "Here is a place of rest; let the tired people come and rest. This is the place of peace." But the people would not listen.

Isaiah 28.12 (NCV)

And in another place Jesus calls,

Come to me, all who labour and are heavy laden, and I will give you rest.

Matthew 11.28 (RSV)

It is the will of God to give rest (which is peace of mind) to His people but many would rather go for it their own way. Drugs are highly addictive and in many cases, expensive. Consequently, drugs can dry up a man's finances within a short period of time and that means poverty. That is why many drug addicts do go into crime to raise money for the drugs. Drug addiction is so bad that it does not only affect one's finances directly, it does so indirectly too. It can break down a man's health while its addictive yoke is still on the fellow. Thus, the fellow will continue spending on his ill health which will never get better unless the addiction is broken.

Addictive drugs are so dangerous that many fellows who sell them don't take them. They only sell them to those who are ignorant and unwise. Moreover, at the end of the day, drug addicts never find rest or comfort in such drugs. Rather they find poverty, ill health, suicide, death, broken homes, more frustrations, mental illness, bad names, imprisonment, criminal records, irresponsibility, etc.

Meanwhile, many people still argue that there is no direct reference to drugs in the Bible but the Holy Spirit teaches us all things (1 John 2.27). And it can never be the will of God for us to leave His offer of rest and go to seek it in something else that would lead us into the list of problems I have just mentioned.

Coming to the side of sexual immorality which includes pornography and all its brothers; it seems to be among—if not the only sin that is addictive expressly condemned in the Bible. The reason is because it is the only sin a man commits against his own body. When its yoke is upon a man, it can bring about many problems of which poverty is only one. The Bible says,

For by means of a harlot
a man is reduced to a crust of bread;
And an adulteress will prey upon his
precious life.

Proverbs 6.26 (NKJV)

It is not uncommon to see people who engage in sexual immorality squander their money. Even in the parable of the prodigal son, Jesus pointed to it as a cause of poverty. Whenever its yoke comes upon a man, it will never leave him until he is reduced to a crust of bread or to the level that he would long to share the feed made for pigs. The yoke of immorality does not just make a man waste his resources but also gives him ill health and distracts his attention from his means of making those resources. At the end, when such a person might have gone down in poverty, he won't still find the love and comfort he is looking for. Instead, he will have great hatred for women. And if such a person is a woman, she will have great hatred for men.

Another addiction that comes with great controversy is that of alcohol. It is very common to see many people who claim to be Christians walking around not knowing that they are slaves to alcohol. Those who desire to drink could easily cite where Paul asked Timothy to take a little wine for his stomach, the miracle of turning water into wine and so on. Some have gone ahead to analyse the alcoholic content of the miracle wine at Cana in Galilee (though they were not there). When Paul was telling Timothy to take a little wine, was he asking the young preacher to give himself to wine in a little measure? Nay! He was only interested in his health since faith in Christ is not ascetic. Even though mere drinking of alcohol is not sin, God would rather that you keep away from it. The Bible says,

Do not get drunk with wine,
which will only ruin you; instead,
be filled with the Spirit.

Ephesians 5.18 (GNT)

Elsewhere, the Bible also says,

Wine is a mocker and beer
a brawler; whoever is led astray
by them is not wise.

Proverbs 20.1 (NIV)

Many Christians do go on to argue about drinking too much and drinking little but at the end of the day they turn into addicts. They think of buying courage and comfort in a bottle instead of depending on the Holy Spirit. And they end up with more frustration. Anybody who has been given to wine does not just spend his money but he also spends his time and capacity to make money. For alcohol reduces a man's sense of judgment and abilities. A man does not need to get in at all, let alone getting to the extremes. Alcohol also destroys a man's health thereby causing him to spend his money on illness. And that can incapacitate him from working to make money. All these point to disasters which poverty is one of them.

Despite the fact that people don't find the comfort they seek in drugs (and tobacco), sexual immorality (and pornography) and alcohol, they find it difficult to give them up because of the yoke of addiction. Even when they have gone down to a very bad state of life—say illness, poverty or frustration, they will still use any smallest opportunity to indulge in such lifestyles. It takes the hand of God to break such lifestyles if the addicts be willing.

Ignorant Addiction

Many people are addicts without knowing it. As long as many people are concerned, once they are not victims of the big three addictions, they are free from addiction. However, that is not always true. And the bad thing about these kinds of addiction is that they are rarely detected at their early stages. It is usually when such an addiction has been well established that some people can identify it. And some people continue with it without knowing it. One of such addictions is gambling (and lottery). Any man who is overcome by it can sell everything he has or even borrow in order to play it. The way it usually puts its ugly hands of addiction on its victim is by allowing him to win some money. Then he will continue with the lifestyle until he finds himself in financial difficulty which can be another name for poverty.

There are many other addictions that do not affect a man's finances directly. But they do so indirectly by taking his time. Such addictions include television, sports or games (especially when that person is not getting any income out of it), internet, some kinds of food, etc. Some of the items in this level of addiction might not be sin on their own but their addiction makes them sinful. They tend to become a god unto their victims and at the same time destroy them. The Bible gives an example of such:

Whose end is destruction, whose
god is their belly, and whose glory
is in their shame, who mind
earthly things.

Philippians 3.19 (KJV)

In conclusion, every human being should be on the lookout for anything tending towards addiction in his life. Of course, the obvious ones like drugs (and tobacco), sexual immorality (and pornography), alcohol and gambling (and lottery) should be avoided. It is better to avoid a problem than to solve it even with an expertise.

SOLUTION

A Word of Advice

Avoiding addictive tendencies remains the best solution for addictions. But in a case in which it is already in existence, turning to God is needed. For God can remove the taste or pleasure of the addiction from the addict. Any person in such a condition should pray to God with sincerity and faith; for God will not abandon such a person. Inviting Christ into one's life as Lord and Saviour will break the lordship of the addiction. Moreover, such a person must be willing to do the physical separation from the things that have to do with the addiction. Whether such a separation will cause some people to hate you or not, you must do it. And you may also have to throw away things you bought with money. Besides, you must set boundaries for utmost safety. Actually, the way to ensure the breaking of an old habit is by introducing a new one. And this time, it is the sure and guaranteed character of Christ. Such character will be enhanced by the study of the Word of God, a lifestyle of prayer and very importantly, fellowship with Christian brethren that call upon God with a pure heart. God doesn't want anyone to exist alone; you must exist in the midst of the brethren and grow in the power of fellowship. The Bible has this to say:

That is, that you and I may
be mutually encouraged by each
other's faith.

Romans 1.12 (NIV)

You should also know that the benefits of fellowship can only get to you if you open your heart to it. One may require the prayers of other brethren—which is still part of fellowship. These principles to breaking addictions are Biblical and thus effective by the working of the Holy Spirit. Make use of them.

Practical Questions

1. Area you addicted to anything?
2. Is there anything that is taking more of your productive time and money?
3. Have you tried to break an addiction without success?
4. Have you given your life to Christ?
5. Have you applied prayer, the Word of God and fellowship in your life?
6. Do you believe you can live without addition?

A Verse for Inspiration

So if the Son sets you free,
you will be free indeed.

John 8.36 (NIV)

CHAPTER

15

Failure to Know the Trends and Times

And of the children of Issachar,
which were men that had understanding
of the times, to know what Israel
ought to do; the heads of them were
two hundred; and all their brethren
were at their commandment.

1 Chronicles 12.32 (KJV)

Failure in this context is a state of not doing something that is expected. To know is to be aware of facts and information concerning something. A trend is a general likelihood of behaving in a particular way by the people while times are periods of existence. Thus, failure to know trends and times is the state of not being aware of facts and information concerning the likelihood of people's behaviours in periods of existence.

It is good to work hard but it is also necessary to understand the trends and times. It will prevent one from wasting his time on something that will earn him no money. Even when such a venture gives him money, it will be far less than the effort he is putting into it. Every human being is supposed to have the knowledge of his business. He should know the past, the present and the future of his business. He should know the past so that he won't waste his time doing what had been done. He should know the present so that he will know what the market wants.

And he should know the future so that he will know what he is expected to do in order to stay in the business.

It is common to see people complaining that they work like an elephant but eat like an ant. Some will tell you that they have read many books and applied the principles, yet nothing seemed to change. But a closer look at what they are doing will reveal that they are doing the wrong things. Following the trend does not in any way suggest the negative in this context. There is always the good trend as well as bad trend. Any man who wants to stay in business must conduct a research to know the trend. If in the process he finds a bad trend, he must continue with the search until he finds the good trend (which is the right trend). If a man wants to buy a pair of shoes of size 45 for his personal use, he won't say because the first trader he meets in the market deals in female shoes, he will go ahead and buy female shoes for himself. Rather, he will continue looking for a trader that deals in men's shoes. That is not even enough; he will continue searching until he finds size 45 of men's shoes. The same is expected for anyone who wants to stay in business.

No matter what you think you have, whether money, skills, energy, information—do your best to know the trend also. And do not be in haste to claim that you know the trend when you know only one time, namely: past or present or future. Trend is all about direction. If you must know the direction of a man, you must know where he is coming from (his past), you must know where he is at the moment (his present) and you must know where his face is turning to (his future). The introductory verse of this chapter says that the children of Issachar had understanding of the times (plural) not time (singular).

Erroneous Confidence

Many people are poor because they have other things and thus neglect the trends and times. Many people are always tempted to neglect the trends and times when they think they are so big in their business to be affected by them. They may trust their money which they deem too big to dwindle just because of changing times. The temptation is always bigger when the person concerned controls a large portion of the market. Nonetheless, even a monopoly can be broken by changing times. Even people with great abilities might not know when they become outdated, irrelevant and obsolete because they trust their skills and undermine the trends. The same is true for information and also, the way the information is passed on. For example, the information one may have about computer technology in 1970 might not be invalid in 2015 but actually obsolete. Coming to mode of passing on of information, you can consider the Bible. Though the Bible is still the same over the years; its mode of presentation changes with time. You have the scrolls, and then the codex, and then the printed paper bound Bible. However, you now have the Bible software applications which can enable one to have numerous Bible versions in one electronic device. A man who knows that he can use his tablet to read the Bible in Hebrew, Greek and English Language (and so on) may not think of buying sixty six scrolls just to read the Bible in one language. However, the paper Bible is still relevant. Thus, trends cannot be overlooked if one does not want to be overtaken by the changing times. The Bible has this to say:

Again I looked throughout the earth
and saw that the swiftest person does
not always win the race, nor the strongest
man the battle, and that wise men are
often poor, and skillful men are
not necessarily famous; but it is all
by chance, by happening to be at the
right place at the right time.

Ecclesiastes 9.11 (TLB)

I know that many people will simply interpret this verse by saying that everything in life is by chance or luck. But they willingly close their eyes to the 'time' written in the verse—they choose only chance. I will like you to understand that life is governed by principles and for any principle, there are exceptions. Exceptions are quite few but cannot as well be neglected. Understanding times is a great principle that will help you to succeed in life. Learn the principles and don't give yourself the headache about exceptions; God will take care of them.

Adamance

Some people fall into poverty because they bluntly refuse to follow the trend. It is not unusual to see people fighting new things, not because the new things are bad but simply because they are so much in love with the old ones. Such fights are seen even where the old things are no longer useful. But in the words of Victor Hugo, 'There is one thing stronger than all the armies in the world and that is an idea whose time has come.' Coming to the side of business, some people try to resist new trends for the fear that the new trends will make them fall apart. But on the contrary, it is their resistance that makes them to fall apart. It is only the wise ones that usually follow the new trends immediately they are discovered. One great secret about excelling in any business is being among the first to discover and follow a new trend.

Some people close their eyes against new trends simply because the old one gave them much profit. They fail to understand that the old trend was once a new trend. For a new trend to come out simply means that the old ones might have finished their usefulness. Some people will continue in a particular business even when it no longer gives them any meaningful income (if at all it still gives them anything). Some men even spend much time in prayer expecting God to change the trends and turn development backwards just because they don't want to change. Such person won't mind doing the same old things the same old ways expecting the same kind of prosperity they once experienced despite the changing times.

It is also easy to see some Christians trying to paint the concept of changing trends black, wrongfully from the spiritual angle. As a Christian, it behooves one to check every new trend to know whether it is ungodly or not. It will be very wrong for anyone to see the general concept of changing trends and times from the negative point of view. Even the Bible tells us:

The steadfast love of the LORD never ceases, his mercies never come to an end; they are new every morning; great is thy faithfulness.

Lamentations 3.22-23 (RSV)

As a Christian, one can live a lifestyle of being a trail-blazer and still continue in faithfulness just as our Heavenly Father is forever faithful.

No well-thinking human being will spend his money on goods and services that will not give him a commensurate benefit with respect to the present time. And if any man's business is no longer relevant because of time, let him know that poverty will certainly patronize him unless he changes.

Obsolete Progress

When people refuse to understand the times, they can still make progress—but just a repeat of old time progress. Sometimes you see people with beautiful achievements and works of great craftsmanship but they only attract admirations and applause—but no money. The simple reason is that though people appreciate their intelligence, they will not spend their money on an outdated development. Just think of a good engineer coming up with the type of aircraft invented by the Wright brothers. It will be better for such an engineer to learn how to service a modern aircraft engine than having that achievement. People can clap for him but nobody will buy it from him except those that want to stock their museum. It can take such an engineer many years to come up with such an aircraft and of course; some money. But that will not be sufficient to make him earn a good living from the so called achievement. It would be better for him, if he spends the same time and money to invent only one innovative part of a modern aircraft.

No matter how intelligent and ambitious a man is, if he does not regard timing, his achievements and his business will not help him to live out of poverty. To have true progress, one must learn to do the right thing at the right time. One must be willing to acknowledge and accept change in trends and times.

In conclusion, change is a reality one cannot deny. Whenever there is a change in trends, any man who does not want to struggle with poverty should check the new trend critically to know whether it is good both morally (or spiritually) and financially. If it is good, then no delay should be made before flowing with it.

SOLUTION

A Word of Advice

Don't allow yourself to be willfully stubborn and resist the changes that occur due to time, only to bring poverty upon your life. Don't wait for change in trends and times to come upon you. Rather be on the lookout and act by foresight. Being a trial-blazer even only once in your life can be enough for you to raise a huge capital that you will need for the rest of your business life. Don't waste your life cherishing old things. Always look out for new things, for that is even the nature of God.

Practical Questions

1. Do you cherish any business such that you won't like to change it even when time demands so?
2. Have you seen people or business organizations that fell apart because they tried to resist change?
3. Do you think trends and times respect any man?
4. Do you believe that innovation can lead to financial breakthrough?
5. Do you believe that the new things of today can be rendered obsolete tomorrow?

6. Do you believe that any business, service or product can be rendered obsolete by changes in trends and times?
7. Are you willing to follow the trends and times as long as they are sensible and not against the Word of God?

A Verse for Inspiration

Forget the former things;
do not dwell on the past.

Isaiah 43.18 (NIV)

CHAPTER

16

Indebtedness

Keep out of debt and owe
no man anything, except to
love one another…

Romans 13.8 (AMP)

Indebtedness in this context is the state of owing money to somebody or a legal entity.

Anyone who does not limit himself to his earnings but takes credit whenever it is available or borrows whenever it is possible would likely end up frustrating his finances. Some people are so given to indebtedness such that even when they have the resources to pay back they will not do it—and at that point it becomes a sin. One may now ask, 'Does it mean that it is sin to be in debt?' The main concern of the Bible is for us to be faithful in paying back our debts and more also, for us not to give ourselves to a lifestyle of indebtedness. When a man gives himself to such a lifestyle, he spends his future earnings today. He does not consider the fact that if his complete earnings cannot be sufficient for the present; he will not be able to cope in the future with incomplete earnings. He does not understand that continuing with such a lifestyle can degenerate to the point that he must borrow to survive. At such a point he will become a slave to others. The Bible says,

Poor people are slaves of the rich. Borrow money and you are the lender's slave.

Proverbs 22.7 (GNT)

Many people now believe that borrowing is part of life. And for such persons, if they are not in debts, it seems to be an abnormality. A lot of ideas exist about borrowing, many of which are wrong. Let's see some things about borrowing and how they affect not just the borrower but the lender also. Indebtedness can make a borrower, as well as the lender, poor. And the earlier a man decides to live by the Word of God, to keep out of debt, the better for him.

Spending the Future

Any man that borrows spends his future. No matter how strong or sensible a reason might be, it still does not deny the fact that borrowing is an act of withdrawing from one's future earnings. Another issue is, 'Will the borrower be able to pay back by the agreed future?' If he defaults, then he will be ready to face any music from the creditor, which most of the times is not friendly. Thus, the first thing you must know about borrowing is that it is never the best option.

Now, there might be situations in life in which borrowing might be considered. The best of such situations is when borrowing is meant for business. Nonetheless, in such a situation, the borrower should be certain about the business. He shouldn't borrow to try a new venture. He shouldn't borrow for a business with a high level of risk. He shouldn't borrow such an amount that will make him to stake all he has as collateral. He shouldn't borrow an amount that is beyond his capacity. He shouldn't borrow if he is not certain that the business will be able to pay back the loan before the agreed future time. And of course, he shouldn't think of borrowing to do a business prohibited by law. One thing about the temptation of borrowing for business is that if a man does not take time to think over it, he will yield to the temptation which may finally frustrate his life.

It is advisable that any man going into a business as a freshman should do so without borrowing. The reason is simply because he is still under trial. If he starts succeeding, then he can think of borrowing. But if he fails, he will learn his lesson but his loss will only be limited to the amount he has invested in the business. Failing with borrowed money will be more frustrating. If a man can do a business without borrowing, that will be the best option. He will have more peace of mind. And in case there is a loss, he will likely see something to fall back upon. On the other hand, if he borrows and encounters a loss, what would have acted as a cushion for him will be used to settle his debts and he will likely go down to the zero level (which means serious poverty).

Other situations one may consider borrowing is when they have to do with adding value. One can borrow to build a house but not the kind that will make him a slave for life. One can borrow to pay for acquisition of knowledge for that is a form of investment. However, it is wrong for one to borrow to pay his children's school fees when he could comfortably take care of that in another school. In the same way, it is very wrong for someone to borrow for his recurrent expenditure.

Most of the times, people borrow for lack of discipline. Discipline makes a man to live within his means. A man who goes borrowing for none productive reasons and for recurrent expenditures—how will he survive when the future comes, having spent the resources meant for the future before it comes? That is a simple introduction to a life of poverty. Availability of loans and credits tempts men to take them and live beyond their means. At that initial time, they are sweet but at the end they turn bitter. The best remedy for them is not to take them in the first place; for once taken, one might not be able to get out for a long period of time. And somebody who is struggling to pay his debts doesn't talk much about prosperity. This is why for some people, immediately they lose their job, they will become frustrated.

Meanwhile, despite all these, there might be some other pressing needs that are not productive that may cause someone to borrow. One of them is hospital bills and things like that. However, that still does not make borrowing a good venture. It is good to live one day at a time. The Bible admonishes us thus,

> *Keep your lives free from the love of*
> *money and be content with what you*
> *have, because God has said,*
> *"Never will I leave you;*
> *never will I forsake you."*
>
> Hebrews 13.5 (NIV)

Harsh Borrowing Conditions

Some people borrow without considering the conditions only to be frustrated later. Most of the time borrowing goes with interests and some other conditions which may be harsh. But for the fact that the borrower is at the mercy of the lender and has lesser bargaining power, he may go ahead to accept the conditions. However, he could as well say 'no'. It is only when the payback time has come that some people come to discover the trouble they have entered into.

At the initial time, ambitious borrowers will usually believe that they can pay back. They only consider the positive side and neglect the negative. Even though it is good for one to have a positive mindset in everything he is doing, it is also expedient to always have a look at the negative side. Even in some situations when things work as expected for the borrower, he may still find it difficult to meet all the conditions when the time comes.

Doubtless, I know that there can be situations where borrowing seems to be inevitable and even finding a person who will lend with harsh conditions seems to be a miracle. Nevertheless, care must be taken in order not to sell oneself into slavery. It is good for a man to borrow on terms he can easily honour for that will make him a faithful borrower. The truth is that if a man is counted faithful, many people will be willing to lend him their money. Thus, he will have many options to choose from and can easily stay away from loans with harsh conditions.

Risk to the Lender

Indebtedness can also frustrate even the lender. Though it is quite obvious that indebtedness can impoverish a borrower, it is also obvious that even banks do close down because of bad debts. The Scripture warns us,

A wicked person borrows, but
he does not repay.

Psalm 37.21 (GW)

Thus, a man should not only keep away from borrowing, he must also be careful about lending for that also can lead to poverty. Meanwhile, the Bible says,

Give to him who asks you, and
from him who wants to borrow
from you do not turn away.

Matthew 5.42 (NKJV)

Now, the question is, 'How are we going to go about giving and lending?' In order to answer the question, I will give some rules about lending.

The first rule is to avoid lending as much as you can and do only giving. It is better for you to give freely and spare yourself the trouble of lending and borrowing which usually comes at the repayment time. Many people can appear as saints when they come to borrow but when the time for repayment comes they won't mind painting you black before others. And for the fact that you may find it difficult to predict, it's better to give the amount you can give freely and prevent the heartbreak. Moreover, some people resort to such ungodly behaviours when they see that they cannot pay back—they use it as a defense.

The second rule about lending is if you must lend, then you are to lend to the limit you can forgo should the borrower default. There can be situations when the amount you can give freely might not be sufficient for the need of the borrower and you may consider lending. Nevertheless, if a default can lead to your own frustration, you should refrain. Don't begin to say that you can trust that person. The truth is that the same person can be frustrated and thus can default. I will like you to imagine the kind of frustration you can get yourself into should the borrower default. When you get the picture in your mind—just know that such a picture is possible if you lend in such a situation. This does not call for a stingy lifestyle. If you are truthful to yourself you will know when a default can lead to frustration and when it will not.

The third rule is that if you are to lend, lend only to those you trust; unless you call it a free gift by which you can give to any kind of person, even a stranger. But if you call it lending, you must trust the borrower. Don't lend by assuming that the person might be trustworthy. Rather, lend because you have a conviction that the person is trustworthy. If somebody comes to borrow and you find out that he is lying, then it will be expedient for you to refrain from lending. If there should be any option again, then that is free giving unless you will consider the money so lent as gambling.

The fourth rule is that if you are to lend your money to somebody, try and know the purpose for the borrowing and the person's capacity to pay back. When people borrow for the wrong reason, they find it difficult to pay back and you won't like to fall a victim. Again, when people borrow beyond their capacity, they find it difficult to pay back.

The fifth rule is that it is wrong (if not sin) for you to lend when you should give freely. Some people can be in need and it is certain that they don't have any means of paying back. In such situation, if you have the ability to give freely, that will be the only option God wants from you. The Bible says,

Blessed is he who considers
the poor; The LORD will deliver
him in time of trouble.

Psalm 41.1 (NKJV)

The sixth rule is that it is sin to lend at interest to the needy. You can decide on terms of agreement with a man when you are talking about business and investment. However, it becomes sin for you to mention interest for a man when he comes to borrow because he is needy.

Risk to an Innocent Man

Indebtedness can also frustrate an innocent man who is neither the lender nor the borrower. When the Bible says that you are to keep out of debt, you should do that both directly and indirectly. Sometimes, in order to please friends and relatives, some people who would always keep away from borrowing fall victim of the same. This happens when one stands as a surety. A man should know that if the borrower defaults, he might be affected as a surety. And no one will like to be frustrated financially because of a loan he did not take.

However, there can be situations where one can consider standing as a surety. One can do that if the borrower is known to him to be trustworthy. He should also know the borrower such that he would be able to locate him should there be a need. He should know the purpose for the borrowing and be convinced about the capacity of the borrower to pay back. Above all these, it is wrong for a man to stand as a surety for an amount that will lead to his frustration should the borrower default. If a man does not consider these things before presenting himself as a surety, he may end up in poverty even when he did not enjoy the loan. The Scripture says,

My child, be careful about giving
a guarantee for somebody else's
loan, about promising to pay what
someone else owes.

Proverbs 6.1 (NCV)

Apart from standing as a surety, some people go the extent of borrowing to give to their friends or relatives. Some do that without proper considerations—which can result to their own frustration.

In conclusion, do your best to live by what you have. Don't spend your future income today—when that future comes, what will you do? Borrowing can be sensible when it has to do with business and not for merriment. If you must lend, be wise. However, it is better to be a lender than a borrower.

SOLUTION

A Word of Advice

I will like you to know that sometimes even when you don't like to borrow; the offer will come looking for you. That is when discipline and determination come in. I want you to understand that borrowing can make you ineffective. If you believe in living each day by what you have and the day's resources seem insufficient, necessity will push you to work hard. But if you resort to borrowing to maintain a certain standard of living, you will end up postponing the evil day. And a time will come when you will lack the capacity to postpone it again. At that time, poverty will attack you like a monster. It is not sin to borrow but do your best to live by what you have.

Practical Questions

1. Are you presently in debt?
2. Do you live a lifestyle of borrowing?

3. How do you feel when paying back a loan for the things you used some time ago while there are many needs to be met at present?
4. Have you ever been embarrassed because of debt?
5. Have you ever lent money to somebody who never paid back?
6. Do you easily stand as a surety for people without asking questions?

A Verse for Inspiration

The LORD your God will bless you,
as he promised. You will make loans
to many nations, but you will not
have to borrow from any of them. You
will rule many nations, but no nation will
ever rule you.

Deuteronomy 15.6 (GW)

CHAPTER

17

Distraction

But the Lord replied to her by saying, Martha, Martha, you are anxious and troubled about many things.

Luke 10.41 (AMP)

Distraction is anything that stops somebody from concentrating on what he or she is doing.

Whenever a man is not careful to pay close attention to one or few things at a time, he may end up being carried away by one thing that is meaningless or many things that are meaningful. But he will end up catching nothing except poverty. Whenever the word 'distraction' is mentioned, what usually come to the mind of many people are things that are not useful. But the truth is that things that are ideally useful could become great distractions. For this reason, a man should always decide on the things necessary for his financial progress at any point in time. Anything that is out of context should be termed distraction. It was Thomas Fuller that said, 'He that is everywhere is nowhere.' Even having a new wonderful vision can become a distraction if it will hamper the progress of the ongoing vision. The usefulness of such visions can make them irresistible but proper definition of terms can put such visions in a waiting list. Human beings have limited time and resources, thus spending them on many things can only start those things with none completed.

On the other hand, some things which are ideally bad still distract a host of individuals. Some of them come in disguise. Some of them appear normal. Some of them appear negligible. Some of them appear pleasurable. They can come in different ways but their work is to make sure that the foremost vision is not accomplished.

Distraction is one of the causes of poverty that is silent and many poor people who are its victims can't even identify that. Likewise, many rich people who are moving down the slope into poverty because of distraction don't even know it. Distraction is so powerful that giving attention to it even once can be enough to derail a man—just like yielding to temptation even once can ruin a man's entire life. Moreover, distraction can come in form of temptation.

Anxiety

Many people worry a lot without knowing that it is a distraction. A man who is working for a living can decide either to continue his work and think of how to make it more efficient and effective; or to give his time, energy and skills to worrying. When many people worry, they assume that they are thinking but they are wrong. Thinking is all about considering a matter in order to make a decision but worrying is all about troubling oneself because of an unfortunate past or uncertain future. Worrying does not bring any solution; rather it adds health problems to a man. And it also distracts him from making money for his living. Consequently, it does not bring money but rather, it stops money from coming in and creates more avenues for expenses.

If a man knows that he cannot undo the bad things that have happened in the past, why then should he worry? On the other hand, why should a man trouble himself about a future that is yet to come? Why should a man create an image of a burden concerning the future and allow it to weigh him down? Hear what Jesus says,

Therefore do not worry about
tomorrow, for tomorrow will
worry about itself. Each day
has enough trouble of its own.

Matthew 6.34 (NIV)

When a man packs the troubles of many days and put them on himself in one day, they will definitely bring him down. He can then begin to see frustration even where there are opportunities. That also invites sickness—and a sick man cannot work effectively (if he can work at all). You should remember that poverty does not ask a man whether he is sick or not. It only follows the rule: if a man does not work, he should not eat (or rather, let poverty strike him).

Good Things

Good things can distract even the wise. At every point in a man's life, some things are needed and many things are not. Among the things that are not needed can be good things. And if care is not taken, such good things can become powerful distractions. This contributes a lot to the reason why some people are busy and hardworking but are still struggling with poverty. Some people pursue a lot of goals at the same time only to have the individual goals as distractions to one another. Such persons usually have wonderful curriculum vitae but no fortune. Only if such persons could focus on one thing or few things at a time and finish them, they will prove to be efficient and effective. Financial returns don't come to a man because of how many things he has started but because of how many things he has finished. Whenever a man is starting something he should always take a look at its completion by foresight. Having this mindset will stop him from starting a new project when the current one is struggling to reach the completion stage with the available resources. The Bible says,

Something completed is better
than something just begun…

Ecclesiastes 7.8 (CEV)

Sometimes, people are tempted to abandon their visions for new ones that seem to be better. Although it might be sensible, it is also expedient to consider if the available resources will be enough to accomplish the new vision. Lest the old and new visions would be stopped along the way and the resources invested in them might be wasted. As a result, the new vision will end up working as a distraction to the old vision.

Early Life Distractions

Distractions faced early in life can derail a man into a lifelong poverty. The early days of a man are his formative days and if he gets it right at this stage he will go far in prosperity in life. In the same way, a closer look at the life of many poor people will reveal that they got distracted early in life. Now, in this context, early life might refer to early childhood, youthful age, early days in business, early days in career, etc. Among all these, the strong one I will like to consider is the youthful age.

The youthful age is the beginning of the time of responsibility. Even the early days of business life, career life, marital life, etc. are usually in this age. It is very easy for youths to be distracted by good and sensible things of life just because of wrong timing. Moreover, poverty never asks of timing, it only fits in whenever there is a poverty-shaped hollow. It might come as relationship, bandwagons, etc. Mistakes made during childhood could be easily corrected but not those made as a youth. Many bandwagons that carry away the youths only present their fascinating aspects but at last they throw off their victims into a life of despondency and of course, poverty.

Bad Things

The rule has not changed; bad things distract many people into poverty. Many bad things have distracted many people and threw them into poverty, yet many people are still falling victims of such things. You can even see situations where a man will fall victim of the same thing over and over; and whether consciously or unconsciously, people still fall victims of such things. The main reason for that is because such things come as baits in a package called temptation.

Now, temptation comes only in three ways, namely: the lust of flesh, the lust of the eyes and the pride of life (1 John 2.16). That was all that the devil used to tempt Eve likewise Jesus Christ. And that is still the pattern of temptation. You can have a look at the temptation of Eve in Genesis 3.6: *So when the woman saw that the tree was good for food*—the lust of the flesh, *that it was pleasant to the eyes*—the lust of the eyes, *and a tree desirable to make one wise*—the pride of life, *she took of its fruit and ate.* (NKJV)

Again, you can take a look at the temptation of Jesus Christ in Luke 4.1-13. The tempter asked Jesus to turn a stone to become bread—which is lust of the flesh. Again, he took Jesus to a high mountain and showed Him all the kingdoms of the world in a moment and asked for worship—which is the lust of the eyes. Finally, he asked Jesus to jump down from the pinnacle of the temple to fulfill the Scripture—which is the pride of life.

One thing that makes a man to give in to the distraction of temptation is his own desire. If a man could keep his heart with the Word of God he will do well to overcome temptations. The Bible says,

Everyone is tempted by his own
desires as they lure him away
and trap him.

James 1.14 (GW)

In conclusion, having good focus and concentration can keep one from distraction. Besides, everyman should be conscious of the fact that distraction can come from anywhere. Finally, a man should be mindful of the things to which he gives attention for they can influence him and can distract him as well.

SOLUTION

A Word of Advice

You should understand this fact that distractions come in everyday life in different forms and capacities. Nonetheless, you should monitor your movements to know when you begin to derail. The greatest problem about distraction is for one not to know that he is being distracted. And another problem is for one not to know where to return to after discovering that he had been distracted. Whenever you discover that you have been distracted, don't waste your time recounting your loss—just return to the right track.

Practical Questions

1. Have you ever been distracted?
2. Have you seen any distracted person who never recovered?
3. What are the things you can list as distractions that can lead to poverty?
4. What has ever distracted you?
5. Can such a thing or things distract you again?
6. Do you have boundaries against distractions?

A Verse for Inspiration

But Jesus told him, "Anyone who lets himself be distracted from the work I plan for him is not fit for the Kingdom of God."

Luke 9.62 (TLB)

CHAPTER

18

Immediate Gratification

...Think of farmers who wait
patiently for the autumn and
spring rains to make their
valuable crops grow.

James 5.7 (CEV)

Something is immediate when it is happening or done with no delay. And gratification is the act of giving satisfaction or pleasure. Thus, immediate gratification is the act of giving satisfaction or pleasure with no delay.

Love for immediate pleasure squanders one's seed which means no harvest. Poor people are always not willing to sow their seeds and watch them grow to maturity. Many people will rather enjoy their present day instead of setting aside some of their resources for the uncertain tomorrow. To them, it is 'Do not plan about tomorrow; for tomorrow plans for itself.' They might be praying for an opportunity to make money but when it comes they will neglect it if it will not yield money immediately. They will always envy the success of others but will not like the endurance part of success. The time of endurance is always like eternity before those people. But the truth is that those days will come and pass and such persons will remain the way they are. It is only during their old age that some of them will begin to recount how they had been faithful to God but received no blessing. However, God gives opportunities for financial breakthrough to all His children, only that many do not like the 'Patience' part of the Fruit of the Spirit. See what the Bible says,

For God is not so unjust as to overlook your work and love which you showed for his sake in serving the saints, as you still do.

Hebrew 6.10 (RSV)

This same character is the reason why some people will read a lot of books and learn many principles but no positive change in their financial lives simply because the principles will take time to yield returns. This same character is the reason why men can leave and die in poverty in the midst of vast arable land without planting trees. They will tell you that it takes five to seven years for a tree to grow and start yielding fruit, thus they can't wait. Meanwhile, they might have lived for seventy years.

Comfort Driven Life

Love for comfort enhances immediate gratification and thus, poverty. Actually, it is normal and good for someone to desire comfort but when it goes for obsession it leads to error. It is at this point that a man longs for immediate comfort with no consideration for the future. However, the irony of it all is that a man could be said to be living in comfort when it is continuous. And another truth about it is that every man that is carried away into poverty because of immediate gratification has the capacity to enjoy continual comfort—even better comfort; but he lacks knowledge. There is this principle in life, and that is; a portion of every harvest is a seed. Thus, for every comfort available to a man, there is a seed of comfort. Only if a man could learn this principle he would have comfort as a lifestyle.

Immediate gratification entails immediate enjoyment of long hours of sleep, long hours of leisure, sumptuous daily feasting, expensive clothing, etc.—all these with no consideration that they would not continue as a lifestyle.

Many times, comfort potentials come our way with no prior announcement. And when they come at times when one is in need of relief, he might be carried away to enjoy the whole comfort including the seed portion of it. It only takes a cautious mind to spare the seed. It is common among many people who have suffered in the hands of poverty to say that they must enjoy comfort to its fullest as soon as it comes their way. Little do they consider that enjoying the seed portion of the comfort may keep them back in the poverty-waiting-line until I-don't-know-when.

Impatience

Immediate gratification abhors patience. In the quest to get everything immediately many people have missed their financial opportunities and some ended up in the hands of fraudsters. It is only fraudsters that promise huge financial returns within a very short time with little or no effort. However, a man that understands the principle of patience and hard-work will hardly fall victim of such. In the words of Charles Spurgeon, 'By perseverance the snail reached the ark.' The truth about strong financial entities is that they are built over time. Sometimes, people will only notice them when they start booming. Sometimes, the owners might have been training for a long time. They might also be doing one work or the other which are not seen immediately by others. The introductory verse of this chapter talks about the farmer—how he waits patiently for the rain to fall on his crops. He does not rush to harvest the crop just because he wants to enjoy them immediately. And he does not refrain from sowing his seeds just because they would need the early and the latter rain to mature.

Many people are poor simply because they spend their time looking for businesses that will give quick returns and end up finding none to satisfy their taste. Sometimes they will wish they had started doing something all those years they have wasted, yet they won't be willing to start immediately. Little do they understand that though the best time to plant an oak tree was twenty years ago; the second best time to do it is now. The time of sowing and waiting might be unpleasant but they surely result in better continual comfort. The Bible says,

He who continually goes forth
weeping, Bearing seed for sowing,
Shall doubtless come again with
rejoicing, Bringing his sheaves
with him.

Psalm 126.6 (NKJV)

In conclusion, though the bud might taste bitter, with time, the fruit will appear with sweetness. The time of sowing and waiting are set by God to maintain order in the world. Any attempt to go against the rule will be walking down the path of poverty. It is in the character of the poor to quit. Meanwhile, winners don't quit and quitters don't win. The fifth stanza of the hymn 'God Moves in a Mysterious Way' by William Cowper (1731-1800) says,

His purposes will ripen fast,
Unfolding every hour;
The bud may have a bitter taste
But sweet will be the flower.

SOLUTION

A Word of Advice

Enjoy comfort whenever it comes your way but make sure that you keep the seed portion of it. Don't live your life today believing that tomorrow will plan for itself or assume that God will plan everything for you with you making no effort. The Bible says,

Ask the LORD to bless your plans, and you will be successful in carrying them out.

Proverbs 16.3 (GNT)

Have this in your mind that in every true prosperity there is an element of patience. Prosperity does not start on the day you get the harvest, it starts the day you sow the seed.

Practical Questions

1. Do you believe that we all work hard in order to enjoy comfort?
2. Do you believe that comfort is a harvest?
3. Do you believe that farmers keep back a portion of their harvest to serve as seed?
4. Do you believe that delaying gratification is like sowing a seed?
5. Which one is easier; to quit or to persevere?
6. Which one is better; to quit or to persevere?

A Verse for Inspiration

Then instead of being lazy, you will imitate those who are receiving the promises through faith and patience.

Hebrews 6.12 (GW)

CHAPTER

19

Wrong Priorities

Wherever your treasure is, there your
heart and thoughts will also be.

Luke 12.34 (TLB)

Something is said to be wrong when it is not right or is derived from an error. And a priority is something of more importance and urgency above others. Thus, wrong priorities are things regarded to be of more importance and urgency out of error.

What people regard to be important determines the flow of their expenditures, time and energy. And when such things are not properly evaluated, a man may end up wasting his limited resources and thus end in poverty. Though a man can hardly be perfect with his spending, a closer look at the spending history of the poor will reveal that they spend more of their resources (i.e. money, time and energy) on things that do not add to their financial capacity. Every time is precious and should not be neglected, likewise money and energy. However, a man's level of wisdom defines the things that are precious to him. It is left to the discretion of a man to decide the things that are important to him and things that are not, likewise the urgency of every matter in his life. He is the one that will separate his needs from his wants. If he fails to determine these things his life will be subject to the demand and supply of resources—that is a life without control. And the Scripture says,

Those who do not control themselves
are like a city whose walls are
broken down.

Proverbs 25.28 (NCV)

It is obvious that such a city is not safe. In the same way, a man like that is highly prone to poverty. This is why many people spend their lives on achieving a particular goal but at the end, such a goal will not be able to contribute to their wellbeing.

Waste of Resources

If a man fails to identify his needs and prioritise them over his wants, he will finally discover that though he has his wants, they won't be able to satisfy him. However, his unmet needs will be calling for attention. It is at that time that it will dawn on him that he has wasted his resources doing the wrong things. In many cases, people will have to sell the things they bought wrongly in order to meet their needs. And in some cases, they will go to the extent of selling some of the things they need in order to meet the more pressing needs. Meanwhile, at this point, such persons will be struggling with poverty. Many times in life people spend money on issues or problems that actually don't need money and they end up wasting their resources. Having money in one's hands does not mean that every issue that comes around must be solved with money; just like having a hammer does not mean that everything that comes around is a nail.

It is good for a man to ask himself many questions before spending his time, money and energy. He should think of the outcome of such spending and ask himself whether it is necessary, especially when such resources are not much at his disposal. If we take a look at one of the strong factors which is time, we will see clearly that every human being has only twenty four hours in a day. It is limited and also equal for all mankind. However, it is common to hear people complain that they are too busy and thus cannot do some things that are essential to their lives. Many people take pride in confessing it but little do they know that they are just telling others how weak they are in their inability to control themselves with respect to time. They assume that busyness is the same thing as productiveness or effectiveness. Occasionally, one can become too busy because of emergencies and situations beyond one's control but when it tends to become a lifestyle it becomes a weakness. Many people go about with the burden of being busy but they are actually busy doing the wrong things.

If I can use this opportunity to talk a little about time management, I will like you to understand that God does not expect any man to be busy more than he ought to be. The Bible says,

...for so he giveth his
beloved sleep.

Psalm 127.2 (KJV)

The problem is that many people don't manage their time properly and fail to see it as a weakness. Time continues to go on and on, it is only left for an individual to arrange his activities within time. Sometimes even successful people fall victims of time mismanagement. They fail to observe their activities as they grow until they become burdensome. They fail to understand that at each point in a man's life, he should know the activities that are still needed and those that are wanted. It is not a new story that many Christians expect God to reward them for being so busy while God is whispering in their ears, 'Delegate some activities to others.' We can see a picture of that in the life of Moses until his father in-law intervened. Also, the Bible says,

...every branch that bears
fruit He prunes, that it may
bear more fruit.

John 15.2 (NKJV)

It is normal that as a man becomes more productive, his activities will tend to grow but it is the will of God that some activities will be cut off to ensure more effectiveness. Any man that wants to manage his time properly must categorize his activities into things that are necessary, things that he can delegate to others and the urgency of all the activities. Many people live with the fantasy that if they are not there, nobody will be able to do it. But they fail to ask themselves who had been doing it before they were born. It is when people fail in time management that they can gradually slip into financial struggles. Meanwhile, it might be difficult for them to detect it since they are busy but producing waste.

It will be difficult to separate time from energy. Generally, energy, time and money go together and the same principle of waste from wrong priority applies to all of them.

White Elephants

Wrong priorities produce white elephants. A white elephant is a kind of waste—but a higher level kind of waste. In the case of an ordinary waste, an individual will incur a loss based on the cost of the project or activity he engaged in. The cost can be in form of money, time or energy. But in the case of a white elephant, the individual will lose the initial cost and also continue to spend for the sustenance of the project or activity which gives him nothing in return. One white elephant is enough to send a man into poverty let alone when they are many.

You can take a literal view of a white elephant as an elephant (i.e. the big animal) that is white in colour. Indeed it will be a good sight to behold and many people will like to have it. But look at the bad side of it: it will be consuming a lot of food from the owner's purse but will not be giving him anything in return. The beauty, the prestige, the admiration, etc. are the attractions but the poverty is the ultimate result. The truth is that white elephants can come as things that are useful but are wrongfully prioritized. For instance, a car is good but can be a white elephant to an individual; for a car must be maintained. Another example is a big mansion; it is good but can become a white elephant to an individual because of its cost of maintenance. Many other examples abound but the main issue is that a man should ask himself the benefit of any endeavour to him and its cost (including running cost) before spending his resources on it.

If a man discovers a white elephant in his possession and does not want to end in poverty, he should sell it or give it away or destroy it. For some cases, the only option will be to kill the elephant. However, if the owner decides to cherish it, one day, he will come to poverty and the white elephant will still die of hunger. But this time, the owner will be left in poverty. The Bible asks,

Why spend money on what does
not satisfy? Why spend your wages
and still be hungry...

Isaiah 55.2 (GNT)

Lifestyles

Lifestyles go with priorities. As a man's lifestyle determines his priorities, his priorities also determine his lifestyle. Those that are given to fashion are carried away by fashion. To them, fashion comes before any other; likewise those that are given to tourism, cars, food, trendy things, etc. A man's lifestyle influences his judgment on the things that are his needs and the things that are his wants. However, no matter a man's judgment concerning his needs and his wants, his real needs still remain his needs and his real wants still remain his wants. Human beings are created to leave a balanced life but a skewed mindset can lead to a skewed life. That invariably will lead to deficiency in some parts of a human life. As it happens with the human health, when a man is deficient in some nutrients, he will spend more money to restore it to balance than he would have done to keep it in balance in the first place. The same thing happens with a skewed lifestyle. It takes more for a man to be restored to a balanced lifestyle than he would have done living a balanced life in the first place. Sometimes people might not be able to come out of the deficient life they bring upon themselves. The truth is that the struggle to restore to a balanced life might mean a struggle with poverty which might be quite difficult.

It is better for a man to do all the struggling and balancing and evaluations in his mind—that simply means thinking. If he gets it right with his thinking, life will be easier. Every man should do his best to get the right knowledge especially the knowledge of the Word of God to make his thinking efficient. The Bible says,

For as he thinks in his
heart, so is he.

Proverbs 23.7 (NKJV)

A man is as good as the way he thinks likewise his priorities. In the same way, a man's expenditures are the description of his priorities.

In conclusion, many human needs are more objective than subjective and many human wants are more subjective than objective. Do your best to identify those objective needs and meet them first; for no matter how you neglect them, you will definitely be compelled to attend to them.

SOLUTION

A Word of Advice

Always consider the cost and benefit of anything to you before spending your money on it. Also do the same consideration before spending your time and energy on anything. Always differentiate your needs from your wants whether in little things or in big things. Understand that no matter how long you have travelled on the wrong road it will not lead you to your destination.

Practical Questions

1. Do you know that needs are different from wants?
2. Do you presently have a pressing need?
3. What are the cost and benefit of your present topmost need?
4. How urgent and how important is your present topmost need to you?
5. Do you still think it is a need or a want?
6. Are you too busy every day?
7. Do you think you do well in managing your time?
8. Do you consider God in your needs?

A Verse for Inspiration

Remember this: If the owner of the house knew what time a thief was coming, he would not allow the thief to enter his house.

Luke 12.39 (NCV)

CHAPTER

20

Spiritual Matters

Simon Peter said to them, "I am going fishing." They said to him, "We are going with you also." They went out and immediately got into the boat, and that night they caught nothing.

John 21.3 (NKJV)

Something is spiritual when it is immaterial and has to do with the supernatural. And matter, in this context is a situation under consideration. Thus, spiritual matters are situations that are immaterial and have to do with the supernatural.

Many people are poor because of issues beyond physical interpretations and such situations defy physical solutions. Such situations can be as a result of sin, curses, witchcraft, etc. The main point is that they are spiritual. Most of the time, they look natural and there might not be any hand to write on the wall that they are spiritual cases. It takes the knowledge of God for one to understand that they are spiritual. And it takes the hand of God to break such a yoke of poverty.

The victims of such circumstances might be hard-working like the apostles in this chapter's introductory verse. They might be obeying all the financial and business rules like the apostles that went fishing in the night. But they will end up working like an elephant and eating like an ant or end up with nothing like the apostles. As I said before, it can appear as natural and normal like in the case of the apostles. But a man of understanding will ask, 'Why didn't the apostles catch even a single fish throughout the night?' The Bible did not tell us the reason why it was so. Nevertheless, a good consideration of the situation will suggest that it was not normal.

It is quite unfortunate that many people live in such a situation for a reasonable part of their lives and some even die in it. For some persons, when they have struggled enough they might give in to other causes of poverty. And some observers can easily conclude that such things are the cause of their poverty. In some cases, it only takes a revelation from God to know that they are spiritual matters. That is why God says,

Call to me, and I will answer you. I will tell you great and mysterious things that you do not know.

Jeremiah 33.3 (GW)

Many people, in a bid to solve the problem of this poverty of spiritual nature, end up with more spiritual problems. Some do resign to fate and some continue struggling with their physical strength but to no avail. Nonetheless, God still delivers those that turn to Him with all their heart.

Sin

Sin can lead to poverty. Whenever people begin to lift their own will above the will of God—that becomes sin. If a man can avoid sin, a greater percentage of the spiritual causes of poverty would have been dealt with. Wherever there is sin, it creates an open door for the devil to strike. Normally, sin fascinates and presents its sweet part to men but at the end it destroys. Poverty is just one of the outcomes of sin. Sin does not only attract the attacks of the devil, it also attracts the punishment of God. The Bible says,

But it shall come to pass, if you do not
obey the voice of the LORD your God...
You shall carry much seed out to the
field but gather little in, for the locust
shall consume it.

Deuteronomy 28.15 and 38 (NKJV)

The Bible is full of examples of consequences of sin—how people were subjected to extreme poverty because of sin. Some had to eat their own children out of poverty and hunger. And some were taken captives as slaves. Sometimes, sins might seem silent and unpunished but the truth is that they will definitely lead to losses. The Bible says,

Some people get caught in their sins
almost at once, even before the time
of judgment. But other people's sins
don't show up until later.

1 Timothy 5.24 (CEV)

A good look at many causes of poverty shows that many of them are sinful acts, namely: dishonesty, addiction, pride, fear, etc. Nevertheless, some carry more spiritual implications than others. For instance, the sin of sexual immorality doesn't just have a physical implication which is more of squandering one's resources; it has a strong spiritual implication. Many evil covenants go with sexual immorality and it is difficult for one to part with it. The Scripture makes us to understand that it is such an act in which a man can lose a lot for just an insignificant momentary pleasure. The Scripture says,

Be careful that no one takes
part in sexual sin or is like
Esau and never thinks about God.
As the oldest son, Esau would have

received everything from his father,
but he sold all that for a single meal.

Hebrews 12.16 (NCV)

The sin of immorality is so strong that the best remedy a Christian should use against it is to flee from every opportunity that can lead to it. The same also goes for any other kind of sin, for sin is a destroyer. People who are poor because of sin don't only suffer from poverty but they also suffer from lack of peace of mind and frustration.

Curses

Curses can keep a man poor with strong hands. Curses are strong spiritual hindrances that can keep a man in poverty even throughout his life time if nothing is done to break them. It is also quite unfortunate that some people are born into curses. A look into the Scripture reveals that the number one cause of curses is sin. The Scripture says,

'Cursed is the one who does not
confirm all the words of this law.'

Deuteronomy 27.26 (NKJV)

One example is Reuben—his father cursed him that he will not excel for his sin and it affected him to his descendants. Another is Canaan, son of Ham, the son of Noah who was cursed to become a low level servant to his brethren. In fact, the Bible makes us to understand that a curse cannot stand without sin (Proverbs 26.2). However, it is not pleasant for parents to be cursing their children; that is not the best thing.

On the other hand, some people find themselves as victims of curses even when they have done nothing bad. Examples are the descendants of Ham and Reuben. Another set of persons were the first and the last sons of Hiel—a man that rebuilt the wall of Jericho and the gates in the days of King Ahab. Joshua had earlier placed a curse that any man that does such would lose his first and last sons. And it happened to Hiel even though the curse had stayed for a very long time.

From these examples, we can see that a man can be cursed directly by another because of sin. And we can see also that a man can be cursed if he breaks a law that goes with a curse.

The only solution to curses is turning to Christ. It may also take another Christian to pray for the victim but the victim must be willing to turn to Christ. A curse (and other spiritual problems) is like a burden which a man will like to be lifted from his life. If the victim is like a child, he will find it difficult to lift on his own and in such a case he will need the help of another Christian who is like a grown man with greater strength. Moreover, if the victim continues in the Lord, he will grow to become a man with enough strength to lift the burden on his own. Nonetheless, there can be some cases where God will demand reconciliation or restitution like in the case of Abraham and Abimelech (Genesis 20.6-7) and also in the case of Job and his friends (Job 42.7-9). Some curses can be easily broken while some are heavier especially those that go with a (blood) covenant. However, if a man turns to Christ and continue with Him (growing in grace and knowledge); any curse in his life will be broken. The Bible says,

In that day their burden will be lifted from your shoulders, their yoke from your neck; the yoke will be broken because you have grown so fat.

Isaiah 10.27 (NIV)

The Bible also says,

Christ has redeemed us from the curse of the law, having become a curse for

us (for it is written, "Cursed is everyone who hangs on a tree"),

Galatians 3.13 (NKJV)

Curses and many spiritual problems can fall away from a man's life if he grows in the knowledge of the Word of God (John 8.31-32). Remember the Levites, they gave themselves to the Word of God spoken by Moses and ended turning their curse into blessing. But it was not so with the Reubenites and the Simeonites.

The problem with many people who are victims of curses is that they are not willing to give their lives to Jesus Christ and continue with Him to grow thereby. They only want the curse removed so that they can continue with their own lifestyle. Elsewhere the Bible says,

Thou wilt keep him in perfect peace, whose mind is stayed on thee: because he trusteth in thee.

Isaiah 26.3 (KJV)

There might not be a one way formula for breaking of curses but prayers, fasting and above all continuing in Christ are effective answers. I said there might not be a one way formula because I can't tell the kind or the amount of prayer needed for any specific curse. I can't tell the kind or amount of fasting needed. And I can't tell how long it will take to break the curse. But I can tell from the Scripture that when one grows in the Lord, the anointing will break the yoke. A victim of a curse should not think of giving up until it is broken.

Witchcraft/Demonic Activities

Witchcraft or demonic activities can bring about poverty. Though many people will argue that there are no witchcraft activities and some will assign every misfortune to witchcraft, the truth is that witchcraft activities exist but are not responsible for every misfortune. They exist in some places more than others and since they are of the devil and are for destruction, they can also cause poverty. The Bible says,

I know where you live—where
Satan has his throne.

Revelation 2.13 (NIV)

Elsewhere, the Bible also says,

The thief comes only to steal
and kill and destroy…

John 10.10 (NIV)

Even though some demonic activities are carried out entirely by demons, witchcraft activities are mainly initiated by human beings who work with demons. Sometimes, they will specifically cast a poverty spell on their victims and at other times poverty will only be a part of the fallout of their evil domination. They can manipulate a sinner easily and they can also manipulate any man who is not holding unto Christ with tenacity. When they manipulate a sinner they claim to be right unlike when they suppress a man sitting on the fence because he is weak in spirit. The Bible has this to say,

Shall the prey be taken from the
mighty, Or the captives of the
righteous be delivered?

Isaiah 49.24 (NKJV)

Some witchcraft activities seem to be stronger and more devastating than others. They don't mind making an entire community, state or even a country to be poverty-stricken. But the Bible also has this to say,

But thus says the LORD:
"Even the captives of the mighty
shall be taken away, And the prey
of the terrible be delivered…

Isaiah 49.25 (NKJV)

Nevertheless, a man cannot sit down and fold his hands and wish them away. He must turn to God in serious prayers to stop such activities. However, a daily walk with God is a strong immunity.

Acts of God

Sometimes God can bring poverty for a purpose. If we take a look at the apostles that went fishing and caught nothing, it will be wrong to attribute their failure to sin, curse or witchcraft. We can only assume it to be an act of God for a purpose. Sometimes, God can use poverty to move people from their comfort zone; especially people who are satisfied with mere survival level. If you take a look at many rich people's testimonies, you will notice that many of them excelled in their quest to defeat poverty. Though, unfortunately, many people would rather die than rise to fight poverty.

On the other hand, God can send poverty for reasons beyond our comprehension as human beings. The Bible says,

I form the light and create
darkness, I bring prosperity
and create disaster; I, the
LORD, do all these things.

Isaiah 45.7 (NIV)

Nevertheless, this does not call for a man to become lazy and blame God for his poverty. The Bible tells us that the apostles did not give up. They struggled through the night and caught nothing but they continued until Christ came to their help and they ended with a big catch. God is sovereign and He does whatever He wishes but always for our own good.

Many people are poor because they don't pay tithe or give offering. It is common among many poor people to think that their income is small, thus they will not pay tithe or give offering. They don't know that it might be their reason for being poor and they go about believing that they are on the Lord's side. However, it is the same Lord that said,

"Will a man rob God? Yet you have robbed Me! But you say, 'In what way have we robbed You?' In tithes and offerings.
Bring all the tithes into the storehouse, That there May be food in My house, And try Me now in this," Says the LORD of hosts, "If I will not open for you the Windows of heaven And pour out for you such blessing That there will not be room enough to receive it. And I will rebuke the devourer for your sakes, So that he will not destroy the fruit of your ground, Nor shall the vine fail to bear fruit for you in the field," Says the LORD of host.

Malachi 3.8,10,11 (NKJV)

Even when some people think they pay their tithe, they are only paying what they like. Tithe is the one-tenth of one's income. A man can decide to pay more but not less. On the other hand, offering is any other thing one can give to God apart from tithe. It is when people fail to pay their tithe that the devourer comes around on their finances.

In conclusion, spiritual causes of poverty are realities. I chose to treat them at this point in this book so that many people will not use them to justify their poverty. Moreover, if a victim of such things turns to Christ, he will be set free.

SOLUTION

A Word of Advice

The main reason why people fall victim to spiritual causes of poverty is going out of the will of God. And such things are usually manifested as sin. Turning to Jesus Christ is the only solution; for then a man's sins will be forgiven, he will be delivered from darkness into light and he will receive grace to live a righteous life. If you have not given your life to Christ, I will like you to use this opportunity to do so. I will like you to pray this prayer:

Father, I turn to You today
I acknowledge that I am a sinner
and now ask for forgiveness. I repent
from all my sins and ask for your
grace to live a righteous life. Lord Jesus,
today, I accept you as my Lord and
Saviour. I believe that you died and
resurrected for my salvation.
Deliver me from all powers of darkness
and transfer me into Your kingdom
of light. Have your way in my life. Thank You
Lord in Jesus name I pray. Amen.

Now that you have given your life to Christ, you need a lifestyle of prayer and Bible study. Also, you need to join a living Church and be committed to it. When people give their lives to Christ, the Holy Spirit gives them wisdom which also helps in good financial management. Above all, do consciously pray to God to bless you financially.

Practical Questions

1. Have you given your life to Christ?
2. Do you believe that sin can open doors for poverty?
3. Do you think that one should resign to fate because of spiritual causes of poverty?
4. Do you believe that poverty of the spiritual nature can also be stopped?
5. Do you believe that a man can live without the influence of evil?
6. Do you believe that God cares for the spiritual needs of His children?

A Verse for Inspiration

Blessed be the God and Father
of our Lord Jesus Christ, who
has blessed us in Christ with
every spiritual blessing in the
heavenly places.

Ephesians 1.3 (RSV)

PART TWO

WHY SOME PEOPLE ARE RICH

The man became rich, and his wealth continued to grow until he became very wealthy.

Genesis 26.13 (NIV)

Presently, about one third of the world's populations are rich. They are rich in the sense that they have more than enough. Though it could be said that some people are born into riches, some acquire riches but no one can force riches upon a man.

In the context of this book, the main interest is not in people who steal other people's money or those who make money through other dubious means. The main interest is in people who have a right standing with God as far as their means of riches are concerned. Again, such persons are those who have more than enough, not just at a point in their lives but those who have it as a lifestyle. The points mentioned here are not hard and fast rules for becoming rich. But other things being equal, within an average seed time and harvest time of five to seven years, they can prove to be true. I will say again, this book considers matters of principles and not exceptions.

It is a common trend to see the rich getting richer and the poor getting poorer. Most times many people do complain against the trend, including Christians. They always point out how corruption contributes to it. But the fact is that even if corruption is removed it will continue unless the poor decide to change their habits that make them poor. The Bible says,

For to everyone who has, more will be given, and he will have abundance; but from him who does not have, even what he has will be taken away.

Matthew 25.29 (NKJV)

The trend is a principle and principles don't respect any man. Above all, it is the Word of God. The best thing a man can do for himself is to look for those principles that make the rich what they are than argue with the Word of God.

It is quite unfortunate that many Christians read the Bible and choose to leave out some things but God knows that we need them and included them in the Bible. Many will like to remain silent on issues concerning finances in the Bible but they will still need money to survive. Some people also believe that God has already appointed some people to be rich and some people to be poor. Perhaps, to deal with such a mentality, the Bible says,

Lazy people should learn a lesson from the way ants live.

Proverbs 6.6 (GNT)

If ants can survive and prosper; how about human beings? If God can direct lazy people to learn from the ants, believe you me that God has deposited some principles of prosperity in ants which ought to be known, not just by the lazy ones but also by anyone who cares about prosperity.

The Biblical secrets of riches discussed in this book are practised by the rich both consciously and unconsciously. However, those who practise it unconsciously can stumble out of it. That is why some people who are rich can become poor—never to rise again. Though a man can face an adversity in life, those who are conscious of these principles can easily come back but not so with those who are unconscious of it. Thus, it is expedient for one to learn the principles whether he or she is already rich or planning to become rich.

CHAPTER

21

Positive Mindset

Jesus said to him, "If you can believe, all things are possible to him who believes."

Mark 9.23 (NKJV)

To be positive is to show confidence and expectation for the best in all possible ways. A mindset is someone's way of thinking formed by nature and nurture, and it determines his or her behaviour and perception. Thus, a positive mindset is a way of thinking that shows confidence and expectation for the best in all possible ways.

One common trait of rich people is their belief that they can make it. A positive mindset is the fundamental seed of greatness. It is only when a man believes that something can be done that he will go to make it happen. Most times, people make their riches by venturing into new grounds where there are few or no competitors. The word 'Innovator' simply defines it all. Innovators do what has not been done. They move out in the first place because they believe they will make it. They don't get discouraged that nobody has done it before. And they don't listen to their doubts and fears. Rather they look on to the brighter side. They believe that where their strength stops the grace of God will complete the rest. The same is true with entrepreneurs and great achievers, they don't settle with the majority who are satisfied in the valley and feel at ease to use the word 'Impossible'. They look up to mountains and say, 'It is possible' and they end up making it a reality.

Such people don't see problems as difficulties that have come to stop their dreams. They see problems as challenges they have to overcome on their road to success. They don't see mountains as the end of the road; rather they understand that if they can stand on the mountains, they would become outstanding. They don't give themselves to failure myths; rather, they pay more attention to success stories. Even when things seem to be falling apart, they believe that those things are falling into place. They understand when the Bible says,

And we know that all that happens
to us is working for our good if we love
God and are fitting into his plans.

Romans 8.28 (TLB)

People with such a mindset understand the meaning of the word 'Breakthrough'; for they will continue hitting until they break their way through. For them, it is not yet over until they succeed.

It Starts from the Mind

Positive mindset (not money) makes and keeps people rich. A lot of people believe that what they need to become rich is a large sum of money. And consequently, they spend their time looking for that free money which may never come. But the truth is that those that get the free money still don't succeed with a negative mindset. Jesus gave an illustration of this in the parable of the talents (Matthew 25.14-30). One of the servants received one talent which worth twenty years wages of a labourer. That was actually a large sum of money but negative mindset did not allow the servant to make any investment with the money. This even happened in a situation where it was a trend for other servants to multiply their talents by two.

Another example was Jacob, son of Isaac. When he went to Laban his uncle, he did not go with any large sum of money to start a business. He only believed that God would prosper him (thus he promised to pay a tithe of the future blessing) and it finally became a reality. One can say that when God blesses a man, he is blessed (he will become rich) whether he has a positive mindset (i.e. believe it) or not. That will imply that Jacob prospered irrespective of his mindset. But that is not true. Now let's look at the nation of Israel which was Jacob more than four centuries later. Of them the Bible says,

We have heard the message, just as they did. But they failed to believe what they heard, and the message did not do them any good.

Hebrews 4.2 (CEV)

A man with a positive mindset moves out with what he has. No matter the amount of money in his hand, he sees it as his capital. He doesn't sit down wishing for free money if he only has a little amount of money. Rather, he will believe that the little money can grow to become bigger if he invests it in a business. He understands the secret of growing money as revealed by Jesus Christ in a parable which is,

...'Do business till I come.'

Luke 19.13 (NKJV)

A positive mindset makes a man to have a dream which he moves out to achieve. The dream can be the kind that happens when one is asleep or while he is awake; the point is that it is the picture of the desired destination. It is the beginning of a success journey. If we look at the beginning of the success story of Joseph, son of Jacob, the Bible says,

Joseph had a dream.

Genesis 37.5 (The Message)

Inward Assurance

The rich believe in their abilities. Positive mindset becomes effective when it starts from oneself. It is easy for people to trust the ability of others and also easy for them to be disappointed and discouraged. Some people can boast of their faith, their hope and optimism but they put all these in other men. The truth is that they are either uninformed or hiding their fears. They want to hide behind another man's ability to make their wealth but they have no power over the spirit of that man. The Bible says,

This is what the LORD says: "A curse
is placed on those who trust other
people, who depend on humans for strength,
who have stopped trusting the LORD.

Jeremiah 17.5 (NCV)

On the other hand, the rich have faith in God that they can succeed with their own abilities. They place no limitation to themselves. They agree with St. Paul when he said,

I can do all things through
Christ who strengthens me.

Philippians 4.13 (NKJV)

This is not an issue of pride but of one acknowledging the ability God has bestowed upon him. Actually, it is even a sin for one to limit the manifestation of God in his life. The sin of the Israelites that made them not to enter the Promised Land at the right time was that they limited God—they called themselves grasshoppers before their problem. If a man agrees with St. Paul that he can do all things through

Christ, he receives more grace and fear flees from him. When a police man stands on the road to control traffic with his uniform, he believes in his ability to control traffic but ultimately, he believes that the authority of his government will make the motorist to obey him and not to run over him. The same is true with the man who believes in his abilities and has faith in God—all things, both animate and inanimate will definitely fall for him. For the Bible says,

...with God all things are possible.

Mark 10.27 (KJV)

A man can hide many things but it is difficult to hide one's fears. Even a lamb can scare a timid lion once it identifies the element of fear in the lion. However, for a man with unwavering faith, he does not consider failure to be an option; for he knows fully well that wherever there is a will, there will definitely be a way. Such a man does not focus on what he does not have; he only considers what he has. Truly, a man may have many wants or may want to have a lot of things but what he has is the only thing he needs to succeed (Exodus 4.2, 2 Kings 4.2 and Matthew 15.34). Having this knowledge enhances improvisation. It gives birth to creativity which is the ability to make something to come into existence especially out of nothing. A creative man is an imitator of God for the Bible says that God calls into existence things that are not as though they were (Romans 4.17).

Dignity

Positive mindset gives a sense of honour. Many people want to be honoured by others and go the wrong way to get it, only to end in dishonour. But a positive mindset gives a man a positive self-worth and makes him to first of all honour himself which makes others to follow suit. He doesn't pursue honour from others; he knows that it is within him. That positive self-worth drives him to do honourable things which end up attracting financial trust to him. His business decisions are all about symbiotic engagements and that is a good secret of keeping and growing a business even in hard times. The parasitic businesses will eat up the hosts without knowing that when the host dies, they die too.

Positive self-worth makes a man not to accept poverty. And the same makes him to move ahead to prevent poverty in an honourable way, for poverty is a thing of dishonour. That makes such a man to be creative and he understands the meaning of improvisation. I will like to consider a man who exhibited a positive self-worth; the Bible says of him,

Jabez was more honorable than his brothers. His mother had named him Jabez, saying, "I gave birth to him in pain." Jabez cried out to God of Israel, "Oh, that you would bless me and enlarge my territory! Let your hand be with me, and keep me from harm so that I will be free from pain." And God granted his request.

1 Chronicles 4.9-10 (NIV)

In the Book of 1 Chronicles, from chapter one through chapter nine, the theme is genealogy. However, the Holy Spirit found the need to inspire the writer of the Book to pause a little for a man of honour. There might have been reasons for him to settle with dishonour from childbirth but he decided to tread the honourable path. He did not blame anybody nor accuse his mother of any wrong. He knew that the path of honour was only between him and God and he took it.

In conclusion, any Christian that is serious about living a life of financial abundance must have a positive mindset—that is faith. Without it, he can spend his life being an observer and a commentator as long as financial matters are concerned. Besides, God won't even see any means to bless him, for faith is like the only receiver in a man that connects with God's signals.

EXHORTATION

A Lesson from the Ants

The ants, though they are small creatures, they believe that they can subdue their world in order to achieve their goals. They move fearlessly and even scare bigger creatures. Not because they have too much power but because they believe that they can survive with their abilities however big or small. Ants can lift up to 50 times their body weight. Just because they believe, they do it.

Recommendation

As a man rises in success (and riches); he should also draw closer to God, lest he will be tempted to ascribe his success to himself and forget God. Every positively minded person should always watch out for this. Above all, prayer is indispensible; for prayer on its own creates a positive mindset.

Practical Questions

1. Do you believe that you can become rich or richer with your present situation?
2. Do you think that those who will be rich will be rich and those who will be poor will be poor?
3. What do you think is your greatest need for financial success: money or a positive mindset?
4. How long do you think it takes to start having a positive mindset?
5. Do you love yourself?
6. Do you believe that you can do all things through Christ?
7. If yes, why not speak it out with boldness?

A Verse for Inspiration

It was by their faith that people of
ancient times won God's approval.

Hebrews 11.2 (GNT)

CHAPTER

22

Sacrifices

Then Isaac sowed seed in that land
and received in the same year a hundred
times as much as he had planted, and
the Lord favored him with blessings.

Genesis 26.12 (AMP)

Sacrifice is the giving away of something valuable in order to get something else considered to be of more value.

Anyone who wants to be rich must be ready to give up something of value in order to gain riches. It can be time, energy, pleasure, unfruitful friendship, sleep, etc. It is called making a sacrifice and it works the same way as sowing a seed. At the initial stage they look like wastage but at the end they turn out to be agents of multiplication. It is a fact that many people don't like making sacrifices and the few that make it end up being successful.

One can wonder why some people were richer in the olden days and some people were poverty-stricken even when there was no specialization or demand for any qualification. At that time, everyone was free to become a fisherman. There was no certification for anyone who wanted to be a hunter. They had land in abundance and everyone was free to be a farmer and so on. In all these, only a few learnt to give up their food and use it as seed. Only a few learnt to give up their pleasure to fish through the nights. Only a few found it necessary to go hunting for games in the forests consistently.

The same rule that worked in those days are still working now. Right from the school days, some students will sacrifice their time, sleep and pleasure studying to excel. Only a few persons can sacrifice their time learning a new skill or trade. Only a few do give up their wants because of higher expectations and such persons end up being rich.

Proportionality

A greater sacrifice leads to a greater success. The rich understand this principle but it is unfortunate that many will not see the sleepless nights but the beautiful mansions. Every man has something he can sacrifice if he needs a breakthrough. And if a man understands the principle of seed and harvest, he should also know that the harvest is proportional to the seed. The Bible says,

Remember this saying,
"A few seeds make a small harvest, but a lot of seeds make a big harvest."

2 Corinthians 9.6 (CEV)

If a student understands that studying for three hours every day can make him to pass his exams easily, adding an extra hour or two for each day can make him to be among the best. If a man finds out that reading a good book in his field in a year makes him better and increases his earnings, what stops him from reading at least three books in a year? In fact, if he does that for five years, he will be qualified for an expert in his field. You can imagine what will happen if he continues with it as a lifestyle.

Some people may have to cut down the cost of their daily food by say 30 to 50 per cent for a year because they want to raise fund for investment. Others may look at them as foolish but after a short time they turn into rich men. Moreover, they may not necessarily starve; they only have to plan their meals with the limited resources.

One may easily admire the pleasures of rich men but it is good for one to know that they have sacrificed their pleasures at one time or the other. And they also continue to make sacrifices whenever it is necessary. Even if you give a lot of money to a man who does not know the way of sacrifice, all the money will dwindle as fast as possible.

The rich don't only make sacrifices, but whenever they discover anything that can serve as a sacrifice; they do it to the utmost.

Effectiveness

Only the right sacrifice gives the right result. No matter the sincerity, the wrong sacrifice cannot give you what you want. Rather, it can lead to more disaster. We can see a picture of that in the lives of Nadab and Abihu—two sons of Aaron. They died because of wrong offering (Leviticus 10.1-2). The rich don't just make sacrifices; they watch their circumstances carefully before determining what to sacrifice. They know that offering a wrong thing will only result in a harmful waste. For instance, a man can be having sleepless nights thinking that he is making a sacrifice for his success, while he only needs to cut down the number of hours he spends on television.

One thing you need to understand is that circumstances play the principal role in determining the sacrifice needed for a breakthrough. You don't have to sacrifice your time for a circumstance just because you take delight in sacrificing your time. Even if you give up the twenty four hours of the day, nothing will happen if the situation demands that you say 'No' to an ungodly relationship.

Usefulness

The relevance of some sacrifices goes with time. Sometimes people complain that they did the same thing with the rich but did not get the same result. But one of the questions they need to answer is 'When?'

There are some situations that accept delayed sacrifices, but of course, their result would have been delayed as well. On the other hand, there are some situations that don't tolerate delayed sacrifices. If you fail to do the sacrifice at the proper time, you will forget about the result as far as they are concerned. A student who decides to sacrifice his time and pleasure a day before his exam might not be expecting a good result, if he had wasted more than six months he should have used for his preparations. The Bible says,

If a snake bites the tamer before it is
tamed, what good is the tamer?

Ecclesiastes 10.11 (NCV)

Circumstances don't just demand sacrifices, they can also demand urgency. One thing that is always at the back of the mind of the rich is that sacrifices are not always pleasant for the moment. Nonetheless, they look towards the returns. When others are still bemoaning the sacrifices the occasion demands, they go ahead to make such sacrifices. They know that failure to make some sacrifices at the proper time can lead to a situation whereby the individual will be compelled to do even bigger things, but this time, at a loss.

Sacrificial Lifestyle

Many powerful sacrifices come as a lifestyle. Even though there might be one-time milestone sacrifices that can make people rich, the ones that keep people rich are usually continuous. The rich don't just make a milestone sacrifice and go to bed; they live a lifestyle of sacrifice. If we consider Abraham whom the Bible considered to be rich, we will see it as one of his secrets of prosperity. The Bible says of him,

And the Scripture was fulfilled which says, "Abraham believed God, and it was accounted to him for righteousness." And he was called the friend of God.

James 2.23 (NKJV)

Abraham believed God throughout his life after he encountered God such that he earned the status of being called a friend of God. He sacrificed his lifestyle for the lifestyle God demanded of him. Elsewhere, the Bible shows more of his relationship with God,

When Abram was ninety-nine years old, the LORD appeared to Abram and said to him, 'I am Almighty God; walk before Me and be blameless.

Genesis 17.1 (NKJV)

There is no doubt that Abraham walked before God and lived a prosperous life. He first of all sacrificed his homeland for a place God would show him. He even went as far as trying to sacrifice his son Isaac. He didn't stop on the way even till death.

In conclusion, sacrifices can look like a waste at the beginning and sometimes painful. Nonetheless, they are essential ingredients for riches. It is only a matter of time, when a man adopts them as a lifestyle they will become normal to him. If we consider Cain and Abel, we will see that Abel was careful to offer the first fruit of his flock and their fat portions in line with the demands of God. But Cain took no care and offered what he liked. Of course, God accepted the sacrifice of Abel and rejected that of Cain.

EXHORTATION

A Lesson from the Ants

In the ant colony, the workers sacrifice their pleasure and energy gathering food for the whole colony and building their homes. In the addition to that, the soldiers and the workers go as far as sacrificing all their strength in protecting their colony against intruders.

Recommendation

Inasmuch as sacrifices are essential for riches, care should be taken to make sure that they are godly. Besides, they shouldn't be harmful to the individual since it won't be reasonable for one to kill himself making sacrifices, while he is expecting to earn a living through the sacrifices.

Practical Questions

1. Can you give up anything because of something of higher value?
2. Do you believe that there are always sacrifices to make for one to get something good?
3. Do you believe that there are big sacrifices and small sacrifices?
4. Do you think a man should neglect some sacrifices if they seem not to be pleasurable to him?
5. Do you think that sacrifices should only be done once in a lifetime?
6. Have you made any sacrifice for your financial prosperity?

A Verse for Inspiration

Cast your bread upon the waters,
for you will find it after many days.

Ecclesiastes 11.1 (RSV)

CHAPTER

23

Time Management

If you obey the king, you will stay
out of trouble. So be wise and learn
what to do and when to do it.

Ecclesiastes 8.5 (CEV)

Time is a period of existence. And management is judicious use of resources to achieve a goal. Thus, time management is the judicious use of a period of existence to achieve a goal.

Rich people are always mindful of their time, since any time wasted is like wealth wasted; for time is wealth. Every human being receives the gift of twenty four hours in each day but what makes the difference is how each individual makes use of it. The rich don't wait for things to happen randomly in their lives—they make things happen. They divide and allot their time effectively to different causes. They don't assume that what will be will surely be. They know that nothing happens without a cause—and the cause can be planned and directed or unplanned and undirected. Thus, they can be the planner of their own time.

The rich don't live with the idea that the supply of time is endless and thus allow their time to waste. Rather, they acknowledge that the supply of time is endless but also understand that they only have a limited time for every purpose or endeavour. They understand that even their lives on earth are limited.

Consequently, they don't use the time they should spend doing something meaningful engaging in frivolities. We can see a picture of it in the life of Nehemiah when he was rebuilding the wall of Jerusalem. Opposition tried to distract him but he exhibited wisdom thus:

So I sent messengers to them,
saying, "I am doing a great work,
so that I cannot come down. Why
should the work cease while I
leave it and go down to you?"

Nehemiah 6.3 (NKJV)

Finally, the work on the wall was finished in fifty two days because Nehemiah did not succumb to distractions.

Proactive Lifestyle

Wise people grab time and manage it. It is normal to hear many people say that they don't have time but it is usually the rich (or the successful) that has something to show for it. Though time is a gift to every human being on earth at the same proportion, it is unwise for one to think that time will just fall out for any purpose. A rich man creates or makes out time consciously for every purpose. He understands that he cannot literally manipulate time, for time is static. But he can arrange his actions and fix them effectively and efficiently into the continuum of time by planning. He orders his actions to know those that will come first to avoid putting the cart before the horse or creating Adam before the Garden of Eden. Also, he goes on to prioritise his actions according to their importance and urgency. By this, I can say that the priority of any action is the function of its importance and urgency. If you can score a list of actions mathematically, priority will then become a product of importance and urgency.

That is: Priority = Importance × Urgency

This is just the main difference between the rich and the poor when it comes to time. From this chapter's introductory verse, we can see that the wise learn what to do and when to do it. It is at this point of evaluation that a man can discover things that are inconsequential and deserve to be moved to leisure. If we consider the Scripture where Jesus refers to the Father as a Husbandman or a Farmer (i.e. a Businessman); we can gain knowledge. He says,

I am the true vine, and my Father is the husbandman. Every branch in me that beareth not fruit he taketh away: and every branch that beareth fruit, he purgeth it, that it may bring forth more fruit.

John 15.1-2 (KJV)

From this place we can see that a good time manager just like a good businessman removes things that are useless in his life and pays more attention to useful things in his life. Even with the useful things, he still works on them to keep away unwanted parts.

Productivity

Good time management increases productivity. From what I have said before, time management removes things that are not needed thereby making much time available for the useful things. It also relieves the individual so that he will have more energy and concentration on things that are important. Sometimes, rich men are not the strongest or the smartest but they use the little strength and skills they have on few useful things. At times, they also tend to be too busy but they are simply busy doing a few useful things. They seem to understand what the Bible says:

Remove the dross from the silver, and
out comes material for the silversmith.

Proverbs 25.4 (NIV)

Wise people don't allow circumstances to manage them in time. Rather, they consciously manage circumstances in time. No matter how highly skillful a man might be, if his daily activities come up randomly and he attends to them like that, he will definitely be less productive. Some activities are related in terms of physical location, some can be related in terms of nature of execution and so on. Good planning can fix the related activities next to each other for greater efficiency. Proper time management also includes when a man should eat his profit. If a man should eat the profit of a work at first, there is a tendency that the fellow will feel reluctant to do the work later. This is because there will not be any gain to drive him. In his mind it will appear as if he is working for free.

More also, lack of time management can lead to ill health which slows down or halts or even ends productivity. This happens when a man fails to consciously allocate time for rest. This reveals the secret of rich men who control large businesses and still stay healthy. They know how to allocate time for rest and stick to it.

Planning

Proper time management can paint the future. In the process of organizing one's activities in time, a man can see the picture of his future and judge how realistic or efficient he can be. If he doesn't see a pleasant picture, he can then adjust his plans beforehand for better results. On the other hand, even if he sees a pleasant picture, there can still be room for improvement. It is actually because the rich plan their time and work towards it that makes them to say 'I am busy', whenever a request that can disrupt their plans comes their ways. Thus, many people like going with the word 'I am busy' because they count it to be synonymous with prosperity.

Sometimes people who are hard-working put themselves under pressure because they want to do a lot of things at the same time. That is because they fail to manage their time. They only think of how to achieve their goals but take no thought of the fact that all those activities take place in time. Most times, the activities will clash with each other and everything will end up in frustration. Just a little planning would make such a frustration to end on papers. The Bible says,

Teach us to number each of our days so
that we may grow in wisdom.

Psalm 90.12 (GW)

In conclusion, time management is a great tool for productivity which cannot be neglected. If we take a look at the story of creation, we can see how God allocated time for each creation and also for resting. It is never enough for one to assume that he is working with time; he must plan it consciously if he wants to make the best use of time. Besides, time management becomes indispensible as work increases.

EXHORTATION

A Lesson from the Ants

Ants know how to number their days effectively, that is why they gather their food in the dry seasons of the year and hide in their nests during the wet or unfriendly seasons of the year.

Recommendation

One thing you cannot neglect in time management is the allocation of time for resting. It may look like a waste but that increases your productivity, and you will also be healthy to enjoy the fruit of your labour. Another thing is for you to know that one of the most effective ways to manage your time is by writing down your activities and assigning time to each of them.

Practical Questions

1. Do you plan your time consciously on papers or do you assume that you are working with time?
2. Do you think that you shouldn't bother about time management any more—having failed to comply by it more than once?
3. Do you think that time management should only be called upon when you are under pressure?
4. Do you believe that planning your time can give you a peace of mind?
5. Do you think that time management is a waste of time or it reduces waste of time?

A Verse for Inspiration

The ants are a people not strong, Yet they prepare their food in the summer.

Proverbs 30.25 (NKJV)

CHAPTER

24

Realistic Goals

Then I answered the king, "If you are
willing and if I have pleased you, send
me to the city in Judah where my ancestors
are buried so I can rebuild it."

Nehemiah 2.5 (NCV)

Something is said to be realistic when it shows a sensible, practical or possible idea of what can be done, based on known facts. And a goal is a result someone wants to achieve. Thus, goals become realistic when they show a sensible, practical or possible idea of what can be done, based on known facts.

Rich people don't just dream big, they set realistic (reasonable, sensible) goals, determine the price for the goals and begin to pay the price immediately. They don't continue dreaming when they are supposed to be awake to face the realities of life. They understand that only those who are no longer sleeping can live their dreams. They don't hide under faith to live in a dream world. They understand very well that even though it is written that angels would carry them when they fall from a height, they should not tempt the Lord their God.

This does not in any way mean a call for pessimism. Though there might be situations in a man's life when he looks up to God for miracles, it will be wrong for any man to think that everything in his life will be by miracles while he sits down doing nothing. Rich men set goals based on principles not on exceptions.

God controls the whole universe and works miracles when needed but He also expects human beings to make use of the abilities He has deposited in them. The Bible says,

The heaven, even the heavens, are
the LORD'S: but the earth hath he
given to the children of men.

Psalm 115.16 (KJV)

Thus, as we go on in solving problems that come our way—and setting goals, we ought to exhibit sound judgment. I know that someone might ask, 'How can we believe that all things are possible and still be talking about goals being realistic or unrealistic?' Now, I will show a few things on how to know whether a goal is realistic.

Price Determinability

The price of a realistic goal is determinable. If a man wants to buy anything in life, he must first of all know the price of it before he can make payment. For instance, a man from Adam's time that wants to buy a computer manufactured in the 21st century would likely end up in frustration; for he won't even understand money itself let alone the amount to pay for the computer. As long as that man is concerned, the idea would be an unrealistic goal. However, that would be a realistic goal for a student in the 21st century even if he is still struggling to pay his school fees.

I know you can say, 'But the man of Adam's time can learn the concept of money and understand how much to pay for the computer.' The truth remains that until he learns those things, his goal is still unrealistic. Another thing you need to understand is that the cost of a goal is not just the financial aspect of it; it entails everything that will make the goal to be achieved. Even when a man thinks that his goal is a simple (and common) one, as long as he cannot determine the cost, it is not realistic. No matter how energetic or empowered a man might be, if he cannot determine the total cost of his goal, his empowerment can only lead to skewed actions. You can relate this with what the Bible says,

What's this? Fools out shopping for wisdom!
They wouldn't recognize it if they saw it!

Proverbs 17.16 (The Message)

I will like you to understand this: determining a cost is quite different from affording the cost. For now, just know that the cost of a realistic goal is first of all determinable. If a man lacks the ability to determine the cost of a goal; that simply means that the man lacks the capacity to attain the goal. Besides, I will like you to understand that a wish is not the same as a goal.

Reasonability

A realistic goal does not defy reasoning. This is actually the place where faith and sight meet. When you talk about reasoning, you are talking about rational thinking or judgement; that is how people see things. And that is also subjective or relative. But the truth is that some people will be wrong and some people will be right. Everybody cannot be right on the same matter and still have diverse (and even contradicting) views. If not, nobody should disturb a thief for stealing since that is his own business concept. Thus, even when a man is fully convinced within himself that he is wise, he can still be a fool. The Bible says,

The fool has said in his heart,
"There is no God."

Psalm 14.1 (NKJV)

This man, the Bible calls a fool might be a wise man in the eyes of many people, but because the Bible is the highest authority we know, he is a fool indeed.

Now, I have tried to establish the two different kinds of reasoning, namely: right and wrong reasoning. The right reasoning is the one that flows with faith and that is the one I will also show that agrees with realistic goals.

Now, when you talk about applying faith in situations, you talk about God multiplying the effects of an input or doing something that is entirely extraordinary. Nevertheless, both agree with reasoning but at different orders. You can see the different orders in what the Bible says about Abraham,

Who against hope believed in hope,
that he might become the father of many
nations; according to that which was
spoken, so shall thy seed be.

Romans 4.18 (KJV)

We can see that the hope Abraham used was higher than ordinary hope—yet it is still hope. This case of Abraham and Sarah having a son at old age is God multiplying the effects of an input. However, it agrees with reasoning though on a higher order, for Abraham still mated with Sarah before she conceived. And that is in line with the principle of procreation.

Now, if you look at the case of the conception of Jesus Christ, you will see hope at a higher level. For Mary believed that she would conceive even without mating with a man. This is an instance of God doing something entirely extraordinary. Nevertheless, it agrees with reasoning but on a higher order. Because for the Word to become flesh (i.e. a man), He has to be born of a woman. And that is still in line with the principle of procreation. If the baby Jesus had fallen from the sky or carried down to the earth by angels, nobody would have the right to call Him 'Son of Man'. In all these things, I am trying to show how faith (or miracle) agrees with reasoning—it is not arbitrary.

When a man wants to set a realistic goal, it must be based on reasoning, no matter the level or the order of the reasoning. Again, the situation at hand will justify the level of the reasoning. For instance, it would be an unrealistic goal for Abraham to expect Sarah to conceive and bear a son even without mating with her. In another instance, it will likely be an unrealistic goal for a young man to make up his mind that he will not marry until he is one hundred years old. Then he will marry a ninety year old lady for them to have a baby boy. God still works miracles but that will be tempting God.

In another example, if a man knows that the fuel in his car will barely take him for fifty kilometers and decides to drive through a wilderness of about three hundred kilometers just because he wants to save his money; that would be an unrealistic goal. However, if by any unplanned circumstance, he finds himself in the wilderness with the little fuel in his car, he can believe God and God will save him from the situation (God can make the fuel to become more than enough for him or send a helper to him). A man cannot claim that he is already pushed to the wall and thus requires a miracle when God knows that it is within the ability of the fellow to plan his goals aright.

Realistic goals flow with sound reasoning in line with one's abilities. No one should confuse faith with greed—i.e. trying to get everything in one fell swoop. Even the journeys of faith as written in the Bible are either 'Walk of Faith' or 'Race of Faith'. The two move in a clear path, though one is faster. But there is no such thing like 'Flight of Faith'. When considering one's abilities, it won't be wrong to think of the possibility of increasing or improving on one's present capacity. Nonetheless, it will still be with sound judgement. For instance, it will still be unrealistic for a man to think that since he is growing in skills, strength and stature, one day, his dream of going to the moon would be achieved by just a gallant jump from the earth. Abraham Lincoln said that the whole world steps aside for the man who knows where he is going.

In conclusion, faith is not a license to live in a fool's paradise. Faith agrees will godly reasoning. One should have faith as a Christian and at the same time set goals that exhibit sound judgement.

EXHORTATION

A Lesson from the Ants

Ants know very well that they are small creatures, thus, they dig their nests inside the ground for safety. They don't count their large numbers as a justification to build their nests on the surface.

Recommendation

Being realistic does not mean that you should forget about faith. It also does not mean that you should only be looking for little or moderate goals you can easily achieve. You can set big goals even beyond your present capacity but such goals should be sensible and could be achieved. You can set big goals and start moving towards them from your present capacity.

Practical Questions

1. Can you determine the cost of your goals?
2. Is your goal like putting God to the test?
3. Do you think that your goal is achievable based on any level of reasoning?
4. Do you believe in dreaming big and sensible?
5. Do you believe that a goal can be unrealistic from the beginning?

A Verse for Inspiration

So the wall was finished on the
twenty-fifth day of Elul, in fifty-two days.

Nehemiah 6.15 (NKJV)

CHAPTER

25

Honesty/Faithfulness

His master replied, 'Good job! You're a
good and faithful servant! You proved that
you could be trusted with a small amount.
I will put you in charge of a large amount.
Come and share your master's happiness.'

Matthew 25.21 (GW)

Honesty is the quality of being characteristically truthful. And faithfulness is the quality of being consistently trustworthy.

Honesty and faithfulness are two factors that perpetuate the flow of financial gains. It is not sufficient for a man to be honest but for him to be consistent in it. One of the things people guard seriously is their money. And for them to let go of it, they must be convinced that they will get the adequate value in return. However, no one becomes rich by staying alone but by meeting the demands of fellow human beings in return for payments. Thus, what makes people rich is when such payments continue over time.

Faithfulness is one of the attributes of the Fruit of the Spirit that has great financial value. The irony of it is that even sinners, fraudsters and unfaithful people are all in the queue looking for faithful and honest Christians. They can condemn and quarrel with a Christian because of his faith but when they want to part with their money, they still look for those faithful Christians. The Bible says,

For the earnest expectation of the creation eagerly waits for the revealing of the sons of God.

Romans 8.19 (NKJV)

All creations are not only waiting for the sons of God to be revealed in eternity, they long to see them now. They long to see the sons of God in business and financial matters. And this is a great advantage to faithful Christians. Most of the time, faithful people are considered foolish at the beginning but as time goes on, they turn out to be rich. However, faithfulness can only yield financial returns if the faithful man is into financial engagements.

Indispensability of Faithfulness

Everyone without exception wants a faithful man. All over the world, people are looking for faithful people to commit the finances into their hands. Employers are seriously looking for such people and they are willing to pay them good salaries. Investors are looking for such persons to be their business partners and so on. The truth is that as these faithful ones continue to show themselves faithful, more people will come knocking at their doors with their money. All these things happen because faithful people are in short supply. And you know that things that are in short supply are always expensive. A good example is the diamond. You should not also be surprised why rich men are fewer in number. The Bible says,

Many people claim to be loyal, but it is hard to find a trustworthy person.

Proverbs 20.6 (NCV)

Honesty and faithfulness are two among the many things that everybody wants but only a handful is willing to give it out. And that has helped in keeping the supply in check—thus making the price high (for the lower the supply, the higher the price). The market is always open; if anyone is willing to give himself to honesty and faithfulness, his value will appreciate. And consequently, his financial capacity will appreciate.

Time-Based Virtue

The profit of faithfulness and honesty grows with time. I want you to understand that it is when a man becomes honest consistently over time that he would be said to be faithful. (Though some people can be faithful in many other things (including bad things), the kind of faithfulness the Bible listed in the Fruit of the Spirit is all about goodness). If a man is found to be faithful only for six months, it will not be obvious or acceptable to everybody that he is truly faithful. But if a man is found to be faithful up to six years, he will appear credible to many. And if he be found faithful for up to twenty years, it will even be difficult for some people not to believe him even when he is wrong. And that is also how people commit their finances to different years of faithfulness.

As a man's faithfulness is still counted in months, people commit their finances to him proportionately. And as he goes on to years, people commit their finances accordingly. However, sometimes, a man can prove his high level of faithfulness within a short time or with respect to circumstances. But such persons may have to pass through difficult temptations to show that they are trustworthy. An example was Joseph, son of Jacob, of whom the Bible says,

The LORD'S promise tested him through fiery
trials until his prediction came true.
He made Joseph the master of his palace
and the ruler of all his possessions.

Psalm 105.19&21 (GW)

In this kind of situation, the later testimony might be palatable but the fiery trials are not. This also does not mean that people who acquire their credibility over a longer period of time may not face a fiery trial. The main point is that whether it is for a short time or for a long time, one must show himself faithful. Every day is a test. People consciously and unconsciously observe you. Whether you know about it or not does not matter as long as you are faithful. When they find you faithful with little things they will be convinced to commit greater things into your hands. The Scripture says,

Whoever is faithful in small matters will be faithful in large ones; whoever is dishonest in small matters will be dishonest in large ones.

Luke 16.10 (GNT)

A Living Virtue

Faithfulness can die but very hard to be reborn in the eyes of others. It can be easier for a stranger to acquire credibility than for a faithful man who betrayed his faithfulness to be trusted again. The reason is simply because people will rather try a new person than rely upon a fellow who has proved himself untrustworthy. Just as the credibility of a man's faithfulness can grow with time, it can also be killed. Though people can conspire to destroy a man's credibility, the effects can only be temporal as long as the man's faithfulness is still alive. But if a man should kill his own faithfulness, his credibility will automatically die as well. And it is always difficult to restore such credibility. The Bible says,

A brother offended is harder to be won than a strong city: and their contentions are like the bars of a castle.

Proverbs 18.19 (KJV)

A man doesn't need to commit a great act of betrayal for people to count him unfaithful; only a little act of unfaithfulness is enough. It can destroy the credibility one has built over many years of faithfulness. Whenever a betrayal takes place, people will start drawing back with their finances for fear of the possibility of another betrayal. They won't waste their time analysing whether the betrayal is big or small. In fact, every faithful man doesn't only watch out for big obvious temptations, he pays a careful attention to those small matters others can easily overlook. And that makes his faithfulness complete. The Bible says,

Dead flies putrefy the perfumer's ointment,
And cause it to give off a foul odor; So does a
little folly to one respected for wisdom
and honor.

Ecclesiastes 10.1 (NKJV)

In conclusion, faithfulness is indispensible in the accumulation of enduring riches such that no rich man can be without it. Even those engaging in illegal and evil businesses are faithful to some extent even to their agents and partners in crime, at least before judgement comes upon them. I also know that you, as a person, always demand some level of faithfulness before giving out your money for any transaction. Above all, continue to be conscious of the fact that every day is a test; even when it seems that nobody is watching, God is watching. Nobody might have seen David when he killed a lion and a bear just because of a lamb but God saw him as a faithful shepherd and chose him to be a king.

EXHORTATION

A Lesson from the Ants

Ants have no king but it is difficult to see them fighting each other. They can live in large numbers in a single nest but because they are faithful to each other, they manage their food very well.

Recommendation

If you are honest and faithful, don't assume that every other person is the same. Also, don't assume that every rich man is faithful; for you don't know those that are bad and their time of divine judgement. Let every man prove his faithfulness to you so that you don't fall victim unnecessarily. However, as long as you live, remain faithful to God and your financial faithfulness will be taken care of.

Practical Questions

1. Can you trust yourself?
2. Do you think people can trust you?
3. Do you think that a little compromise at certain situations is a part of life?
4. Do you believe that you can become faithful till the end of your life?
5. Do you believe that faithfulness has a financial value?

A Verse for Inspiration

A faithful man will be richly
blessed, but one eager to get rich
will not go unpunished.

Proverbs 28.20 (NIV)

CHAPTER

26

Continuous Learning

It takes knowledge to fill a home with
rare and beautiful treasures.

Proverbs 24.4 (NCV)

Something is said to be continuous when it goes on without interruption. And learning is the process of acquiring knowledge. Thus, continuous learning is acquiring knowledge without interruption.

Rich people are always developing themselves. They are always interested in getting new knowledge and skills. They agree with Henry Ford when he said, 'Anyone who stops learning is old, whether at twenty or eighty. Anyone who keeps learning stays young.' They are not just willing to learn, they are also willing to take corrections which enhances their earnings and saves them from losses. Rich people know that what gives them an edge over their neighbours is the knowledge they have which their neighbours do not have. The truth about this life is that we all pay for our ignorance. If you know how to repair your television, you won't need to call a professional who will only spend less than thirty minutes on the faulty television to make it work again; only to collect some reasonable cash from you. People can travel for many kilometers looking for medical professionals. It is not because such persons just want to appreciate the comeliness of the medical professionals but because they need the knowledge of those professionals.

Truly, if you discover the secret of some of the things for which you have been paying heavily, you will shout. And for such things that are known to you, you will not like to pay heavily for them again.

Nonetheless, you cannot know everything. Again, knowing something does not necessarily mean that you have known the best way of doing it. That is why the rich ones keep on improving their knowledge to make sure that they are always ahead of the rest of the society who would gladly pay for their ignorance. They know that if they stop for a little time without acquiring knew knowledge, a host of individuals in the society will overtake them. That will simply mean that they will become ignorant and thus will have to pay the new individuals for their new knowledge.

Deliverance

Knowledge brings deliverance. I want you to know that ignorance is like darkness. Though you cannot know everything in this life in details, you are required to know a few things about many things in life, at least, the basic necessities of life. Now, I will like you to understand that knowledge grows. What you call a new knowledge today can be called obsolete tomorrow. And those who continue to live with that knowledge could be seen as living in ignorance or darkness and thus need deliverance. The Bible says,

In many separate revelations [each of which set forth a portion of the Truth] and in different ways God spoke of old to [our] forefathers in and by the prophets.

Hebrews 1.1 (AMP)

From this Scripture, we will understand that at each point in the time of the forefathers, the portion of the Truth they had would be greater than the portion available to the generations before them. And one thing I will like you to know is that the truth referred to in this verse which is the Word of God, is a complete package. It enlightens us not only on spirituality but also on the way we live physically (including financially). It gives us light and thus deliverance from our ignorance and darkness. The Bible says,

The hypocrite with his mouth destroys
his neighbor, But through knowledge
the righteous will be delivered.

Proverbs 11.9 (NKJV)

The deliverance a man can have through knowledge is not once and for all for every aspect of human life. That of our financial aspect of life is continuous. That is why the rich learn continually.

Timelessness of Learning

No wise person can outgrow continuous learning. What keeps the rich going is their ability to humble themselves and acquire new knowledge. Once pride comes in and they stop learning—it is a matter of time, such persons will be overtaken by ignorance. There is no level a man will attain in this life that will make him to be above learning. Even if he receives abundant revelations from God, learning cannot be overlooked. The Bible says of Daniel despite his great revelations,

In the first year of his reign
I Daniel understood by books…

Daniel 9.2 (KJV)

No one is all-knowing except God. The truth is this; the more we increase in knowledge, the more our ignorance is made known to us. It is in the process of moving out of ignorance that we enter into knowledge.

Sometimes when there is a new knowledge, some people who believe that they cannot learn it will start fighting it. But the wise ones will go ahead and learn it and thus become richer. Most times, it takes only a new knowledge for a man to have a great financial breakthrough. Learning is not an act of weakness but an act of wisdom and maturity. The Scripture says,

Give instruction to a wise man, and he will be yet wiser: teach a just man, and he will increase in learning.

Proverbs 9.9 (KJV)

Continuous Increase

Continuous learning simply means continuous increase in capacity. The reason why we go to school is because we want to acquire knowledge. We start with the knowledge of how to read and write, and then to the knowledge of how to reason effectively in different fields of human existence. Moreover, in each field of knowledge, a man can decide to go further than others and such persons are counted to be more knowledgeable. Other things being equal, you will count a PhD holder in mathematics to be more knowledgeable in mathematics than an undergraduate student of mathematics. The simple reason is because the PhD holder has developed a bigger capacity to understand mathematics more than the undergraduate student.

Now, real life situations may not demand certifications, but it does demand practical knowledge. If a man keeps on increasing his knowledge, he will definitely develop a capacity that is beyond that of his neighbours. If you have a farm and you know a contractor that can cultivate your farm with straight ridges in less time, you will prefer him to others who could do the same with additional one week. Only that one week advantage can make that contractor to become the most preferred contractor among the rest of the farmers. That time-crashing knowledge will set him forth before the farmers as the contractor with the greatest capacity to cultivate their farms. Moreover, this kind of knowledge can come by reading only one page of a book.

From this example, you will agree with me that increasing one's knowledge leads to increase in one's capacity to work and consequently, one's income. It is simply, an act of diligence. The Bible says,

Do you see a man diligent and skillful in his business? He will stand before kings; he will not stand before obscure men.

Proverbs 22.29 (AMP)

In conclusion, continuous learning is what makes the rich to be continuously relevant. There is no mystery about learning; it is only the acquisition of knowledge—especially something you don't know before. It can be attending a training session or a seminar. It can be listening to an audio or video recording. However, the oldest, the simplest, the easiest and perhaps the most powerful, is reading a book. If you can make up your mind to be reading at least twenty pages of a book in your field every day, in thirty days of a month you will be able to finish a six hundred page book. Believe you me, if you can finish five to seven in any area of your interest, you will be talking about being an expert in that area. But wait, don't rush, give the studies and training and practice at least five years if you are indeed interested in becoming an expert. If it requires more books just do it. Five years is not too much for you to become an expert.

EXHORTATION

A Lesson from the Ants

The ants learn every day from their environment and that helps them to keep away from things that kill them. They can abandon their nest for another environment once they discover something disastrous and that keeps them alive. Moreover, it is only those that are alive that can make a living.

Recommendation

Do your best not to postpone your studies. It only takes a start before you finish a book. However do a little research before adopting any study material. Above all, remember to plan your studies and try not to become crazy with studies.

Practical Questions

1. Do you believe that studies add knowledge?
2. Do you believe that knowledge increases one's capacity to function?
3. Do you believe that knowledge can become obsolete with time?
4. Do you believe you can acquire any knowledge if you are willing to do so?
5. Do you think that some knowledge are too small and thus should be neglected?

A Verse for Inspiration

After all, you must make careful plans
before you fight a battle, and the more good
advice you get, the more likely you
are to win.

Proverbs 24.6 (GNT)

CHAPTER

27

Gratitude

A good man is concerned for the welfare
of his animals, but even the kindness
of godless men is cruel.

Proverbs 12.10 (TLB)

Gratitude is the quality of being thankful or recognizing the importance of something.

One good character of rich men who are holistically rich (i.e. in the spirit, soul and body) is that they are grateful to any one that contributes to their life. This character might not be easily found in every man that has material possession at any given time. Truly, some supposedly rich men do not have any other thing apart from their material possessions—that is why such men can commit suicide if their material possessions are taken away from them. However, my interest in this book has been holistic riches.

Rich men know that an act of gratitude is an encouragement unto more good works. They know that the best way to get a man to put his best in a work is to make him happy while he works. They know very well that an atmosphere of joy gives room for creativity. They have respect for their workers, from the greatest to the least, even their animals. They understand that the least among their workers can contribute to their increase or to their devastation.

Rich men know that treating a man who has done something good for them with respect will not diminish their own respect; rather, it will add to their reputation. And you know that people will like to do business with any man that treats them with respect. A lifestyle of gratitude is something that makes both the giver and the receiver to feel like kings. And both as well go home with peace of mind. But do you know; not everybody that receives gratitude bothers to show the same to others. However, the rich don't bother about that. They know that those who show gratitude attract others. Thus, people are attracted to rich men who show gratitude and they end up making them richer. Just like other godly characters, a lifestyle of gratitude is an act of wisdom and maturity. The Bible says,

Good sense brings favor…

Proverbs 13.15 (GW)

Mustard Effect

One act of gratitude can bring a life time opportunity of greatness. I may not need to remind you that gratitude is not shown only to fellow men but also to God. We can see from the Bible that it took Solomon the single act of sacrificing a thousand burnt offerings for God to give him wisdom, wealth and honour. It also took Mary the breaking of a costly ointment for Christ as an act of gratitude for Jesus to make a pronunciation that she would be remembered in the preaching of the gospel. Coming to the side of men in our present time, sending Christmas gifts to one's customers at the end of the year will be enough to secure such customers at least for the following year. And if such gifts should be meaningful enough, believe you me; it can secure such customers for a longer period, especially if such persons have not received such an act of gratitude before. Understand this: the gift which is the object of gratitude might not cost much, but the spirit of gratitude conveyed in the gift is very strong. The Bible says,

A gift opens the way for the giver
and ushers him into the presence
of the great.

Proverbs 18.16 (NIV)

There might be many ways to show gratitude to the people but making it tangible can be more effective. It can be as little as a greeting card. If you want to test it, just get a little gift and give to that man or woman that has done something good for you. With just a little word of gratitude, you will be surprised at the level of motivation you will see in the fellow. You can also try it on your customers, even your president and then tell the story. If not for any other thing; the Word of God says so—just believe it and that settles it.

Humble Mind

It takes humility to express gratitude. Even though many people might not come up openly to request for gratitude, they expect it. Moreover, those who are holistically rich don't wait for such an expectation; they act ahead of time. They swallow their pride and express their gratitude to whomever it is due, whether richer or poorer. One of the reasons why pride hinders financial growth is that when the people to whom gratitude is due look for it and do not receive it, they will go away. And remember that when they go, they go with their money. Truly, it takes a heart of wisdom for a man, especially a rich man to be humble. It is wisdom that teaches a man to forget about his assumed self-worth in order to achieve what he wants to achieve. It was John Ruskin that said, 'I believe the first test of a truly great man is his humility.'

You can think of a businessman who argues with his customers about his rights all the time. It will only be a matter of a short period of time and he will not see any customer to argue with again. It is humility that makes a man to focus on his goal and not to be engrossed in his pride, for nobody can feed on his own pride. Apostle Paul in his own time said,

To the weak I became as weak, that I might win the weak. I have become all things to all men, that I might by all means save some.

1 Corinthians 9.22 (NKJV)

Though it might be quite easy to show gratitude to many people, for some people it might not be easy. It is not just the case of some persons being richer or poor; the point is that some persons are hard to please. However, by humility one can endure to win them over. This does not in any way imply a compromise of one's faith, but an exhibition of wisdom. The ultimate result is that by humility, gratitude will be shown to all to whom it is due and they will be moved to continue putting their money into the hands of the humble rich men. The Scripture says,

By humility and the fear of the LORD are riches, and honour and life.

Proverbs 22.4 (KJV)

Resultant Effect

It takes a heart of gratitude to have a balanced financial system. As a man needs a sound health to sustain his life, a rich man needs a peaceful balanced financial system to sustain his wealth. However, gratitude is one of the factors that maintain order. This is because it gives to every player in the financial system what is due to him. Gratitude makes a man to be satisfied with what he has. It also makes him to be satisfied with the good things others have done for him. It is difficult for a heart of gratitude to harbour greed. Though it is common to associate the rich ones with greed, but greedy men don't have peace. Thus, such riches cannot be holistic. However, it is only a matter of time, when greed succeeds in destabilizing the system everything will collapse and by implication, the riches will vanish. Greed is like a disease that when it affects a man, his reasoning will be highly distorted. Greed makes a man to believe that his actions will be without consequences.

Most times, it takes the touch of God for a man to understand the full meaning of gratitude. The introductory verse of this chapter shows that it takes righteousness for a man to show gratitude even to his animal. Such a heart makes a man to allocate the necessary resources for the maintenance of his means of wealth creation; whether they are human, animals, machines, etc. The mere eyesight of a very rich man with malnourished workers in a poor working environment sends a signal of disorder. Besides, such an atmosphere breeds temptation for the workers. And when they yield to such temptations, the rich man suffers. The Bible says,

When an ox is working in the grain, do
not cover its mouth to keep it from eating.

Deuteronomy 25.4 (NCV)

Understand that the ox will not finish the grain; rather, you will get the best service from it. This does not mean allowing one's workers to squander his resources; it means providing good working conditions. Andrew Carnegie once said, 'No man becomes rich without himself enriching others.'

In conclusion, a heart of gratitude does not just make a man rich; it also gives him peace of mind to enjoy his riches. Gratitude doesn't take much from you; it only takes humility and not humiliation.

EXHORTATION

A Lesson from the Ants

The ants appreciate each other's role in their colony. The workers don't look down on the queens and so on. Thus, there is order in their colony all the time.

Recommendation

In showing gratitude, caution should be taken so that it won't be seen as weakness and thus generate contempt. Again, do your best to judge people by how they respond to gratitude individually. Do not consider others according to one man's response to gratitude especially when it is negative. Above all, always be grateful to God. Always put on a cheerful countenance; for you look better when you smile. Besides, people feel free to interact with those that have a cheerful countenance.

Practical Questions

1. Do you believe that gratitude has something to do with riches?
2. Do you react positively towards people when they show you an act of gratitude?
3. Does it pain you to be humble?
4. Do you like to see people relate with you with humility?
5. Do you believe that a life of gratitude can give you peace of mind?

A Verse for Inspiration

The Lord answered, "Who then
is the faithful and wise manager,
whom the master puts in charge of
his servants to give them their food
allowance at the proper time?"

Luke 12.42 (NIV)

CHAPTER

28

Savings

Joseph stored up grain in huge quantities like the sand on the seashore. He had so much that he finally gave up keeping any records because he couldn't measure it all.

Genesis 41.49 (GW)

Savings refer to the money that is not used or wasted but set aside for the future.

Rich people are known for setting aside some of their earnings, not just for the rainy day but for further investment. They postpone pleasures as long as there is something more beneficial that demands their resources. They save because they make up their mind to save not because their income is overflowing. Human wants are unlimited, thus a man who saves is not doing so because he doesn't know what to do with the money again. Saving is a conscious decision. If a man's income is high and he doesn't believe in saving, he will encourage himself that there will always be money to spend. On the other hand, if a man's income is low and he does not believe in saving, he will encourage himself that he doesn't have enough. However, saving can consolidate the wealth of a man whose income is high and make him richer. It can also raise the income of a man whose income is low and make him rich.

The rich know that even a reliable source of income can collapse at any time. Even if they are expecting a big profit, they still hold on to what they have until the big profit comes. They know that saving reduces the impact of a financial misfortune to the barest minimum. The truth about businesses or any other financial endeavour is that they have their time of boom and low tide period. It is what a man can save during the time of boom that can keep him and the business going even in the low tide period. The rich understand that even a low tide period of one month is enough to destabilize a business and they don't like to take chances. The Bible says,

He who gathers in summer is a wise son…

Proverbs 10.5 (NKJV)

Expansion

The rich save to expand their means of income. The rich know that one of the best forms of capital is the one they get from their savings. The reason is that they don't have to depend on any external factor to raise the fund. Consequently, they don't have to be under any pressure in the process of their investment. You will agree with me that a man gets the optimum performance in decision making when he has an atmosphere of freedom. As such, he will not act out of fear or to please anybody. He takes responsibility of his actions and is also more flexible with them. However, all these constitute some of the powerful ingredients in building a good business.

One thing about savings is that it doesn't discriminate whether a person is a child or an adult. It doesn't know whether a person is a man or woman. Once a person decides to save, he or she will accumulate fund which when invested will multiply into riches. Of an ideal virtuous woman, the Bible says,

She looks over a field and buys it, then,
with money she's put aside, plants a garden.

Proverbs 31.16 (The Message)

There is a point I will like you to note concerning savings that distinguishes the rich from others, many people save only to spend—without investment. But that kind of savings doesn't lead to riches. Of all the savings a man can make, the most beneficial is the portion he invests. Consider the ideal virtuous woman: she plants a garden with her savings.

Contingency Plan

Rich men save for a rainy day. A rainy day in this context does not necessarily mean a bad day. It can be a life time opportunity to make an investment and it can as well be an instance of impending danger, etc. One thing common with all of them is that they are times when something (money) is needed. Normally, before the rain, there would be a moment of ease but history, experience and wisdom teach that the rain would always come. So, having this understanding, the rich ones don't assume that there would be no rain or try to wish it away. Thus, they prepare for it through savings.

At this point, I will like to note that as long as a man is in the flesh, rainy days are bound to come. What makes the difference is how he handles them. And what determines how he handles them is how prepared he is before they come. It is good for a man to gain knowledge by learning and not by experience, for certain things in life. Though there might be some things for which experience is needed, no man in his right mind will like to pass through avoidable grievous pains. However, savings can prevent one from many of such grievous pains.

Another thing I will like you to know is that a man's capacity (i.e. his knowledge and level of preparation) influences what he calls a rainy day. A man who lives in an arid region might not be wrong if he says that it is raining while it is only drizzling. Again, in a region of normal rainfall, as some people will be complaining about the devastating effects of a rain that took place in the night, some will frankly say that they are not aware of the rain. This is what savings can do in the lives of people. In other words, it is not actually what many people count as rainy days are so. And unfortunately, when some Christians see such days they conclude that it is a trial of faith. Moreover, it is just a matter of savings. From the story of Joseph in the Bible, we can see that Egypt had food when others faced famine simply because they saved. Moreover, not every sprinkling of water is a rain. Sometimes when a man has saved a meaningful amount of money, problems demanding the money seem to spring from all angles. Nevertheless, wisdom is highly needed to know when to release one's savings and when to say no.

In conclusion, savings sustain riches in the hands of a man. If a man should have a lot of money in his hands but does not save, he is simply a poor man that is having a moment of respite. Rich men don't see savings as a punishment; they see it as a necessity for riches. They save not because they are rich but they are rich because they save.

EXHORTATION

A Lesson from the Ants

This is one of the most visible characteristics of the ants. They save while they can work and stay back in their nests to eat what they have when they cannot work.

Recommendation

Even though it is good to save, your present life should not suffer unnecessarily. Besides, don't consider putting all your eggs in one basket. You should save in at least three places especially in banks. However, that is for a case of someone who seems not to have a lot of money; the Bible recommends seven or eight (Ecclesiastes 11.2).

Practical Questions

1. Do you believe that people need to save to become rich?
2. Do you believe that rich men still need to save?
3. Do you think that all rainy days are accidental?
4. Do you think that all savings must be spent on solving problems?
5. Do you think that God does not want us to be saving?
6. Do you believe that savings can reduce worries?

A Verse for Inspiration

So you ought to have deposited
my money with the bankers, and
at my coming I would have received
back my own with interest.

Matthew 25.27 (NKJV)

CHAPTER

29

Unity of Purpose

But everything should be done
in a fitting and orderly way.

1 Corinthians 14.40 (NIV)

Unity is the state of being in agreement. And purpose is the reason why something exists. Unity of purpose is the state by which one's many reasons for existence agree together in one main reason for existence.

Rich men make sure that everything they do in life is in line with the attainment of their goals, all of which are driven by a purpose. Even their leisure and resting periods are not arbitrary. If you talk with a rich man for a reasonable length of time, you will definitely find out the direction of his life from his words. And I don't need to tell you that a man dreams about his goals even while he sleeps at night if he is serious about it. This is not a matter of obsession but a commitment to a purpose. Rich men know that for whatever they want to do in life, there are always options that agree with their goals and purpose. When men fail to understand this principle of unity of purpose it does not just frustrate their financial life, it also frustrates any other aspect of their life. That is why you can see some people that desire a good marriage but their favourite marriage television programme they watch for relaxation is organized and anchored by divorcees that know not the Word of God concerning marriage. Or you can see a man that wants to control his weight but he likes spending his leisure at a fast food joint.

A man's ultimate purpose is his actual reason for living. He may have many other smaller purposes showed by his goals. With the smaller purposes, he may still have even more smaller purposes and so on. However, the difference in that of a rich man is that all the smaller purposes agree with the ultimate purpose. Rich men consciously define all such purposes. They don't allow circumstances to throw up such purposes lest they will end up having goals that are opposite of each other. In life, it is normal for one to come across enticing goals but a rich man will always ask if such goals are in agreement with his purpose. When he rejects such goals, if they are not in consonance, it might look like a loss but that is the secret of his riches. The opposite is just the case with those who want to make the most of all such goals. They end up being jack of all trade and master of none. This should not be confused with diversification in which a man consciously decides and makes plans to enter into different businesses. And all such businesses still agree with his purpose.

Sometimes, you can see a man who is starting or about to start a business only for him to see an advert of a scholarship for a post-graduate degree that has nothing to do with his business. He can take the opportunity and come out with a good result but little will he know that he has lost such years. And even if he goes back to his business, he will spend another time updating his knowledge. After that, it might be another wonderful training package, and more incongruous opportunities will continue to present themselves. At the end, the man may have a lot of knowledge but will fail to apply them effectively. This is just an example; it can happen in many different ways. You can see someone with a first degree in accounting, a second degree in engineering, a third degree in law and so on. It takes a coordinated mind to identify a point of convergence and make sure that all his goals and purposes move towards it. The Bible says,

Keep your eyes straight ahead;
ignore all sideshow distractions.

Proverbs 4.25 (The Message)

Explicit Definition

Defining a financial purpose is the first step in financial planning. Rich men decide on their financial purpose for each period of time in their lives and set their goals towards it. It is their clear definition that makes them to know when a goal is congruent or not. Such a definition saves a man from wasting his time and resources pursuing frivolities. If a man is planning to resign from his job and start his own business at the age of forty, he won't find himself struggling with his friends to be the owner of the most expensive car at the age of thirty eight. He won't be among those struggling in his work place to be sent for a two year training programme at the age of thirty nine. In fact, the very day he declares that his purpose of working is to gather experience and capital for his own business at the age of forty, a good sense of financial responsibility will come upon him. A man can easily set a goal but it is the purpose or reason behind the goal that will compel him to move towards it. When the purpose is sensible and obvious, and the goal is visible, it will be difficult to discourage such a man. The Bible says,

The workers' hunger helps them, because
their desire to eat makes them work.

Proverbs 16.26 (NCV)

You now see that the purpose to eat makes a worker to set a goal in his work. This particular purpose starts the planning of his financial journey. He can take up many jobs but the foremost reason for all of them will be to keep him out of hunger. His reason or purpose for taking many jobs while he is still younger might be for a retirement plan, yet it still agrees with the foremost purpose—to keep out of hunger or to eat.

Ultimately, for a Christian, his foremost financial purpose is to serve God with his money. Other purposes and goals must find their place in this foremost purpose. And with that in mind, it will be impossible for such a person to consider making dirty money to give to God. It is as simple as that, the foremost purpose becomes the standard for measuring the usefulness and progress of others.

Synergy

Unity of purpose leads to synergy. When all the purposes are connected to each other, one will act as a stepping stone to the other. In such a situation, a man will not find himself repeating what he has done before. Even worse, he might be working against himself.

Sometimes you see young people that want to be rich but they don't like listening to business news. They would rather cherish entertainment programmes especially when it is full of ungodliness. After everything, they will expect God to bless the application of their knowledge in their business. Meanwhile, there is no good knowledge to bless and there is also no good relationship with God.

The rich understand that unity of purpose saves cost for them, thereby making more resources available for investment. It helps them to order their activities efficiently and effectively. It makes a man to execute his goals in the right order. When a man doesn't have a connection among his many goals, he can easily be carried away and will end up spending all his resources on one goal. Meanwhile, the goal is only a part of his ultimate goal. It is like a farmer who is excited about the efficiency and effectiveness of a tractor and he spends all his money buying tractors and cultivating a large expanse of land. But then he discovers that there is no money left to buy seeds. Definitely, he will end up cultivating his land for weeds. The Bible says,

> *...Every kingdom divided against*
> *itself is brought to desolation, and*

every city or house divided against
itself will not stand.

Matthew 12.25 (NKJV)

In conclusion, it is good to be ambitious and to set many great goals. But if all the goals do not have a central purpose, at best, one can end up achieving all the goals but will not have a meaningful successful life. Moreover, the normal thing is that such a person can find himself executing conflicting goals. Some people are rich because before they adopt any financial goal they ask, 'Does my purpose for this goal agree with my ultimate financial purpose and consequently my ultimate financial goal?'

EXHORTATION

A Lesson from the Ants

The central purpose of ants probably from the human point of view is to grow and sustain their colony. They hunt for food and store them while they could. They reproduce in their thousands even when the males have to give up their lives. Thus, they continue their existence because they don't have any other conflicting goal or purpose. It could also be seen clearly in their movements in definite lines.

Recommendation

Sometimes in life, even when you do your best to unite your goals in an ultimate purpose, there might still be conflicts. At this point, you will have to reevaluate the conflicting goals and your purpose. It might be that one or all the conflicting goals are wrong mainly because of the individual purposes. More also, it might be that your central purpose is wrong. Just make sure that the individual purposes and goals complement each other for optimum results.

Practical Questions

1. Do you believe that every action has a purpose?

2. Do you believe that every financial action has a purpose?
3. Do you think that everybody is obviously conscious of the purpose of all his or her actions?
4. Do you believe that being clearly conscious of one's purpose for any action makes him act wisely?
5. Do you have any ultimate financial purpose?

A Verse for Inspiration

...Be completely united, with
only one thought and one purpose.

1 Corinthians 1.10 (GNT)

CHAPTER

30

Patience

You need to keep on patiently doing God's will if you want him to do for you all that he has promised.

Hebrews 10.36 (TLB)

Patience is the ability to tolerate an unpleasant situation or to continue doing something despite difficulties.

Rich people sow their seeds and wait for them to mature before harvesting. They are not in a hurry for they know that any journey from one point to the other must have a time factor. Even when others are discouraged from embarking on a beneficial long journey because of its time cost, the rich know that the same time must pass whether they embark on the journey or not. Thus, they embark on many life's journeys with patience. And by the end of the day, they will be on the better side of life while those that did not make a move will of course remain where they had been.

In this book, I use the timing of five to seven years in many instances as the period between seed time and harvest time. Ordinarily, it will scare many people away but that five to seven years will definitely come and pass in their lives whether they do anything or not. I know that there is hardly any seed, be it a plant or a tree that will not germinate and be ready for harvesting within the period of five to seven years.

The number five itself is known to be the number of grace and the number seven is known to be the number of perfection or completeness. From the Scripture, during the feeding of the five thousand, Jesus used five loaves and two fishes (making a total of seven). You will also remember the five stones of David. Also, the pool of Bethesda (meaning house of mercy) had five porches and so on. Truly in life, if something happens once, it can be an accident, twice can be a coincidence but thrice is more likely to be a pattern. Also from the Bible, you have the seven days of creation, Seven Spirits of God, seven days of the week, etc. More precisely concerning sowing, the Bible talks about six years by which the Israelites could sow (and harvest) but the seventh which is meant only for harvest. The Bible says,

Six years you shall sow your field, and six years you shall prune your vineyard, and gather its fruit; but in the seventh year there shall be a sabbath of solemn rest for the land, a sabbath to the LORD. You shall neither sow your field nor prune your vineyard.
And the sabbath produce of the land shall be food for you…

Leviticus 25.3,4,6 (NKJV)

Just like many other portions of the Bible, you can see many prosperity codes. And many of them are hidden in the Old Testament laws. For instance there is one of many prosperity codes meant for a people as a whole, and that one is hidden in the laws of apprenticeship (Deuteronomy 15. 12-18). This code does not just empower one or few persons but it ensures a distributed prosperity among the people. However, for the apprentice as a person, his harvest year is still the seventh. I know of a certain group of people in Nigeria that applies this code and its result has been a distributed prosperity. I know that the code can work in any part of the world, anytime.

Now, someone might be of the opinion that some financial endeavours yield profits even within months. That is true but you can only judge that such endeavours have stood in prosperity after five to seven years. You have the seventh year as the prefect standard but starting from the fifth year for some cases because of grace. All these explanations still point to patience. There can be exceptions where one has to wait beyond the seventh year. However, in such cases, one has to check well to see if there is something wrong somewhere. However, one can consciously make a plan that will take more than seven years to be actualized.

A Necessity

The rich see patience as one of the bare necessities to prosperity. When a farmer sows his seed, he knows that there must be some time of waiting before the harvest comes. He does not go about worrying that his seeds did not germinate and bear fruits immediately. If he has sown grain in his farm and goes to check them after one week, he can come back happy even though without a harvest. His joy will be that though the seeds are not yet ready for harvest, they are no longer the way they were on the first day.

In the same way, whenever a rich man wants to invest his money, he asks for the waiting period. That knowledge keeps him from worries and premature harvest. With that knowledge, he doesn't see the waiting period as a misfortune but rather, as a necessity. Thus, the Bible says,

A man's wisdom gives him patience…

Proverbs 19.11 (NIV)

In the parable of the growing seed, Jesus painted the picture of a typical farmer. The Bible says,

Then Jesus said, "The kingdom of God is like someone who plants seed in the ground. Night and day, whether the person is asleep or

awake, the seed still grows, but the person does not know how it grows. By itself the earth produces grain. First the plant grows, then the head, and then all the grain in the head. When the grain is ready, the farmer cuts it, because this is the harvest time."

Mark 4.26-29 (NCV)

Without patience, no man can build holistic riches. Just the way a great house is built with many blocks, one at a time until the big structure is completed. Even though it is possible for a man to fast track some activities, there are always limits to that. Besides, not all activities could be fast tracked. Patience is thus indispensible and normal for wealth accumulation. Abraham Lincoln said, 'I will read and prepare myself and someday my chance will come.'

Two Sides of Patience

Rich men understand the two sides of patience. Many times you see people who could be said to be patient but they linger with poverty and some even die with it. And that can discourage a lot of people from believing that patience is a prerequisite for riches. The truth is that many people do not know the two sides of patience to know which one to adopt at each point in time. The two sides of patience are endurance and perseverance. There are situations in life when a man is required to endure. By that he is expected to hold on despite the unpleasant situation. It is this side of patience that could sometimes be called longsuffering. From the word itself, it simply means suffering something for a long time. The main point is that despite the suffering, the person does not give up. A rich man endures in situations which he cannot change. Actually, the reason why many people who could be said to be patient linger with poverty is because they choose to endure even in situations they can change. That also brings in the issue of the other side of patience which is perseverance. By this, a man is expected to continue working hard until he gets a breakthrough. What makes people rich is their understanding of when to endure and when to persevere. The truth is that poor people choose more of the endurance side of patience while the rich ones choose more of the perseverance side of patience. Sometimes, the three words (i.e. patience, endurance and perseverance) are used interchangeably but they are not the same. Patience implies either of the remaining two at each point in time. Endurance is all about inactive waiting while perseverance is waiting with action.

In conclusion, one of the things that distinguish a Christian from others is his ability to be patient. That is actually the work of the Holy Spirit and it also separates holistic riches from hasty ones which dwindle in no time. Patience keeps a man calm while his riches accumulate. But when men lack patience they can develop a heart problem such that even if their expectations are actualized their joy would no longer be full.

EXHORTATION

A Lesson from the Ants

Whenever the ants want to build their nest, they patiently carry the soil particles to the surface over a long time. Finally, they will have their nest inside the ground and an anthill on the surface of the ground.

Recommendation

I will like you to understand that your patience is not tried when things are easy and smooth. Your patience is tried when it is difficult to wait and when your expectation seems to be uncertain (Romans 8.25) but be assured that it is when you have waited patiently to the end that you will come out with victory.

Practical Questions

1. Do you think that patience is all about pain?
2. Do you think we should always have limits to our patience?

3. Do you believe that knowledge enhances patience?
4. Do you believe that we should endure what we cannot change?
5. Do you believe that we should approach most of life's difficult situations with perseverance?
6. Do you believe that the presence of patience does not mean the absence of hope?

A Verse for Inspiration

Abraham was patient, and so he received
what God had promised.

Hebrews 6.15 (GNT)

CHAPTER

31

Diversification

Invest what you have in several different businesses, because you don't know what disasters might happen.

Ecclesiastes 11.2 (NCV)

Diversification is the act of giving variety to something. And in this context, it is the act of giving variety to one's sources of income.

Rich people do not put all their eggs in one basket. They earn from different means so that if one fails others will keep them standing. On the other hand, they reap from different means at a time. Since the Bible advocates for diversification, rich men don't go for one business and then pray that nothing bad will happen to it. The truth is that the bad things that can happen to a man's business might not necessarily happen to his business alone. It might be the whole line of that business. And you know that though the man is a Christian who is serious with his faith, he is only one of the thousands or even millions of people in that business line. Meanwhile, if a man is serious with God he should also obey the Word of God that advocates for diversification.

No matter how careful a man is, it is not advisable for him to carry all his eggs in one basket. In fact, it is even when he does so that tension and fear will come and push him down. Every farmer prays that none of his eggs will be broken but carrying them in different baskets will save him a lot if there happens to be a fall. This is one of the reasons why a man can be very rich but in the twinkling of an eye—just one mistake, he will become very poor. Making a mistake is something common in life but it will be so bad when only one mistake can ruin a man's life. To give a picture of this, the Bible says,

There is a grievous ill that I have seen under the sun: riches were kept by their owners to their hurt, and those riches were lost in a bad venture; though they are parents of children, they have nothing in their hands.

Ecclesiastes 5.13-14 (NRSV)

A man might not be able to avoid mistakes in his life but he can reduce the impact of a single mistake in his life. And concerning finances, the Bible offers diversification as a solution.

Many Income Streams

By diversification, the rich earn from many sources. Earning from many sources gives one the opportunity to take advantage of the benefits that may arise from those sources at any time. In the world of business, every business line has its own season. Some have their seasons in a particular month or months of the year. Some have their seasons as a particular number of years in time. The good thing about diversification is that when one business line is out of season, another would likely be in its season. But for a man who is only in one line of business, he may enjoy the business during its own season and could be frustrated immediately the season of the business line is over. The Scripture says,

Plant your seed in the morning, and don't let your hands rest until

evening. You don't know whether
this field or that field will be profitable
or whether both of them will
[turn out] equally well.

Ecclesiastes 11.6 (GW)

No matter how comfortable a rich man is with his business, he knows that just as the season of his business came, it can go one day. He doesn't wait for that time to come; he moves ahead.

We can learn from the roots of plants or trees. The root spreads to every direction in quest for water and soil nutrients. And the more it spreads, the better its chances of survival. Though one is not expected to spread into an uncountable number of business lines like a root, the Bible offers some numbers. If you read this chapter's introductory verse in another Bible version, it says,

Give portions to seven, yes,
to eight; for you do not know what
disaster may come upon the land.

Ecclesiastes 11.2 (NIV)

Efficiency

Diversification leads to effective and efficient investment. Just as it is obtained from roots of plants and trees, there is more concentration in areas of the presence of water and soil nutrients. For some plants and trees, there is always a tap root which is the biggest, longest and the principal root. In the process of diversification, a man can see other businesses more profitable than the one he is doing. Such a discovery will make him to allocate his resources effectively across the various business lines. Thus, he will invest more money in the business that will yield the highest return at any point in time. If we look at the parable of the talents as told by Jesus, the master of those servants delivered his goods to them according to their abilities. Even though he knew the one that would perform better and the one that would not, he still went ahead to invest in all of them but proportionately.

Many rich people don't have anything to do with their first business line any more—having discovered something better because of diversification. Some started by working for others until they tried to diversify. It was only then that they discovered financial open doors they had never thought of. It is normal for men to be satisfied with their careers as long as they can see any comfort in it. But after a long time, what seemed to be of comfort may turn out to be uncomfortable. In life, people do have the opportunity to diversity but it takes only a willing mind to accept such an opportunity. Moreover, it takes a willing mind to discover the opportunity when it comes even before accepting it. In the parable of the hidden treasure, though its spiritual side is about giving up everything for the sake of the kingdom of God, we can still gain another kind of knowledge from it. And it has as to do with finance and diversification. The Bible says,

Again, the kingdom of heaven is like treasure hidden in a field, which a man found and hid; and for joy over it he goes and sells all that he has and buys that field.

Matthew 13.44 (NKJV)

Whenever you hear 'hidden', 'found', 'buy' and 'sell' together, you will be talking about financial matters. In this parable, we can see that Jesus used a financial story to portray a spiritual meaning. Now the man in the parable might have been a labourer since the land was not his own but his discovery would probably turn him into a miner or a trader. If he had no desire for a change, he would probably ignore the opportunity and continue to be satisfied with what he had. Besides, he might not even be able to identify the treasure. Financial opportunities are always like hidden treasures but it is only those that venture in their fields that would discover them. Finally, we can see that the man sold everything he had to make a more profitable investment.

In conclusion, diversification opens the doors of many financial opportunities and reduces the effect of a loss in one business line. Any man that is interested in financial prosperity should not see diversification as something he will do sometime in the future but something that must be his immediate character. A man should not try to use faith as his reason against it; for it is the Word of God that says, 'Diversify!'

EXHORTATION

A Lesson from the Ants

The ants don't eat only one kind of food; they gather anything that is available to them. Again, their nests are not just a single chambered hole; they dig multiple channels and chambers that serve for easy escape whenever there is a danger.

Recommendation

It is good for a man to start diversifying while he is still young and flexible—not when he is getting old. One may not have to wait until he gets a perfect option for diversification and a huge sum as a capital. It is even possible that the second option business will be a strong cushion in time of crisis or even grow to become bigger than the first option business. Though the Bible says, 'seven' or 'eight', it is expected and good that you start somewhere. Thus, no matter how difficult you find it, make sure that you have at least two means of income; even if the second means is passive.

Practical Questions

1. How many streams of income do you have?
2. Do you think it is wise to carry all your eggs in one basket with faith that nothing will happen to them?

3. Have you seen a rich man that became poor because his one and only business had a problem?
4. Do you think that diversification is an act of fear or obedience to the Word of God?
5. Do you believe that diversification creates financial opportunities?

A Verse for Inspiration

In a wealthy home there are dishes
made of gold and silver as well as
some made from wood and clay.

2 Timothy 2.20 (TLB)

CHAPTER

32

Responsibility

God spoke: "Let us make human beings
in our image, make them reflecting our nature
So they can be responsible for the fish in the sea,
the birds in the air, the cattle, And, yes, Earth
itself, and every animal that moves on the
face of Earth."

Genesis 1.26 (The Message)

Responsibility is the state of being accountable for something done or for its consequences.

Rich people are always ready to answer for their lives and actions. They don't waste their lives shifting blames from one person to another. They know that no matter what others say or do to them, they are the ones God put in charge of their own lives. They have it fixed in their mind and thus act likewise. They accept the responsibility; for they know that rejecting it might be easy but painful at the end. They don't spend their lives wishing that God would have created them in another way. Such people agree with the words of a writer, Johann von Goethe, who said, 'If God had wanted me otherwise, He would have created me otherwise.' Just as we can see in many Bible passages; it all starts with the mind. The mind of a man is like a mould, his thought is his moulding material and the vessel that comes from it is what he becomes.

It is much easier for someone to use clay as a moulding material but at the end the vessel will be cheap and easily breakable. But if a man decides to use gold as his moulding material, he may not find it easy at the beginning in getting the gold. Again he has to take the pains of smelting it. But at the end, he will have a very expensive vessel for which he will not be afraid of its breakage.

Most times you see rich people that never had rich parents or rich relatives who were of help to them; but they end up being rich. That is because they understand that if they must move into the life of abundance, they must accept the responsibility of their own lives. Even as they progress in life, they don't waste their time preparing wonderful speeches they will render against their government or anyone. Even when the system in which they operate becomes counter-productive, they move out of the loop. They know that even if everybody around becomes poor, that will not make poverty to mean riches. It is only when a society lacks men that think like this that poverty takes over.

Rich men know that sailing with the wrong wind will not only lead them to a wrong destination but it's also a disappointment unto God. The Bible says,

"I commissioned you judges, each one of you,
deputies of the High God, But you've betrayed
your commission and now you're stripped
of your rank, busted."

Psalm 82.6-7 (The Message)

Sincerity

Responsibility makes a man to be sincere with himself. When a man knows that he is in charge, he does not go about with unfounded assumptions or any form of pretense. He knows that nobody will come and make up for such things; it is what he sows that he will reap. A good sense of responsibility makes a man not to build his life on superstitions. Every responsible man knows that there is no such thing as a chest of gold in every cave; if anyone wants gold he should go to the mines. Every responsible man knows that there is no honey in the moon; if anyone wants honey he should go to the beehives.

Rich men don't wait for people to come and enrich them; they know that riches are a payment for responsibility. They live for something—they become in charge of something that the people need and they are paid for it.

A responsible man knows his capacity and works from there. He does not go about deceiving himself that he will do something for which he doesn't have the capacity. If he wants to do something, he first works on his capacity. He does not go about living his life carelessly and without planning believing that God will take the responsibility of everything. He sees himself as a manager that God has appointed to manage the business of his own life. His main assignment is to succeed and not to find reasons to blame God. He understands when the Bible says,

What is man, that thou art mindful of him?...
For thou hast made him a little lower than
the angels…
Thou madest him to have dominion over
the works of thy hands…

Psalm 8.4-6 (KJV)

A responsible man knows that this dominion God has given to him is not a ceremonial appointment but a call to duty. He knows that God that has called him to duty has also made provisions for its execution. Thus, in his bid not to disappoint God, he excels in life. He is not interested in giving God a waste-report or a failure-report or a well analysed breakdown-report. His interest is only a success-report. He agrees with the words of Abraham Lincoln who said, 'A man is not held responsible for the beginning of his life but for the end thereof.'

Accountability

Responsibility leads to accountability. One thing common with any kind of success is accountability. If a man knows that he will present an account of how he spends his time, he wouldn't like to present a report that he spent twenty hours in a day sleeping. If a manager of a business organization knows that he will present a financial account of the business by the end of the year, he wouldn't like to give a report that he spent half of the organizations profit on entertainment. Such accountability comes when a man knows that something has been put in his charge. Thus, if he feels no responsibility, he thinks of no accountability.

It is at this point that rich men are separated from others. They know that even when no man will come to them to demand an explicit account, they are accountable to God. They are also accountable to themselves and also indirectly accountable to humanity. At the beginning of everyday, a rich man asks himself what he intends to do with his time. And by the end of every day, he asks himself what he has achieved with his time. If money enters his hands, he will ask himself if he is justified before God to spend it the way he is planning to do. He will also consider how humanity will judge him after hearing that he spent such amount of money the way he is planning to do. Finally, he will consider the outcome of such a spending, whether he would be able to say, 'I have done well.'

Many people will easily say that God will not judge them by whether they are rich or poor. Thus, they used the resources and opportunities and positions God has given to them as they like. And they will even turn to God to expect more; else they will blame Him for not providing enough. When it comes to being accountable to humanity, many people will even be aggressive towards anyone that tries to call them to accountability. However, the Bible says,

The people curse him who
holds back grain…

Proverbs 11.26 (RSV)

People don't curse such a man because they gave him the grain but because they expect any man that has grain to sell it or give it out. However, such a curse holds, if not, the Bible will not talk about it.

Now some people can try to deceive humanity; they even start by deceiving their employers or relatives and their immediate society. They may think that they have succeeded by that act but they will end up deceiving themselves—achieving nothing in life. A man with a sense of responsibility knows that there is no benefit in trying to deceive humanity, since he cannot lie to God or himself. The highest sense of responsibility is when a man knows that life is a call to accountability. He will no longer be thinking of any external body to appease with eye service, he becomes personally accountable. He sees life as a stewardship and the Bible says,

Moreover, it is [essentially] required of stewards
that a man should be found faithful [proving
himself worthy of trust].

1 Corinthians 4.2 (AMP)

A responsible man knows that he is required to be faithful in every aspect of his life, whether spiritually, physically (health wise), financially and maritally. Thus, for a Christian who is a rich man, he is, among other things, faithful with his finance.

Self-Sufficiency

Responsibility creates a sense of independence. One common thing among rich men is that they don't put the hope of their success in the hands of another man. They see themselves as the major player regarding their success or failure in life. God created man and gave him dominion but it behooves the man to take responsibility for his success or failure, or to blame others. Even when others seem to be wrong, he doesn't wait for everything to collapse simply because he is not the cause. He moves ahead to correct the situation for he knows that failure is failure no matter who causes it. He will rather tell a story of how he did other people's work in order for him to succeed than for him to tell how his failure was caused by other people. To him, if there is a failure, he will accept his own portion of blame.

The truth in life is that not everybody you meet in life will be faithful in playing his or her role in life. In many cases, people are born into the world to meet parents that are not ready to play their role. However, you have testimonies of such people when they have become successful. For some others, it is their governments, schools, relatives, communities, etc. But the common thing is that you will always have successful people from the same condition. It is simply because they choose to be responsible and decide to be independent of their unpleasant condition. If you take a closer look at the testimonies of such persons, it will appear as if the more unpleasant the situation, the greater the success of those that choose responsibility. It all agrees with what the Scripture says,

I was amazed when I looked and saw that
there was no one to help me. But my anger
made me strong, and I won the victory myself.

Isaiah 63.5 (GNT)

This is God Himself speaking in human terms and the same word is true for human beings. It is the anger of necessity that moves many people into action. And that is what leads them into prosperity.

In conclusion, responsibility is what a man chooses for himself; even the son of a highly responsible man must choose to be responsible. God created every human being and made everyone to be responsible for his or her own life.

EXHORTATION

A Lesson from the Ants

The ants, though little, do not wait for any bigger creature to come and help them do their own works. They don't go about a-sorrowing for the way God has created them. They don't go about blaming the weather. Rather, they put all these things into consideration and work for their successful living.

Recommendation

As you decide to live a life of responsibility, you should do your best to acknowledge God; for everything depends on His mercy. You should see a life of responsibility not just as a mere decision but as the will of God for your life. Even though you might have a complaint about something at one time or the other in life, never allow that complaint to become an alibi to live an unpleasant life.

Practical Questions

1. Is there anybody you are currently blaming for any failure in your life?
2. Do you believe that responsibility raises people from poverty to prosperity even when others have resigned to poverty as their fate?
3. Do you believe that preparing failure stories is to some extent like an expression of irresponsibility?
4. Do you believe that God's gift of life is a call for responsibility?
5. Will you rather choose to be responsible or to blame others?

A Verse for Inspiration

Assume your own responsibility.

Galatians 6.5 (GW)

CHAPTER

33

Boldness

Let us therefore come boldly unto the
throne of grace, that we may obtain mercy,
and find grace to help in time of need.

Hebrews 4.16 (KJV)

Boldness is a state of confidence, fearlessness and willingness to take risks.

It is a truism that if becoming rich is easy, everybody would be rich. Another truth is that many people will like to be rich but when it comes to taking bold steps, many will draw back. It goes with the old saying that if wishes were horses, beggars would ride. The reality is that riches are not horses; that is why beggars don't ride. Rather, according to John Dryden, 'Fortune befriends the bold.'

For a Christian, at the mention of the word 'Boldness'; what comes to mind is 'Faith'. In fact, without faith there is no Christianity. The Bible says,

It's impossible to please God
apart from faith.

Hebrews 11.6 (The Message)

You will hardly find a man who never had a business idea or opportunity but fear holds back many. It is only among those that launch out with boldness that you can find the rich ones. When a man moves with boldness that does not mean that he can't fail. But when he fails, he only learns how not to do the same thing again. In other words, he learns how to do it better or how not to fail again. A man that moves with boldness knows that obstacles might present themselves; he knows that everything might not be as smooth as he wished them to be. But he still moves out believing that he will succeed. It is easier for some Christians to have faith for healing, salvation, etc. but when it comes to finance they will begin to draw back due to hidden fear. They believe that God exists but find it difficult to believe that God also rewards those who diligently seek Him [financially] (Hebrew 11.6).

What makes a Christian rich is his ability to apply his faith in the running of his business. He knows that there is no other way to move the hand of God into his business than moving out with boldness believing God to prosper his ways. Even though it is good for one to do good analysis before launching out, unending analysis only breeds fear. There must be a point at which a man must stop analysing and launch out with faith as long as he has seen that the business is worth taking. This is exactly the reason why many educated professionals can work as employees for others or act as consultants to other businesses. But they cannot start and run their own businesses; simply because they have knowledge but no faith. They can use much analysis to cover up their fears but it is only when a man moves out with boldness that he can talk of making profit or becoming rich.

Conviction

Boldness is an outcome of conviction. When a man is convinced before action, he will continue to strike until there is a breakthrough. But those who act without conviction can even stumble where there is no stumbling block. And that will be enough to discourage them. The rich move out in life as if they have seen the complete picture beforehand that they will succeed. Their words and their actions portray that. That is why they go on with many ventures that others will term to be risky. Moreover, any man that wants to buy goods or pay for services will always look for those that are convinced about what they are offering. It is only when a man is convinced about something that he can make another to be convinced of the same.

It is very difficult to find a man who is fully convinced about his business without being bold about it. Even a weakling can turn into a strong man in the twinkling of an eye because of certainty. From the words of George Eliot, 'Any coward can fight a battle when he's sure of winning.' Bankers cannot lend their money to a man who is not convinced or bold about what he intends to use the money for. Even a man himself cannot commit his time and money fully in his own business if he is not convinced about its success. The Bible says,

Now faith is the assurance of things hoped for, the conviction of things not seen.

Hebrews 11.1 (RSV)

From this Bible passage we can see that faith is ever present; it does not wax old. It is either that a man has faith or he doesn't. A man can start up a business with faith or boldness because of his conviction but immediately he loses conviction about the business, his faith or boldness in the business vanishes. It is only when there is conviction that you can see businesses changing with the market trends and going for innovations. The life of every business is the conviction of its owner in its success. As long as the conviction is there, boldness will be there. As long as there is boldness, there will always be a willing mind to break new grounds. For wherever there is a will, there is a way.

Rapid Movement

Boldness enhances speed. The pace of every movement is dependent on the force propelling it. When it comes to human action—precisely financial actions, the condition of the heart comes into play. Whether it is nonchalant attitude or fear, the pace will show. And if it be of boldness, the pace will also show. It only takes boldness for men to enter an aircraft that will be thousands of feet above the sea level, flying at a speed of hundreds of nautical miles per hour—just to get to a destination for which a cautious person can ride on a horse and get to the same place. The question now is, 'How long will it take the horseman to reach the same destination that takes an aircraft only two hours?'

It is obvious that a man who is afraid of any ground walks slowly but a man who has no fear can run. Many people are rich just because they ran while others were crawling. A lot of people have ideas that they can put into use but fear keeps them to be moving very slowly. They can talk about such ideas fluently and convincingly but when it comes to practice they will draw back. Many of such people can continue drawing back until it becomes part of them. They are the kind that will easily tell others that they had been in a particular field for say twenty years and thus will try to prove that no meaningful progress could be made beyond what they have achieved. The reason why their mind is so clouded is because when they had their first opportunity they drew back or trod slowly. And when the second opportunity came, they did the same even up to the third, fourth, fifth, and so on. On the other side, for the rich, when they have their first opportunity, they act with boldness and that makes it easier for them to act upon their second opportunity and much easier for the next and so on. Boldness increases with each action taken even when the action is not successful. However, when the action is successful boldness increases more.

The point is that when someone acts upon seemingly little ideas that usually present themselves at the beginning of one's life, the individual will develop more boldness. Thus, at each point in his life, while others are fearful or moving slowly, he will come and run with a great speed because of boldness. From the Bible, we can see the story of David when Goliath taunted the Israelites. David was bold enough to face Goliath because he had earlier defeated a lion and a bear. He said to King Saul,

Your servant has killed both lion and bear; and this uncircumcised Philistine will be like one of them…

1 Samuel 17.36 (NKJV)

It is also good to note that David did not imagine the scene of his fight with Goliath, he saw the giant as one already defeated. That could be easily seen in his words; for he asked only of the reward of killing Goliath and not of how to fight the giant. This is what boldness can do in the life of a man.

In conclusion, boldness is the actual force that makes a man to put all his wonderful thoughts into action. A man's level of boldness increases as he exposes himself to practical. There is always a first time to doing something. Boldness understands this fact and also discovers that for the second time it comes with less anxiety.

EXHORTATION

A Lesson from the Ants

The ants go about their business with boldness; that is why they are not intimidated by the presence of other bigger creatures while going about their business.

Recommendation

Even though boldness is good, that does not call for uncalculated actions. Acting without wisdom can lead to discouragement and fear. Wisdom itself will become a form of control on the power a man can exert because of his high level of boldness; for power without control can become a disaster.

Practical Questions

1. Have you ever had any business idea?
2. Have you ever engaged in any business venture?

3. What do you think is withholding you from executing any business idea in your mind if you have not done so?
4. Do you think that people are only bold if they are born with it?
5. Are you willing to start living with boldness?
6. Do you believe that it takes boldness to become a business owner?
7. Do you believe that it takes only a step to start a journey?

A Verse for Inspiration

Now there were four leprous men at the entrance of the gate; and they said to one another, "Why are we sitting here until we die?

2 Kings 7.3 (NKJV)

CHAPTER

34

Giving

Give, and it shall be given unto you;
good measure, pressed down, and shaken together,
and running over, shall men give into your
bosom. For with the same measure that ye
mete withal it shall be measured to you again.

Luke 6.38 (KJV)

Giving is the act of causing someone to receive something by providing or offering it to him or her.

Givers never lack. Giving is the actual proof that one has love—not necessarily having more than enough. It involves giving to God and to humanity. If a man wants to conquer money, then he must give it out. It is possible to count a man to be rich but unless he is a giver he is not a rich man; he is only pretending to be rich. If a poor man who doesn't have enough can give, then a rich man should give even more. To be a rich man simply means having more than enough. Thus, giving is one of the simplest criteria to identify a rich man. However, the interest of this book is to show that giving—as an attribute, can make a man rich.

When some people see a rich man giving, they can easily conclude that the man is giving because he is rich. But the reverse is true; the man is rich because he is giving. That is why some people will wait till eternity to become rich before they start giving. They don't know that the simple thing they are supposed to do is to start giving. Many Christians pray that God will bless them and that is good. But there is something better than that; it is what God seeks in Christians and that is blessing them until they become blessings themselves. The Scripture says that when God called Abram, He said to him,

I will make of you a great nation, and I will bless you, and make your name great, so that you will be a blessing.

Genesis 12.2 (NRSV)

In essence, God gives money to people so that they will become money givers themselves. And the easiest way to tell God that you won't fail Him if He gives you money is to start giving immediately. I can say that there are two kinds of financial blessings God gives to people. One is what I call financial provision and the other is financial empowerment. In the case of financial provision, an individual has more than enough to take care of his bare necessities of life. He can also give to others and for various causes but in a limited form. However, he plans for all his expenses including those of his bare necessities of life. Nonetheless, he is rich. On the other hand, for financial empowerment, an individual is so rich that his riches have turned into a source of power to him. This kind of individual no longer bothers about his bare necessities of life. In his financial planning, he only allocates money for such expenses without caring about the breakdown of the expenditures. His giving to others is more of accomplishing something in their lives. His giving to various causes is not limited; when he gives, he sees to the accomplishment of a goal. For example, when he wants to give for the building of a Church, he sees to it that the Church building is completed. An example of financial empowerment was seen in Isaac. The Bible says of him,

He had so many flocks and herds and servants that the Philistines envied him. Then Abimelek said to Isaac, "Move away

from us; you have become too powerful for us."

Genesis 26.14&16 (NIV)

When a Christian is financially empowered by God, it is expected of him to live his life as a giver. It is only when such a man misses the mark that the empowerment will turn to become a problem to him. That is when money will turn him into a corrupt man. Truly, money can bring power and power on its own has the capacity to corrupt a man. Money can corrupt a man when he lacks the knowledge of the purpose of the money. It is like when you pour water into an elastic container that supposed to be allowing water to flow through it. If the container does not allow water to flow to the right place, it will mess up the environment. On the other hand, if the container decides not to be allowing water to flow through it, it will expand until it reaches its limit and burst. A natural phenomenon that portrays giving is the flowing of rivers and streams. There is this particular water body in Israel that refuses to allow water to flow through it and it ended up having a large concentration of salt in it. Today it is known as the Dead Sea; for no living thing can survive in its salty water.

The Word of God

Givers are rich because the Word of God says so. Besides any other reason one may have for why givers are rich, the Bible expressly declares it,

...and the scripture cannot be broken.

John 10.35 (KJV)

The Bible clearly says,

Whoever gives to others will get richer;
those who help others will themselves
be helped.

Proverbs 11.25 (NCV)

There are many things a man may argue about but it is disastrous for a man to argue with the Word of God. It is God's own decision to make it that every giver will be blessed. Those who understand this live a life of giving and end up being rich. This is not just a physical matter, it has a spiritual dimension. This is one of the reasons why some people who seem not to be quite smart or hard-working end up being rich. Some people can violate some causes of poverty and still end in riches just because they are givers. This is not an invitation to that kind of life but it is a reality. Even in some cases, you can see some people who never gave their lives to Christ but this same principle of giving makes them rich. Again, this is not an invitation to that kind of life for dying without Christ means spending eternity in hell even with the riches.

In all these, the point I am trying to bring out is that giving on its own attracts God's financial blessing. God blesses the giver so that he will continue with his giving. Actually, giving is God's own lifestyle; for God is love and there can be no love without giving. The Bible says,

For God so loved the world that
He gave His only begotten Son,
that whoever believes in Him should
not perish but have everlasting life.

John 3.16 (NKJV)

You can tell someone that you love him or her while you don't but if you give to that person, you may not need to tell the person that you love him or her. Giving is love demonstrated. Giving is so powerful that even a deaf man can hear its language and even if a blind man sees nothing else, he can see it. In the Book of 1 Corinthians chapter thirteen, in which Apostle Paul talked much about love, the translators of the King James Version of the Bible found no better word for the Greek word 'AGAPE' but 'CHARITY'. We can see clearly that God rewards the life of love which is found in givers. Giving does not just make a man rich; it attracts many other blessings to his life.

Religious Giving

Giving to God leads to financial empowerment. Even though it is good to give to fellow human beings and to various causes, the priority should be giving to God. When we give to God, it is not that God needs our money to spend; it is an act of worship. People can be blessed for various acts of giving but when it is an act of worship, God picks a special interest in it. It might not be a surprise to know that the first act of faith as recorded in the Bible was giving. The Bible says,

Faith led Abel to offer God a better sacrifice
than Cain's sacrifice.

Hebrews 11.4 (GW)

We can see that later, when Abel was killed by Cain, his act of giving caused God to avenge his death. Though one can say that God avenges the blood of innocent people, we cannot also deny the fact that the Bible expressly says that it was by faith (expressed by giving) that Abel cried to God for vengeance, even though he was dead.

There are many acts of giving exhibited by men of old in the Bible. Many of them are acts of covenants and obedience to eternal principles. And among such powerful financial principles is tithing. Tithe is simply one tenth of a man's income and tithing is the act of paying tithe. It can be to a minister of God or more especially to the Church of Christ. The main issue is that the tithe is paid towards God. Some people are of the opinion that tithing was an Old Testament practice that ended with the Old Testament. But such people fail to understand that tithing had been in existence even before the Old Testament. Tithing is an eternal principle of financial prosperity.

Abraham paid tithe to Melchizedek hundreds of years before the Old Testament. God in His infinite wisdom deemed it fit to make it part of the law He gave to the Israelites. That only acknowledges the importance of tithing, not an introduction of something new. Thus, nobody should expect it to end with the Old Testament. Rather, people should be asking for who taught Abraham to pay tithe, if not the Spirit of God.

As a matter of fact, all the Old Testament laws that are not stopped in the New Testament are still valid. Concerning the issue of tithing, Jesus Himself said,

But woe to you Pharisees! For though you are careful to tithe even the smallest part of your income, you completely forget about justice and the love of God. You should tithe, yes, but you should not leave these other things undone.

Luke 11.42 (TLB)

It has been the character of some Christians that when the Word of God is against their lifestyle, they will look for an alibi. And if such a word is only written in the Old Testament part of the Bible, they will feel at ease to say, 'It is the Old Testament.' In other words, they mean, 'It is no longer valid.' So it is also not a surprise for folks that like poverty to say, 'Tithing is only in the Old Testament.' However, when such people see something they love in the Old Testament, they will still hold on to it.

There is this story of a boy whose mother was a Baptist pastor. The boy had no special talent and the mother who was the only parent there for him was not rich. However, the woman knew the Word of God on prosperity and taught his son tithing at his tender age. The boy continued with that lifestyle until he became the first billionaire and the richest man in his country, United States of America. His name was

John D. Rockefeller. Moreover, he did not lose his faith because of riches.

Another strong aspect of Christian giving is firstfruit. If we look at the story of Cain and Abel, the only thing that the Bible expressly mentioned about the offering of Abel was that he gave the first born of his flock (Genesis 4.4). In another place, the Bible expressly says,

Honor the LORD with your wealth, with the firstfruits of all your crops; then your barns will be filled to overflowing, and your vats will brim over with new wine.

Proverbs 3.9-10 (NIV)

God always delights in anyone that makes Him the first in any aspect of his or her life. He went on to make it known to men that if anyone worships Him with his firstfruit, then He (God Himself) will bless that man beyond measure. Most times, when men honour God with their firstfruit, they find it easy to continue honouring him with their wealth for the rest of their lives. Honouring God with one's wealth involves many other forms of giving including sacrificial giving. Once a man wants to start a lifestyle of giving, nothing will be able to stop him (2 Corinthians 8.12).

In conclusion, to be a rich man, one has to adopt a lifestyle of giving. If any man is interested in a sustained life of financial abundance, he should also sustain a lifestyle of giving. One-time-giving is not enough. It can attract a blessing but a lifestyle attracts more blessings until one becomes a blessing himself.

EXHORTATION

A Lesson from the Ants

The ants live peacefully in their nests because each of them is always willing to give as much as it could for the good of their colony. None of them spends its life thinking of how to receive only, rather their interest is in giving for the good of all.

Recommendation

Giving is a practical financial principle that you cannot neglect if you are interested in living a life of financial abundance. Moreover, you must be committed with tithing. You should understand that God does not give you money just for you to pile it up. Rather, it is for you to use it in serving and worshipping Him. It also involves giving to fellow human beings. Nevertheless, in giving to fellow human beings, it should be for meaningful things, lest one will become a victim of careless lifestyles lived by others.

Practical Questions

1. Do you live a lifestyle of giving?
2. Do you have reasons that make you not to be a giver at the moment?
3. Do you believe that giving starts from the heart and not in the resources?
4. Do you believe that giving is an act of worship?
5. Do you think that giving is not meant for everybody?

A Verse for Inspiration

One man gives freely, yet grows all the richer;
another withholds what he should give,
and only suffers wants.

Proverbs 11.24 (RSV)

CHAPTER

35

Discipline

It is better to be patient than powerful.
It is better to win control over yourself
than over whole cities.

Proverbs 16.32 (GNT)

Discipline is the ability to live a controlled lifestyle even in difficult situations.

Rich people always do what they ought to do even when they don't feel like doing it. It is important to note that rich people face the same tiredness, discouragement, weakness, etc. that others face. It is their rule over themselves that makes the difference. Among the attributes of the Fruit of the Spirit, it is called self-control. It is the ability to live by design and not by default. When the default of your body system is saying, 'Sleep', the design of your inner man might be saying, 'Study for you have an exam tomorrow'. When the default is saying, 'Spend', the design might be saying, 'Save'. When the default is saying, 'Relax', the design might be saying, 'Work'. It is always easier to listen to the default; that is why many people do so. But when men live their life by design, their success is always highly organized. The inner man is always there with his building plan but the flesh is ever ready to justify the easy life. That is why Jesus said,

...The spirit indeed is willing, but the flesh is weak.

Matthew 26.41 (NKJV)

To be disciplined does not in any way mean that a man will not rest or feel tired. It only means resting at the right time of rest not any time one feels tired. Discipline is all about training and character development. You have parental discipline, God's discipline, school discipline, etc. All these are meant to mould an individual unto self-discipline. Even though God disciplines His children, He goes ahead to put self-control as an attribute of the Fruit of the Spirit. It is when a man becomes self-disciplined that he could be said to be a disciplined human being.

Seemingly Painful Beginning

Discipline does not start with enjoyment. One of the things rich men understand about discipline is that no form of discipline is pleasing at the moment though they can yield positive results. Starting from parental discipline which can involve spanking, it is not pleasing at the time of spanking but later in life; they might prove to be fruitful. Another is the disciple of the Lord which is all for our good, people can even think that God hates them at the time. But later, they testify to the glory of the Lord. The Bible says,

We do not enjoy being disciplined. It is painful at the time, but later, after we have learned from it, we have peace, because we start living in the right way.

Hebrews 12.11 (NCV)

With all these, it is also obvious that self-discipline is not without pain. And because it is discipline emanating from one's self, it is always tempting to avoid it. For someone to be able to discipline himself simply means maturity. Self-discipline does not just lead to financial prosperity but it sustains it. Even if you put money into the hands of a man without self-discipline it will be wasted and can even destroy the man. Prosperity of any kind without self-discipline can destroy the prosperous.

In life, when a man is expected to have self-discipline but fails to do so; he will definitely be disciplined, but this time, by life itself. This is the most painful of all. Parental discipline, school discipline and God's discipline might be painful for they are usually without one's consent. Self-discipline also might be painful but less severe because of one's consent. But life's discipline usually has no human face or sympathy. And it doesn't mind if the person dies in the process. Self-discipline is usually the last opportunity to prevent life's discipline. When it comes to financial matters, life's discipline can mean poverty. And it is not expedient for one to experience poverty before he starts to work against it.

Rich men know that if not for any other reason, they should discipline themselves in order to avoid life's discipline. This issue of life's discipline applies to every aspect of human life and in some cases the outcomes are irreversible. St. Paul in his own days, has this to say,

But I discipline my body and bring it into subjection, lest, when I have preached to others, I myself should become disqualified.

1 Corinthians 9.27 (NKJV)

One of the truths about the human life is that all the aspects of life are related and dependent on each other. Lack of marital discipline can lead to poverty. Lack of health discipline can lead to poverty. Lack of spiritual discipline can lead to poverty; of course this book is all about spirituality and finance. An example of this interrelationship is a man that fails to discipline himself healthwise. He will likely fall sick and end up spending his time and money on treatment. And if it is protracted, he may end in poverty. No matter how painful self-discipline might be in any aspect of human life, life's discipline is always more painful.

A Growth Necessity

Discipline is essential for development. In the book of Hebrews chapter twelve, the Bible explains how indispensible it is for one to be disciplined. In fact, it is impossible for God not to discipline his beloved children; for He is interested in their growth and welfare. Rich men understand the importance of discipline and that makes them even to subject themselves to discipline. In other words, it takes self-discipline for one to subject himself to discipline. Discipline is a sacrifice one must make in order to enter any new level of life. Right from childhood, one has to endure school discipline if he must go to school to acquire education. And if one must work to earn a living and acquire experience, he must subject himself to workplace discipline. The Bible says,

If you love learning, you love the discipline
that goes with it—how shortsighted to
refuse correction!

Proverbs 12.1 (The Message)

Any man who wants financial success must be ready to subject himself to financial discipline. It is not a matter of choice but a prerequisite. If it is not there, many other efforts might only be described as wishes. Financial prosperity lifestyles always start by the reason of discipline until they become part of the individual. Whether it is saving, paying of tithe, reducing one's expenditures, commitment to one's goals, etc.; all these are enforced through discipline. Something good about discipline is that even in the future, it will be difficult for an individual to derail.

An outsider will first of all see the pain in discipline (and that keeps many out) but those that see the good in it, enter. It is when people have entered into one level of discipline that they would be able to see a higher level. And when they continue climbing the ladder, it won't be long for them to become highly effective and successful. Discipline is all about training the individual; it is all about bringing out the best in an individual. Discipline takes an individual to a height which he will ordinarily not believe he could achieve. There can be no training of any kind, whether financial or non-financial that does not go with discipline. Perhaps, that is the reason why fields of studies are called disciplines.

A Lifetime Virtue

Discipline never ends in life. There are many things a man can decide to stop at one point or the other in his life and it will still be in line with sound reasoning. In many cases it might even be a professional advice or a counsel from a man of God for one to stop some things. But discipline is what a man must live with if he wants to be healthy, wealthy and wise. A man can even outgrow some kinds of disciplines but God's discipline and self-discipline are always there. No matter how old a man is, once he decides to give up self-discipline with regards to finance, he must be ready to plunge into poverty. Even if he is old and dependent, if he decides to do away with discipline, he can cause his benefactors to become tired of him and abandon him. The only time a man might be exonerated from discipline is when he becomes unconscious of life. At that time he doesn't have to make any decision for his life.

A man cannot say that because he had exhibited a high level of discipline in school and workplace, he won't be disciplined as a business owner. A man cannot say that since he had been disciplined for many years, he would start living a life free of discipline. The Bible puts the Words of Jesus this way,

Then He said to them all, "If anyone desires to come after Me, let him deny himself, and take up his cross daily, and follow Me.

Luke 9.23 (NKJV)

Jesus is not interested in following Him today and forgetting Him tomorrow. It is a daily affair. The same is true about a man's financial life. Of course, a man's financial life is connected to his spiritual life. As a matter of fact, many Christians face great temptations when their finances are frustrated. However, it takes financial indiscipline to have some kinds of financial frustrations. If any man is interested in walking with the Lord faithfully, he should do his best to keep out of financial frustration. It is a wise counsel to keep out of temptation. Jesus asks us to pray thus,

And do not lead us into temptation…

Matthew 6.13 (NKJV)

It is better to avoid temptations than to willingly walk into one. Even if you overcome it, you might sustain injuries.

In conclusion, the way a man cannot be sustained today with the air he breathed yesterday, that is how he needs discipline daily. Every successful life is an evidence of a disciplined life. And a little time of indiscipline can destroy a man's life. Discipline is not about pain but training.

EXHORTATION

A Lesson from the Ants

It takes discipline for the ants to gather food during the dry seasons for they know that a time will come when it will be difficult to work.

Recommendation

In everything you do make sure you have discipline; for it is like your control system. Discipline helps you to place limits to your actions and inactions. Do not neglect discipline both for small things and for big things. And do not be ashamed or too proud to subject yourself to discipline.

Practical Questions

1. Do you think that a man can outgrow discipline?
2. Do you believe that discipline should be part of your daily life?
3. Do you believe in setting limits?
4. Do you believe that discipline produces good character?
5. Can you say you are disciplined?

A Verse for Inspiration

Some of you say, "We can do anything
we want to." But I tell you not everything
is good for us. So I refuse to let anything
have power over me.

1 Corinthians 6.12 (CEV)

CHAPTER

36

Meticulous Mind

I glorified you on earth by completing down to the last detail what you assigned me to do.

John 17.4 (The Message)

A man is said to be meticulous when he shows the character of exactitude, carefulness and great attention to detail. On the other hand, the mind is the center or part of a man where reasoning takes place. Thus, a meticulous mind is a man's center of reasoning that is characterized by exactitude, carefulness and great attention to detail.

Rich men pay attention to everything that concerns their finances. They do not neglect small things since they are the things that come together to make big things. They know that one little thing neglected can destabilize the whole system. Rich men hardly afford the luxury of numerous assumptions. They always demand some levels of exactitude in everything they do with regards to finances. This is not a matter of fear that is caused by ignorance, it is carefulness. Whereas fear runs away from moving ahead, and if at all it agrees to move it will faint with each step until it dies; a meticulous mind moves at controlled pace. It does its calculations before each step and none of the steps is made without boldness.

Rich men don't wait for things to go completely wrong before they start acting. They know that waiting until such a time can be disastrous. Truly, no matter how careful a man is, that is not a guarantee that financial loss will not come knocking at his door. However, being on his guard can keep away a lot of losses from entering his house and if at all any enters, it may not do much harm before it is stopped. The Bible says,

If the owner of a house knew the
time when the thief would come, you can
be sure that he would stay awake and
not let the thief break into his house.

Matthew 24.43 (GNT)

The truth is that just like thieves, financial losses don't make any formal announcement before their arrival. And the only way to find them out on time is by paying attention to little things. It is very easy to see people laughing at the meticulous ones. But at the end, the meticulous ones will prevent many losses while others will cry for it.

Careful Attitude

Meticulous minds don't neglect even a minor loss. The main reason why rich men don't ignore a minor loss is not because it is enough to frustrate them immediately. It is simply because a minor loss is a potential door to a major loss. A meticulous mind sees a minor loss as a sign of a major loss. They are just like the dropping of little stones that can lead to an avalanche. It can be a case of few little stones that will lead to the avalanche or the continuous falling of the little stones that will ensure the weathering of the rock. The main point is that the rock will be broken down.

Jesus showed the pictures of a meticulous mind in the parable of the lost as recorded in Luke chapter fifteen. In all the three parables namely the parable of the lost sheep, the parable of the lost coin and the parable of the lost son, not everything is lost. The father of the prodigal son will not give up on his younger son even though the older son is still available. The woman will not give up on one coin even though she has nine left. More significantly, the shepherd will not give up on one sheep even though ninety-nine are left. Jesus said,

What man of you, having a hundred sheep, if he loses one of them, does not leave the ninety-nine in the wilderness, and go after the one which is lost until he finds it?

Luke 15.4 (NKJV)

In other words, Jesus is saying that this character is expected from any man who wants to live a meaningful life. Now, a good question is how the shepherd discovers that one sheep is missing out of a hundred. You should also know that if he wastes time, the sheep will perish. It only takes a meticulous mind. Of a truth, not everybody can easily notice that ten sheep are missing out of a hundred but in this case, it is one out of a hundred. The good shepherd does not encourage himself with the ninety nine still available in his business. He goes after that one sheep in order to restore his business to its best form. He knows that if he allows one to go like that, one day he will wake up to see an empty pen. This is God's own character and successful people follow it.

Precision

Meticulous mind leads to accuracy. One of the things common in life is that people always like to get the full benefit of the money they spend. Thus, they go for anyone whose work has to do with accuracy. Just imagine what will happen to a bank in which their customers gather every day to argue over their account balance just because the bank owners are not interested in accuracy. The same thing applies to any other business.

Accuracy does not start with big things; it starts with little things. It is the little ones that come together to produce one big accurate work. A man will easily go for something of lesser capacity but accurate, than something of higher capacity but inaccurate. Just think of a train whose speed is one hundred kilometer per hour with an accident rate that is less than one per cent, and another train whose speed is three hundred kilometer per hour but with accident rate of fifty per cent. In life we may not see two situations as obvious as these ones but we face similar options every day.

In virtually every industry, you will see rich men, both in the sophisticated and the simple ones. However, you will also see those who are not doing well. One of the reasons for the successful ones is because their products do what they claim. If a producer of wrist watches claims that his products can last only for two years, people won't mind going back to his shop after using his products for two years. They will go back simply because the life span of the products is accurate, not because two years is the best life span for wrist watches. You can also think of a shoe brand whose sizes are always inaccurate. Just imagine what will happen if you order for three pairs of shoes of the same size only to find out that one fits you, one is bigger and one is smaller than your size. You will agree with me that such a brand cannot do well in e-commerce where people order for goods without testing them.

Rich men understand that just as they are not willing to pay anyone for something that is not accurate, nobody will be willing to pay them for such. That does not mean that they will be carried away by perfectionism but they always try to be free from every known error as much as they could. Even though a man might not be perfect, sensible men move on towards perfection every day of their lives. No one can mention the list of the greatest men of the Old Testament without mentioning Moses. Many people will like to be like Moses before God but his secret of success was accuracy in faithfulness. The Bible says of him,

Moses did everything just
as the LORD commanded him.

Exodus 40.16 (NIV)

Moses was not faithful only in some things or nearly faithful in everything. His faithfulness was met with accuracy. In fact, it is only when faithfulness is mixed with accuracy that you can have complete faithfulness. You may not be surprised that later, in the book of Hebrews chapter three from verse one through six, the Bible talks about the faithfulness of Jesus Christ and that of Moses is also mentioned. We can see that one thing common with the mediator of the Old Testament and the Mediator of the New Testament is accurate faithfulness. In the introductory verse of this chapter, we see Jesus confirming the accuracy of His faithfulness to His assignment. This should be the goal of every human being. Erma Bombeck also confessed the same: 'When I stand before God at the end of my life, I would hope that I would not have a single bit of talent left, and could say, 'I used everything you gave me.' '

Understanding

Meticulous mind is a secret to understanding. As we know that understanding means knowing the interacting units of something and their relationships; it only takes a meticulous mind to see those units. Without understanding, riches can only be transient. The Bible says,

Through wisdom a house is built, And
by understanding it is established.

Proverbs 24.3 (NKJV)

Rich men know very well that they are not truly rich until they are established. Thus they do their best to understand everything about their finances as much as they can. You might not be surprised to notice that it is usually the big businesses that care more about proper accounting in their activities. It is also the big businesses that care about quality control. The result is that they continue to produce things that are consistent with a particular quality. Of course people will always go for products for which they can predict the quality. On the other hand, proper accounting helps the big businesses to manage their activities for better profitability.

In conclusion, a meticulous mind is indispensable if anyone is interested in nipping losses in the bud. The same is also needed if anyone is interested in identifying his success points for optimization.

EXHORTATION

A Lesson from the Ants

Ordinarily, the size of ants makes them meticulous since they don't need any aid to see little things. Besides, being meticulous is seeing things from their little units. The more little the units are, the more meticulous ants would be.

Recommendation

Do your best to pay attention to the details of your finances and avoid many costly assumptions. It might seem to be boring at the beginning but it can save you from a lot of losses. However, you should always apply moderation lest you become a victim of perfectionism.

Practical Questions

1. Do you think that being meticulous is a waste of time and energy?
2. Do you think that being meticulous is the same thing with perfectionism?
3. Do you believe that making a lot of assumptions can lead to frustrations?
4. Do you think that only fearful people are meticulous?
5. Do you believe that a little financial leakage can frustrate a man's entire financial system?
6. Are you ashamed to admit to be meticulous?

7. Will you be ashamed to stop a financial loss at an early stage even when others are falling victims?

A Verse for Inspiration

He telleth the number of the stars;
he calleth them all by their names.

Psalm 147.4 (KJV)

CHAPTER

37

Love for Their Work

Hard work means prosperity; only
a fool idles away his time.

Proverbs 12.11 (TLB)

Love is an intense feeling of affection for something or somebody. And work in this context is an activity in which a man puts his own effort in order to earn a living. Thus, rich men's love for their work is their intense feeling of affection for the activities in which they put their efforts in order to earn a living.

The most visible thing about rich men is that they have a work and they love what they do. Every other principle of riches might not see the light of the day if a man is not working; whether he is working for somebody or working for himself. Looking at the Scripture, starting from Genesis, it is obvious that God didn't create man to be without work. Even before the fall of man, God gave Adam a work to do. The Scripture says,

Then the LORD God took the man and put
him in the garden of Eden to tend
and keep it.

Genesis 2.15 (NKJV)

This kind of first work God gave to Adam is the kind full of grace. That is the kind by which a man puts in a little effort and gets big results. The 'little' here doesn't mean that of near laziness, but in comparison to the result, it would seem to be small. This is what is obtainable especially in the lives of men that are very rich. However, even with this level of grace, the man involved still has to work with all his heart in order to reap the benefits. As we can see in the life of Adam, even though he was so favoured that God had to come down to have fellowship with him and his wife, he still had to work. And since the Bible did not record that he complained about the work, he must have done it with all his heart. Thus, no matter the level of grace a Christian will receive from God, God still expects him to work.

Another example is the people of Israel and the Promised Land. Even though God promised to give them a land flowing with milk and honey, they still had to fight the giants before taking over the land. Presently, Israel as a country is one of the best in the world when it comes to agriculture. Nonetheless, I will like you to know that a good portion of that Promised Land could be described as arid. The simple secret is that the people of Israel understand this secret of prosperity and they subdue their land through irrigation. In the Christian journey of grace and prosperity, God is saying,

Rule your enemies who
surround you.

Psalm 110.2 (GW)

On the other hand, we can see another kind of work God can give to a man. That was seen in the second kind of work He gave to Adam after the fall of man. The Bible recorded it this way,

In the sweat of your face you shall eat bread till you return to the ground, For out of it you were taken; For dust you are, And to dust you shall return.

Genesis 3.19 (NKJV)

This second kind of work is the one that lacks grace. In this case, a man must put in enough labour before he eats. His labour will be directly proportionate to his results. No labour, will mean—no result. Small labour will mean small result. Big labour will mean big result. However, it is quite obvious that there is a limit to the amount of labour a man can put into anything. Thus, the result or riches obtainable from this kind of work is limited. Moreover, in this second kind of work, there are those at the extreme. They are the ones that will put in much labour but get results that are less than their inputs. They tend to work like elephants but eat like ants.

The main point I want to bring out here is that God created man to work, no matter how highly favoured that man is before God. The Bible says,

Idle hands are the devil's workshop; idle lips are his mouthpiece.

Proverbs 16.27 (TLB)

From this Bible verse, we can deduce that busy hands are God's workshop; i.e. the avenues through which He releases His blessings. One of the men that received great grace in the New Testament was Paul but see what he said,

Yes, you yourselves know that these
hands have provided for my necessities,
and for those who were with me.

Acts 20.34 (NKJV)

He would have given many reasons not to work but he laid them aside. Even Jesus Christ our Lord, when He was on earth, He had His own occupation. Many Christians today know that His father, Joseph, was a carpenter (Matthew 13.55). But only few are conscious of the fact that Jesus Himself was also a carpenter. When the Jews took offence at Him, they said,

Is this not the carpenter, the
Son of Mary, and brother of James,
Joses, Judas, and Simon? And are
not His sisters here with us?

Mark 6.3 (NKJV)

Now, rich men understand the importance work is to man. And they know that a man cannot excel in anything he does if he does not like it. Thus, for rich men, anything that becomes their work, they make up their mind to love it; for that is the only way to get the best out of it.

Availability

Rich men love the right things their hands find doing. It is normal to hear people say that the secret of success is to follow your passion. This theory is first of all not Biblical. Again, it is not absolute, it is only a gamble; it can work for Mr. A but not for Mr. B. First of all, concerning passion, the Bible says,

The heart is deceitful above all things,
and it is exceedingly perverse and corrupt
and severely, mortally sick! Who can know

it [perceive, understand, be acquainted with his own heart and mind].

Jeremiah 17.9 (AMP)

A man's heart can lead him to something that is sinful and totally against the Word of God. Even if he makes money from such a thing, that will be an unholy success. Another point is when the passion is not a sinful one but the question is whether the business is a right one. No matter how passionate a man is concerning a business, if it is a financially wrong business he cannot prosper with it. You will agree with me that no matter how passionate a man is about selling ice to the Eskimos he won't prosper with it. Most times, our passions are influenced by where and how we grow up. And by the time one is ready to go into business, some of those passions will be outdated and some actually come out of ignorance. Thus, before any man should think about following his passion for business, he should consider God and the financial viability of the idea.

Another thing wrong about following one's passion absolutely is that some people will spend their lives pursuing their passions and end up doing nothing. Even when the passion is godly and viable, there is no guarantee that it will be available. A young man can be passionate about becoming an aeronautic engineer. He can even study an engineering course that is related to it in the university. But there is no guarantee that he can get close to the engine of an aircraft throughout his life time. One may ask, 'But all things are possible for them that believe?' Yes, that is true but you can never tell what God has planned. Remember that Jonah was passionate about Tarshish while the plan of God was Nineveh. From the story of Jonah we can see that the plan of God for a man's life always presents itself. Now, here is the secret of success concerning work as recorded in the Scripture:

Whatever presents itself for you to do, do it with [all] your might, because there

is no work, planning, knowledge, or skill
in the grave where you're going.

Ecclesiastes 9.10 (GW)

In this place, the Bible says whatever presents itself; of course, it will be godly and financially viable but not necessarily what you have been passionate about. If what you have been passionate about comes your way—that will be wonderful. But the point the Bible is making here is that you can become passionate about anything that comes your way. The only thing required is love for the work you are doing. If you consider the lives of many rich men you will discover that some of them are doing what they love (i.e. their initial passion) and thus love what they are doing. On the other hand, you will see that some of them never had an idea about their business until it presented itself to them. The principal thing remains that they now love what they are doing.

Subjectivity

Love for any work is subjective. Just in line with the point I was discussing, a man can move his passion from one work to another. This is always necessary when what one is passionate about is not godly or financially viable or available. You may ask, 'What about innate abilities? How can one succeed in those things for which he lacks the abilities?' The answer is,

I can do everything through Christ who
strengthens me.

Philippians 4.13 (GW)

The truth is that even with innate abilities, you will still need to improve on them if you want to excel. Just on the same premise, you can improve on any skill. I want you to understand that every human being has a trace of any skill that could be conceptualized and applied on earth. The ones that are obvious are the ones that have been fanned into flames. The ones that seem nonexistent are those left dormant.

Even that wonderful mathematician you know, if he didn't go to school he will know nothing called mathematics. An illiterate may spend five minutes just to tell you how many oranges that will be left in the basket if you take seven oranges out of the twenty two in the basket. That is just a trace of mathematics, and if such a person doesn't go to school, algebra will be a strange word to him. If he goes, he can even become a professor of mathematics with specialization in abstract algebra. The point I want you to understand is that anyone can learn anything as long as he is willing. It is very difficult to see a rich man who did not learn something from somewhere. Even a man that is highly skilled and is following his passion successfully, he will still need to know how to make money from that skill. To be highly skilled in anything does not guarantee financial skills.

Now, if a man has a passion for something, he already has a motivation for it. The same thing is obtainable for a man who is talented or simply put, a man who has fanned his innate ability into flames. If such persons want to increase their skills to a particular level, it will be easier and faster for them. But you should know that a man who has neither a passion for the same thing nor talented can get to the same level of skills if he is willing. It is only a matter of time. He can use time to buy both the passion and the talent until he gets to the new level of skills. The Bible says,

If the ax is dull and its edge unsharpened,
more strength is needed...

Ecclesiastes 10.10 (NIV)

Even if it takes the dull man three years to achieve what the passionate and talented man achieved in one year; by the end of the three years there will be no difference again. If you consider the parable of the talents as recorded in Matthew chapter twenty five verse fourteen through thirty, you will discover that the only problem of the unprofitable servant was that he did not put his talent into use. If he had traded with it, it would have been possible for him to increase his capital to two talents. And it would only be a matter of time for him to increase his capital to ten talents which was the achievement of the servant with five talents.

Rich men understand these principles; that is why it is difficult for them to be idle at any point in their lives. It is a truism that at each point in any man's life, something must be available for him to do. It only takes a willing heart in obedience to the Word of God for a man to do what is available to him with passion. And he will begin to see financial prosperity. The Bible says,

If you are willing and obedient,
you shall eat the good of the land.

Isaiah 1.19 (RSV)

One truth I will like you to understand at this point is that there is no single profession that has the monopoly of making people rich. It is what you sow into a profession that can determine the outcome. It was Oliver Wendell Holmes, a physician and also an author that once said, 'Every calling is great when greatly pursued.'

In conclusion, rich men don't bother themselves about having a prior passion for any business. Their main interest is doing any business that is available to them with passion. Even though it is good to do what you like, you should understand from the Scripture that the most important thing is to like what you do.

EXHORTATION

A Lesson from the Ants

One of the things visible among ants is their love for their work displayed by their dedication to duty. You can hardly see any ant getting itself involved with frivolity when they are working. Right from birth, every ant becomes passionate about their work. Though ants love sweet things, they still go after any food that makes itself available to them.

Recommendation

It is good for you to become more passionate about the skills for which you have comparative advantage and motivation. It will be easier to excel in such skills, other things being equal. However, you should ensure that you don't become enslaved to such skills. You can do everything through Christ.

Practical Questions

1. Do you have any business idea for which you are passionate?
2. Do you love what you are doing now?
3. Do you believe that a man will hardly excel if he does not love his work?
4. Do you believe that a man can develop love for any work?
5. Do you believe that you can learn any skill?
6. Do you believe that it is possible for a man to be passionate about a wrong business idea?
7. Do you believe that even though you have a talent you still need to learn more in order to improve upon it?

A Verse for Inspiration

In all the work you are doing, work the best you can. Work as if you were doing it for the Lord, not for people.

Colossians 3.23 (NCV)

CHAPTER

38

Resilience

Merely a scent of water will make it sprout
and grow branches like a plant.

Job 14.9 (GW)

Resilience is the ability to recover quickly from a misfortune. However, the word 'quickly' in this definition could be applied mainly in the mind. It is when there is recovery in the mind that it could finally be made manifest openly.

Rich people never give up. They never say die. They know that as long as they keep their hope alive, they will always recover from any misfortune. They know that the first and foremost step to recovery is staying alive. Now, resilience works together with patience but it is not patience. Whereas patience is all about staying alive in the midst of trouble even to the end of the trouble; resilience goes ahead to restoration. Patience is like a platform on which resilience stands. Or one can say that patience is part of resilience. Without patience to keep alive, there would be no life to be restored. However, a patient man doesn't mean a resilient man. A patient man stays alive but a resilient man stays alive while retaining his mind. It is in his mind that the specifications for his former state are retained and thus could be called upon for full restoration. A resilient man keeps his internal structures so that when his problems are over, he could be fully restored.

A man can be patient until his troubles are over but that is not a guarantee that he would become as he was before the trouble began. You can see a rich man that encounters a financial crisis that sends him into a life of poverty. He can survive the crisis but that doesn't necessarily mean that he will become rich again. At this point, the man would have proved to be a patient man. But if he is interested in becoming rich again, he has to employ patience for the second time with the purpose of restoration. All these can happen within a long (or very short) time. However, what distinguishes the rich is that they recover at the shortest possible time.

Most of the time, when patient people are celebrated; it is usually those that are resilient. If we look at the life of Job, we can see that he endured his losses (that is patience at work). But come to think of it, if Job died maybe three days after he was healed of his sickness we can still celebrate his patience. However, the story might not be of much encouragement to us when we are passing through troubled times. We get much encouragement from his life because he was more than fully restored. Even during his trials, his mind was sustained. We can also see the role of resilience in his life because after his restoration the Bible did not say that he lacked the ability to manage his wealth. God Himself is not just interested in seeing people, becoming patient, He also wants to see them being restored; that is seeing them resilient. The Bible says,

But the people who trust the LORD will
become strong again.

Isaiah 40.31 (NCV)

Maintenance of Structure

Resilience maintains shape. A lot of people pass through financial crises in their lives but the reason why some return back to riches is that they retain their invisible structure. They still retain their skills, they still know the rules of business and the Word of God still appears wholesome to them. We can see a picture of it in the Bible,

Many are the afflictions of the righteous,
But the LORD delivers him out of them all.
He guards all his bones; Not one of them
is broken.

Psalm 34.19-20 (NKJV)

This Scripture applies to Jesus Christ whose body was wounded and pierced but His bones were not broken. They were kept because He would still need them after His resurrection (and also as a Passover lamb). Now, come to look at it in another way, that while God delivers His people from their numerous problems, He also sustains their shape. He places a limit to which the problem can affect their lives. He is not just interested in delivering them from their problems but He is also interested in their internal structures for total restoration.

Physically, on the side of rich men, since they do not have the power to place a limit for problems in their lives, what they do is to enlarge their coasts to contain the over flowing waters until the flooding is over. They know that even if they could not make any progress because of the flood, at least they can sustain their cities from being carried away. They know that if the flood should carry their cities and they survive, it might be very difficult to build another city. To put this point in a simple way, rich men increase their ability to adapt to their problematic situations until it is over.

A Source of Strength

Resilience strengthens rich men. For the fact that rich men maintain their internal structures during their times of financial crisis, when they recover, their experience makes them smarter. They learn many lessons that theory won't be able to teach them and such lessons cannot be easily forgotten. You might not be surprised that if a similar problem comes their way again, they will end up laughing at it. This is because the structure with which they fought the first problem is still there. That is also joined with the experience they got from the problem which is like the weakness of the problem that had been made known to them. Let's take a look at the words of a resilient man from the Scripture,

> *There's more to come: We continue to shout our praise even when we're hemmed in with troubles, because we know how troubles can develop passionate patience in us, and how that patience in turn forges the tempered steel of virtues, keeping us alert for whatever God will do next.*
>
> Romans 5.3-4 (The Message)

We can see in this passage that St. Paul was not just interested in coming out of problems but in the benefit that comes out of it. And I will like you to understand that when a problem breaks a man on the negative side, there might not be any container to forge the tempered steel of virtue. It takes resilience to keep the structure of the container for any development to take place. Rich men don't see failure as the end of everything, rather, they agree with Henry Ford who said that failure is only an opportunity to begin again more intelligently.

In conclusion, the utmost purpose of resilience is restoration. Moving out of poverty does not necessarily mean living in wealth. The structure of wealthy living must still be sustained if moving into wealth would be achieved. Rich men adapt to circumstances and in that way they survive difficulties without losing their shape.

EXHORTATION

A Lesson from the Ants

Despite the ease with which ants are killed or with which they die, they are still seen everywhere. They know when to run and when to hide in their nests. They don't allow the fact that something once killed them in large numbers to make them throw away their gregarious life. They know that their unity is their strength.

Recommendation

No matter any financial problem that comes your way, don't allow it to change your Biblical principles on finance. So that when you recover you won't be turned into a financial monster. Do your best to increase your capacity to adapt to different financial challenges so that when they come you won't be broken.

Practical Questions

1. Do you believe that when a man's mind is still intact his recovery from a financial crisis will be faster?
2. Do you believe that it is only a sustained mind that can make full recovery?
3. Do you believe that patience is perfected in resilience?
4. Do you believe that a man can wrestle to retain his shape in the midst of a financial crisis?
5. Do you think that even if a man is broken negatively by crisis that time only will definitely heal everything?

A Verse for Inspiration

But he knows the way that
I take; when he has tested me,
I will come forth as gold.

Job 23.10 (NIV)

CHAPTER

39

Right Company

Keep company with the wise and you will become wise. If you make friends with stupid people, you will be ruined.

Proverbs 13.20 (GNT)

Something is said to be right if it is free from error and is consistent with sound morals. On the other hand, a company in this context is the people with whom someone associates or spends time. Thus, a man is said to have a right company when the people with whom he associates are free from error and are consistent with sound morals.

Rich people move along with people of right mindset. This does not mean that rich men only move about with people that are rich like themselves but they move with people that have good sense of judgement. They move with people that live responsible lives. They move with people whose lives will influence their own positively. Whether their friends are richer or not is not consequential. Whether their friends are wiser or not is also not consequential. Even wise kings and leaders still need wise advisers around them. In fact, wise people don't go about comparing their wisdom with each other. Their main interest is the existence of wisdom in the other person. Once there is wisdom in a man, there will always be a time when his contribution will be highly valuable if not the best.

Rich men don't believe that they are all-sufficient. They know that God did not create men to be islands. If a man decides to be on his own, no matter how spiritual he is, he may not know when he begins to drift away from sound gospel. In fact the Bible condemns a solitary lifestyle. The Bible says,

...woe to him who is alone when he falls,
For he has no one to help him up.

Ecclesiastes 4.10 (NKJV)

The same principle holds when it comes to financial matters. That is why some people that are rich—when they face any financial crisis, they will fall completely with no one to give a helping hand financially or otherwise. When things go well with some people, they might be easily deluded that they can't face any financial crisis. And they go ahead to separate themselves from friends and relations only to realize what they have done to themselves when a problem arises. An example of such persons was the man by the Pool of Bethesda. When Jesus asked him for his healing, his response was,

...I have no one to help me...

John 5.7 (NIV)

He had been so obsessed about having no helper that he didn't even know when a question about his healing was asked. The sound of the question in his mind was 'Why are you not healed?' instead of 'Do you want to get well?' One may begin to ask now about the man's friends and relatives. The answer might not be obvious but we saw that Jesus later warned the man of a sinful lifestyle. It might be that the friends and relations that moved around with him when all was well were sinful as he was. And of course, such persons could not be there for him when the need arose. On the other hand, it might be that he separated himself from good friends and relatives when things were well with him. And of course it would be difficult for such persons to come to bear him as a burden when he became sick.

Time and Companionship

Rich men get good companions on neutral grounds. Even though it's possible for a man to get good companions when he has become rich or during the time of crisis, it can be difficult but not advisable. It is usually when things are neutral that a man can find genuine friends or companions. Such persons don't come around because of money or fame but out of sincerity. The truth about this life is that when a man starts making a financial progress, it is not compulsory that all his friends will be making financial progress too. It is always tempting to abandon such friends that are not making financial progress during a man's time of prosperity. But it should be obvious to everyone that when a rich man chooses another rich man to be his friend just because he is rich, their friendship would likely continue as long as both of them are rich. Besides, being a rich man does not qualify a man to be a good friend. Nonetheless, it is quite possible to get a friend who is a rich man but the foremost consideration must not be riches.

Now, if a man chooses a friend just because he is rich, he runs the risk of choosing wrongly. Besides, when a man becomes rich, many wrong personalities will like to come around him. The consequence is that all such wrong friends will either be parasitic or will always come up with financially destructive counsels. Whereas a good friend sees his companion as his own person, those wrong friends are after their own benefits. They are not bothered about the financial condition of the man; their major concern is what will flow from the man into their own purse. Jesus Christ addressed such persons in a man's financial life as hired workers. He said,

Hired workers run away because they
don't care about the sheep.

John 10.13 (CEV)

The value of companions is mostly significant during the times of need. And it is also at this time that the wrong friends run away. From the Words of Jesus Christ, hired workers run away with their lives when the need to stand against a wolf arises. In life's applications, it might be the time when a man is in need of financial advice or finance itself. Just be assured that such persons will always run away with their own interests.

Strong Influence

Characters are contagious. Rich men know that anything that is contagious doesn't need the consent of the other person before affecting him; whether positively or negatively. We may not have the power to stop things that are contagious but we can control our level of exposure to such things. I will also like you to know that of all the agents of contagious things, the most effective on a man are his human companions, especially those he loves. It is obvious that the characters a man allows to be around him all the time has the capacity to change him gradually even without him knowing it. An example is Jesus and His disciples; the Bible says,

The members of the Council were amazed to see how bold Peter and John were and to learn that they were ordinary men of no education. They realized then that they had been companions of Jesus.

Acts 4.13 (GNT)

Someone can say that he is out to influence or change the characters of his friends, but before such a thing becomes a reality, the person must be fully conscious of it. And also, he must be stronger in his character than that of the friends he wants to change. According to George Washington, the first president of the United States of America, 'It is better to be alone than in bad company.'

Rich men are always mindful of the character of those around them. They know that no matter how negligible a character might seem to be, the fact that it is consistent in the life of a man is enough to prove that it is strong. They know that bad characters would normally infiltrate into a man's life even without invitation unlike good characters that need a conscious building effort. However, a consistent exposure to good characters is on its own a conscious character building process. Rich men know that exposure to bad characters is like setting a trap for oneself. For example, the Bible says,

Don't hang out with angry people; don't
keep company with hotheads. Bad temper
is contagious—don't get infected.

Proverbs 22.24-25 (The Message)

Many characters have direct effects on one's financial life and a good number of them have indirect effects. The truth remains that no bad character spares a man's life unlike the good ones. When we talk about exposure to characters through companionship, it might not necessarily be directly physical. A man can consistently expose himself to a particular character through the books he reads, the things he listens to, the things he watches, the role model he cherishes in his heart, etc. That is why those that have the Bible as a true companion always have their lives transformed.

Marital Companion

Rich men understand the position of a marital companion. Rich men know that the closest of all companions to a man is his wife. Thus, her character will have an influence on the man, whether in a big or small measure. They understand that the marriage union unifies every aspect of life of a man and a woman especially spiritual life, health life and financial life. Moreover, they understand from the Scripture that God created the marital union to be permanent,

"For the LORD God of Israel says That He hates divorce, For it covers one's garment with violence," says the LORD of hosts.

Malachi 2.16 (NKJV)

Thus, rich men are always careful when making the choice of a wife. They know that a wife can help build a man's life and she can also help to frustrate it. They know that a good wife can give a good advice. They know that a good wife means a good character around a man. They know that—

The man who finds a wife finds a good thing; she is a blessing to him from the Lord.

Proverbs 18.22 (TLB)

Now, I will like you to understand that the wife the Bible is referring to in this verse is a good wife. And just as a man needs a good wife for his prosperity, a woman needs a good husband for her own prosperity. In marriage, it only takes angels to appreciate and live with angels. And if a man marries not because of the Christ-like character in the wife, let him not assume that marriage will produce a Christ-like character in her. The same also applies to a woman. However, it takes only a God fearing man to identify a God fearing woman and vice versa. I will also like you to understand that financial prosperity is only a part of wholesome prosperity. A man cannot be said to be completely prosperous if he has money without happiness and godliness. A good wife can help to lift a man from poverty to wealth. She is a good financial adviser and manager to her husband. She is a good source of encouragement to her husband during the time of financial crisis. Besides, she shares the favour of God upon her life with her husband.

In conclusion, the people a man allows around his life can influence him. Thus, if a man is interested in financial prosperity, he should choose those that will help to make it possible. Constant exposure to such good people will affect his financial life positively. He will not just become financially prosperous, but he will also observe and learn the secrets of financial prosperity.

EXHORTATION

A Lesson from the Ants

It is quite obvious that ants keep company with ants. Even when a new ant is born, it grows to have the character of ants. It is not just because of its innate composition but because of its companions.

Recommendation

As you are looking for good companions, I will like you to know that many people out there are also looking for good companions. Thus, become a good companion first, and your life will attract good companions. You should make conscious efforts to have good lives and characters around yourself. Don't expect it to happen by chance, it does not happen like that always.

Practical Questions

1. Do you have friends?
2. Who are your role models?
3. Can you identify your role models with Christ?
4. Do you think that characters could be changed with ease?
5. Do you make constant effort to build your own character?
6. Do you believe that your wife or husband has a role to play in your financial prosperity?
7. Do you have the Bible as your daily companion?

A Verse for Inspiration

When Saul and his servant arrived at
Gibeah, Saul met a group of prophets.
The Spirit of God rushed upon him,
and he prophesied with the prophets.

1 Samuel 10.10 (NCV)

CHAPTER

40

God's Favour

John answered and said, "A man can receive nothing unless it has been given to him from heaven.

John 3.27 (NKJV)

God is the Supreme Being, from whom came all in existence and the Controller of all in existence. On the other hand, favour is a preferential act of kindness. Thus, God's favour is God's preferential act of kindness.

Of all the secrets of riches, God's favour remains paramount. When the favour of God is strong upon a man's life, it may seem that all other principles of riches are of no consequence. Truly, all the other principles are always relevant since they are all from the Word of God. If they are inconsequential, God won't bother to add them in His Word, the Bible. Now, what the favour of God does is that even when a man fails any of the principles (though not intentionally), God's favour will make up for his weaknesses. The favour of God directs a man in the paths of riches which he would ordinarily not know. It gives a man insight that would be beyond his normal level of thinking. God's favour also causes a man to be favoured before men. The Bible says,

When a man's ways please the LORD, he maketh even his enemies to be at peace with him.

Proverbs 16.7 (KJV)

Now, whenever God's favour is mentioned, what comes to mind is what the Bible says in a place like this,

For example God said to Moses, "I will be kind to anyone I want to. I will be merciful to anyone I want to." Therefore God's choice does not depend on a person's desire or effort, but on God's mercy.

Romans 9.15-16 (GW)

Someone can say, "If that is the case, why will God give us all the other principles of riches?" Maybe, everyone should resign to fate and take whatever comes his or her way. And if that is just the case, we might not need the entire Bible any more. We may only need a portion of it as we continue to live a life that is resigned to fate. But wait, even before the last two verses, the Bible had earlier said,

What can we say—that God is unfair? That's unthinkable!

Romans 9.14 (GW)

If God has given us principles to follow and at the same time favours those He wills, our duty will be to follow the principles and leave God to do His will. It is God's function to choose whom to favour. It will be foolishness and wrong for us to abandon our own function and try to do or interpret God's function for Him. It will be difficult for us to know or determine where the effort of man ends and where the favour of God starts in a man's financial prosperity. You can see a man that put in a little effort to attain a great level of prosperity. At the same time, you can see a man that put in a greater effort to attain the same level of prosperity. Sometimes, it might seem that another man attains that same level of prosperity even without an effort. The truth is that such a man has his own effort but it is not known to others.

The reason for including God's favour as a secret to riches in this book is not just for acknowledgement but to show some things on how it works as written in the Bible.

Righteousness

God favours the righteous. Of all the things that can attract God's favour, righteousness is the foremost. Righteousness is having a right standing with God. It doesn't depend on place and time like morality. It depends on the Word of God. It begins with believing in God and in His son Jesus Christ and the finished work of Christ on the cross and His resurrection. Righteousness is manifested through good works by the working of the Holy Spirit. The kind of prosperity that righteousness attracts in the life of a man is a wholesome prosperity that has financial wellbeing as part of it. The Bible expressly says,

For thou dost bless the righteous,
O LORD; thou dost cover him with
favour as with a shield.

Psalm 5.12 (RSV)

One of the advantages of righteousness is that a man that lives by it automatically practises most of the principles of riches and avoids the causes of poverty. Another one is that even when he is in error, God's mercy sees him through. The Bible is full of people who prospered exceedingly because they were righteous before God. We can see Abraham, Isaac, Jacob and Joseph who even prospered as a prisoner. The Scripture says of him,

The keeper of the prison paid no heed to anything that was in Joseph's care, because the LORD was with him; and whatever he did, the LORD made it prosper.

Genesis 39.23 (RSV)

Later, he became the second-in-command to the king in a country not his own. The list goes on and on even to our present generation.

Prayer

Prayer attracts God's favour. When a man prays, he shows his dependence on God. Prayer is so powerful in attracting God's favour that many people wrongfully decide only to pray without working. Sometimes, even in their error, God still grant them favour out of His mercy (though I am not saying you should do like that). Nonetheless, in such situations, the favour comes as a gift and an opportunity to work. The Biblical principle is: work and pray. Prayer is having fellowship with God and the deeper the fellowship, the more favour one can receive from God. Louis Evans once said, 'Man is never as tall as when he kneels before God, never so great as when he humble before God. And the man who kneels to God can stand up to anything.' In the midst of prayer, a man can receive divine financial counsels that will make him to prosper beyond measure.

The Bible is full of people that prospered because they prayed. A good example was Jabez in 1 Chronicles 4.9-10. It is also written expressly in the Bible that by prayer a poor man can receive deliverance from all his problems (of course including poverty). The Bible says,

Here is a poor man who called out.
The LORD heard him and saved him from all his troubles.

Psalm 34.6 (GW)

Even if a man does not know how to do a lot of things, if he turns to God with sincerity, the Holy Spirit will help him to pray effectively.

God's Discretion

God favours people for reasons not obvious to men. There are people that are rich but when you look at their lives, it does not show any righteous living. For this kind of people, I don't mean those that committed one thing or the other in order to make wealth. I mean those whose wealth could be said to be clean even though other aspects of their lives are sinful. This kind of people could fall into various categories as recorded in the Bible. First, they could be among God's general blessings. The Bible says,

That you may be sons of your Father in heaven. He causes his sun to rise on the evil and the good, and sends rain on the righteous and the unrighteous.

Matthew 5.45 (NIV)

Actually, many rich people who live unrighteous lives fall into this category. You can see communities that don't believe in God and some are even hostile to Christianity, yet, you will see many rich people in their midst.

Another category is those blessed because of the good deeds of others. If you look into the Bible you can see kings of Judah that were sinful but God did not remove the kingship from their lineage because of King David—a man after God's own heart. Of such kind of persons, the Bible says,

Praise the Lord! For all who fear God and trust in him are blessed beyond expression. Yes, happy is the man who delights in doing his commands. His

children shall be honored everywhere,
for good men's sons have a special heritage.

Psalm 112.1-2 (TLB)

Some people receive favour and open doors in many places just by mentioning that they are children of good men. If you take a look at the families of old time ministers of the gospel who walked faithfully with God, you will always see God's favour upon their children.

The next category is those that are completely weird. They may look like those in the category of God's general blessings or those blessed by the reason of others' good deeds. The main point is that their prosperity could be great and thus confusing. Only God can interpret the reason for allowing it to be. The Scripture says of such,

There is something else meaningless
that occurs on earth: the righteous
who get what the wicked deserve, and
the wicked who get what the righteous
deserve. This too, I say, is meaningless.

Ecclesiastes 8.14 (NIV)

We can only say that God is abundantly merciful.

Blessing of the Fathers

God's favour comes by the blessing of the fathers. By this, I don't mean only the fathers but the mothers also. And it is not restricted to biological parents; it includes spiritual fathers, mentors, teachers, people of higher placements, etc. This is so serious that the fifth commandment says,

Honor your father and your mother…

Exodus 20.12 (NKJV)

However, the efficacy of the blessing pronounced by the fathers depends to a large extent on the life of the person pronouncing it. A man that has a right standing with God would have his words honoured by God than a man who does not regard God. Again, a man who is spiritual would likely pronounce effective blessings through prophecy by the Holy Spirit. For example, when Jacob wanted to bless his sons, he did not call them to make his wishes upon their lives, the Bible says,

Then Jacob called his sons, and said,
"Gather yourselves together, that I
may tell you what shall befall you
in days to come.

Genesis 49.1 (RSV)

Now, I will like to consider his blessing on Asher for that has more to do with prosperity. Jacob, as his biological father said,

Asher's food shall be rich,
and he shall yield royal dainties.

Genesis 49.20 (RSV)

Sometime later, Moses, as a spiritual father to the Israelites (and of course to the tribe of Asher) blessed the tribes:

And of Asher he said, "Blessed
above sons be Asher; let him be
the favourite of his brothers, and
let him dip his foot in oil.

Deuteronomy 33.24 (RSV)

When Jacob blessed Asher and said that his food shall be rich, it would be simple to say that the man would have enough good food in his days. But the blessing went beyond an ordinary imagination. During the time of Moses, he made the blessing more specific by saying that Asher would dip his foot in oil. Our human sense would easily point to olive oil since it is abundant in Israel especially in the land allotted to the tribe of Asher. Even though all these assumptions might be true, the blessing was beyond them all.

As time went on, men began to appreciate the crude oil. Some used it for medicinal purposes and others used it for lighting. In 347 AD or earlier, men began to drill oil wells in China about 800 feet. In 1859, in North Western Pennsylvania USA, one of the successful oil wells was drilled for the sole purpose of finding oil. In 1935 the Iraq Petroleum Company (IPC) which is an oil company jointly owned by some of the world's largest oil companies, opened oil pipeline to the Mediterranean at the Haifa harbour. In 1968, the Eilat Ashkelon Pipeline Company (EAPC) was formed as a 50/50% Joint Venture between Israel and Iran to transport crude oil from Iran to Europe. And that was through the Haifa harbour. Presently, Haifa bay is a center of heavy industry including petroleum refining. Haifa refinery processes 66 million barrels of crude oil a year. Haifa was part of the portion allotted to the tribe of Asher when the Israelites entered into the Promised Land. Besides, Haifa is still mentioned in the discoveries of oil and gas deposits in Israel.

This shows the need for fathers to sanctify their lives in order to pronounce an efficacious blessing upon their children (John17.19). Fathers should consider blessing their children and leave out curses.

In conclusion, it might not be in the hands of a man to bestow the favour of God upon his life but with some principles written in the Bible, a man can attract God's favour upon his life. It is the function of men to plant seeds and water them. But it is the function of God to cause the growth.

EXHORTATION

A Lesson from the Ants

Ants are little creatures that would easily fall victims of their environment but God sustains them. They neither own farmlands for planting seeds nor livestock of smaller creatures but they don't die of hunger. However, they still go out to hunt and gather food.

Recommendation

The role you have to play in attracting God's favour into your life is to live a righteous life and observe the Biblical principles of riches and avoid the causes of poverty. Don't consider living an unrighteous life since some people live like that and still prosper. You never know what God has in place for such persons and you will not like to end like them.

Practical Questions

1. Have you seen a man favoured by God?
2. If yes, is such a man an idle man?
3. Will you prefer God's favour as a righteous man or as an unrighteous man?
4. Will you like to end like a righteous man or an unrighteous man?
5. Will you like to have blessed children or cursed children?
6. What easily comes out of your mouth, blessings or curses?
7. Do you believe that a man is not completely blessed until his children are blessed?
8. Do you believe that it takes God's favour to make you rich?
9. Are you ready to receive God's favour?

A Verse for Inspiration

Every good endowment and every
perfect gift is from above coming
down from the Father of lights
with whom there is no variation
or shadow due to change.

James 1.17 (RSV)

CONCLUSION

The main purpose of this book is not for mere acknowledgement of the causes of poverty and the secrets of riches. It is also not for mere awareness. The main purpose of this book is for practical applications in daily life. Many people have read many wonderful books but nothing has changed in their lives simply because they are not willing to apply the knowledge they acquired from the books. It is so serious that some people read even the Bible and still close their hearts against the Words written in it. The secret of success is to discover the Word of God and apply it in one's life. It is only when the knowledge is applied that one could see the results.

Next, every Christian who is interested in making money should ask himself his purpose for making money. I want to make it categorically clear that money is not an end in itself but only a means to an end. A Christian acquires money to use it for good works and not because he loves money. The Bible makes us to understand that all the evil that men commit on earth could be traced to the love of money (1 Timothy 6.10). The easiest way for one to know if he loves money is if he is ready to compromise his faith for the sake of money. Remember that Judas did not betray Jesus because he was financially broke during that Passover, but because he had loved money before then. Those who love money start with little compromises until they enter the big ones. At that time money controls them and they become slaves to money. Then they degenerate to avarice and of such the Bible says,

Whoever loves money will never be satisfied with money. Whoever loves wealth will never be satisfied with more income. Even this is pointless.

Ecclesiastes 5.10 (GW)

This does not suggest that a man should stop working when he makes big wealth. No, such a man should increase his good works. This verse of the Bible is saying that the desperation of avarice does not abate even with more riches. Even though God wants you to be rich, He also wants you to live a righteous life and be in good health (3 John 2). It won't make sense for you to have all the good things of life money can buy in this life and when you die, you end up in hell like the rich man in the story of the Rich man and Lazarus. A great life is enjoying a life of abundance here on earth and continuing with the enjoyment in the life beyond. The Bible says,

For what will it profit a man if he
gains the whole world, and loses
his own soul?

Mark 8.36 (NKJV)

Truly, all the principles covered in this book could be easily activated by living wholesome righteous lifestyle. It includes humility, honesty, generosity, etc. For example, a man who is selfless and loves his neighbours could easily activate what I call the Levitical prosperity code. That is when one becomes very rich by making others rich. God did not allow the Levites to cultivate lands to make a living like other tribes. He rather made them to serve other tribes before Him. In return, the eleven tribes were to pay tithes to the Levites which were only 10 per cent of their earnings. Now, 10 per cent into eleven places will give 110 per cent. If you look at it, each tribe would gladly pay 10 per cent of the wealth they made because the Levites were faithful with their duty. But by the time the Levities finish collecting the tithes, they would end up richer. All the tribes would be rich and happy while the Levities would be richer and happy as well.

If a man should think of how to make people rich in return for a little portion of the riches they make, the man will end up richer when he helps many people to be rich. Many other examples abound as acts of righteousness. It is not just the will of God to give you financial prosperity; He wants to give you a wholesome prosperity which includes financial prosperity, peace, good health, good family, etc. My utmost prayer is that God gives you this wholesome prosperity, in Jesus name. Amen.

So now, brethren, I commend you to
God and to the word of His grace,
which is able to build you up and
give you an inheritance among all
those who are sanctified.

Acts 20.32 (NKJV)

Shalom.

APPENDIX

AMP: Scripture quotations taken from The Amplified Bible. Copyright © 1954, 1958, 1962, 1964, 1965, 1987 by The Lockman Foundation. All rights reserved. Used by permission. (www.Lockman.org)

CEV: Scripture quotations marked (CEV) are from the Contemporary English Version Copyright © 1991,1992, 1995 by American Bible Society, Used by Permission.

GNT: Scripture quotations marked (GNT) are from the Good News Translation in Today's English Version – Second Edition Copyright © 1992 by American Bible Society. Used by Permission.

GW: Scripture is taken from GOD'S WORD ®, © 1995 God's Word to the Nations. Used by permission of Baker Publishing Group.

KJV: Scripture quotations are from the King James Version

NCV: Scripture taken from the New Century Version ®. Copyright © 2005 by Thomas Nelson. Used by permission. All rights reserved.

NIV: Scripture taken from the Holy Bible, New International Version ®. Copyright © 1973, 1978, 1984 by International Bible Society. Used by permission of Zondervan. All rights reserved.

NKJV: Scripture taken from the New King James Version ®. Copyright © 1982 by Thomas Nelson. Used by permission. All rights reserved.

NRSV: Scripture quotations are from the New Revised Standard Version Bible, copyright © 1989 the Division of Christian Education

About the Author

Bright Okoye is a preacher and teacher of the gospel. He holds a degree in mathematics and has other qualifications in management and project management. Presently, he lives in Asaba Delta State, Nigeria.

Made in United States
North Haven, CT
04 November 2026

21765354R00206